RAISING YOUR SPIRITED CHILD WORKBOOK

RAISING YOUR SPIRITED CHILD WORKBOOK

MARY SHEEDY KURCINKA

HarperPerennial
A Division of HarperCollins*Publishers*

To all of the parents and children who have taught me so much!

HarperCollins books may be purchased for educational, business, or sales promotional use. For information please write: Special Markets Department, HarperCollins Publishers, Inc., 10 East 53rd Street, New York, NY 10022.

FIRST EDITION

Designed by Helene Wald Berinsky

ISBN 0-06-095240-7

98 99 00 01 02 ❖/RRD 10 9 8 7 6 5 4 3 2 1

CONTENTS

ACKNOWLEDGMENTS

This book exists because of the encouragement, support, and insights of many. To them I am very grateful and must say thank you. In random order as always:

All of the parents, professionals, and children who have shared their stories with me, asked the tough questions, offered tips, and tested strategies. Thank you so much!

Lynn Jessen, Jenna Ruble, Marietta Rice, and Kim Cardwell, my friends and colleagues who have seen me through every stage of this book, from the moments of doubt to the celebration of a completed project. Their insights, stories, and support have been invaluable.

Brenda Zirbel, Sandy Moline, Kelly Olson, Judi Marshall, Patricia Lee, Rosann Sowada, Mike LaVallie, Teresa Danielson, ECFE teachers and teaching assistants who taught the curriculum with me, let me observe them work, and helped me catch the "holes."

Heide Lange, my agent, the "dream maker" who put this project together and is my favorite cheerleader.

Megan Newman, my editor, who is delightful to work with and who, most important, has brought clarity and order to the manuscript.

Hillary Epstein, Megan's assistant, who always greets me warmly and keeps the details in order.

Mary Darling, Ph.D., and Megan Gunnar, Ph.D., of the University of Minnesota; Jerome Kagan, Ph.D., and Bob Rosenthal, Ph.D., of Harvard; Elizabeth Murphy, Ed.D.; Craig Ramey, Ph.D., of the University of Alabama; Marianne Daniels Garber; Jim Cameron, Ph.D., of An Ounce of Prevention; Nancy Melvin, Ph.D., of Arizona State University, all very busy professionals who allowed me to interview them for this book.

Patti Labs, Mary Boozell, Lana Hanson, Susan Reppe, Marcia Sosso, and Danielle McCluskey, who answer my calls at ECFE with such warmth and joy.

Pat Francisco, friend, writer, and teacher, who helped me figure out how to create characters.

Sharon Wentzel, the computer whiz who helped me first "see" the potential workbook design.

Gary Smolak, fellow writer, who was willing to go through every chapter of this book word by word with me.

Joanne Burke, friend and creative genius, who brought me books of poetry.

The staff of Paidea, who have taught with me, shared ideas and stories with me, and let me watch them work with kids.

The staff of Highland ECFE, and the Jewish Community Center in St. Paul, who also taught with me and shared their insights.

Carol Roan from the Jewish Community Center; Ada Alden of Eden Prairie ECFE; Debbie Eck and Ann Lovrien of the St. Paul ECFE; and Peggy Gilbertson of Southlake Clinic, who helped me organize groups in the community.

Tom, Lindsey, and Kellen Fish, who are the best neighbors and friends a person could ever want. Your encouragement has meant so much.

Tim Payne, who keeps my computer going.

Vicki Cronin, friend and colleague, who cheers me on.

Lydia Peterson, who helped me figure out the embryo of the workbook.

Jean Illsley Clarke, author, and Joan Comeau, Family Information Services director, who shared their professional experiences and lots of lunches with me.

Terry Bedard and Linda Buchanan, who kept my house in order and me focused.

Joshua and Kristina, my children, who delight me and challenge me to continue to learn and grow.

Richard and Beatrice Sheedy, my parents, who have always believed in me.

Barbara Majerus, Kathy Kurz, Helen Kennedy, and Suzanne Nelson, my sisters, who have sold lots of books for me.

Joe Kurcinka, my husband, best friend, and most favorite spirited adult in the whole wide world. Thank you for your intensity, perceptiveness, sensitivity, energy, and caution. My life is richer, my work better because of you.

Thank you!

GREETINGS

Welcome to *Raising Your Spirited Child Workbook.* Remember me? I'm Mary, your guide, licensed teacher of parents and children, fellow parent of one spirited and one spunky child, both now adolescents. In 1991 HarperCollins published my first book, *Raising Your Spirited Child.* My life hasn't been the same since.

I've been allowed to hear the tales of spirited kids and to learn effective techniques and strategies from parents and professionals across the United States and Canada. I've been a guest in homes, churches, synagogues, schools, hospitals, colleges, businesses, classrooms, child care programs, family centers, and professional meetings. I've seen spirited kids in action and learned from them—children who have invited me to try their personal trapeze built into the garage (I was tempted) and to feel that special spot on their "lovies." I've listened to spirited adolescents who have channeled their sensitivity and perceptiveness into a keen sense of humor capable of breaking the tension at just the right moment.

During this time my mailbox has become a treasure box filled with letters. Many are warm and funny. Others bring that big lump into my throat. I read every one. Frequently I don't even bother to wait until I get into the house with them. I stand right there at the box and read them until my kids come looking for me. Other times I sit at my kitchen counter to enjoy them amidst the smells of dinner cooking. Sometimes I leave them there on the counter for a few days and reread them when I need a little lift. I save them all. Every one of them is here, tucked away. My heirs can throw them out. I never will.

Then there are the phone calls. Sometimes it's amazement that leads a parent to phone. "Have you been in my home with a video camera?" they'll ask. Sometimes it's appreciation: "I feel like you're my friend." Others simply tell me, "I knew you'd understand." And not infrequently it is deep sadness or total frustration that impels them to pick up the phone. There are no words when I answer, simply a sob and a hiccup before a voice asks, "Is it really you?"

I love hearing from every parent. Even though I've now been talking about spirited kids since 1984, the topic never grows tiresome for me. Now as the mother of two adolescents I also know what happens when spirited kids get the keys to the car and a midnight curfew.

So I'm back, in response to your questions and frustrations. I've heard the common woes of getting stuck. The need for help managing your own intensity and a desire for more practice and strategies. I'm eager to share new insights and tools to help make raising your spirited child just a little bit easier. I've also learned you'd like to have someone to talk with or even to come to one of my groups, which is great if you live in Minnesota but challenging otherwise.

I've decided to offer a group for you. It's going to require a little creativity on both of our parts as I take you with me into a composite of my groups. This one is based on the Minnesota Early Childhood Family Education model, in which parents and children come together through their local school district. These programs serve parents and their children from birth to kindergarten, so I've stretched this fictionalized group to include composites of parents with older kids who participate in classes I teach at community and child care centers and through hospitals and health organizations.

As we go along, allow yourself to be a learner. I've discovered over the years that learning new skills is a lot like toilet training. Sounds silly, but it's true. You see, there are actually three stages to toilet training, and each one is tied to neural development and builds on the one before it—the second stage can't be accomplished until the first is finished, and the third one won't work until the second one is in place.

During the first stage of toilet learning a child announces, "I went!" You give her a big high five and exclaim, "Wow that's great! *Soon* you'll be able to tell me when you're going." Sure enough, a few weeks or months later that same child looks up at you red-faced or quizzical to announce, "I'm going!" The frustration may growl in your throat, but this is a moment to celebrate. This is the second stage of neural development—knowing when you're in the middle of it. So you hug your child and say, "All right! *Soon* you'll be able to tell me *before* you have to go."

A few days, weeks, or months later that child comes running to tell you, "I have to go!" Together you make the mad dash for the bathroom and share this moment of success. Of course there'll be a few accidents and setbacks, but once the third stage is in place, toilet learning is just about complete.

The same is true for learning new skills as a parent. Initially you'll catch yourself *after* you've responded the old way. But instead of feeling frustrated you'll celebrate your awareness that you used your old techniques and promise that next time you're going to try to catch yourself in the act. Sure enough, a few weeks or months later you'll find yourself about to lose it as you struggle to get your child out the door, but you'll stop yourself midsentence and change to your new and improved tactics. Now you've got stage two down: you can catch yourself. It's only later, maybe months, maybe years, before you find yourself able to face a situation and say, I need to do it this way. When it happens you'll know you've accomplished stage three. The process is nearly complete. That skill is yours to keep forever.

So grab your pen or pencil and turn the page to meet others who understand what it's like to live with spirit. Others who know that "Progress, Not Perfection" is our goal!

And if you enjoy what you find, I'd like your help. I hope that someday there will be a class like the one you are about to experience for all parents, no matter where they live. If you have a little bit of extra energy, call a friend and share this book with her. If you've got a bit more time and energy, call your local school, child care center, church, synagogue, hospital, or community center, and convince the staff to help you start a group there.

If you're ready to be part of a social movement, contact

The Minnesota Department of Children,
Families and Learning
550 Cedar Street
St. Paul, MN 55101-2273
(612) 296-6130

and find out how you can influence your legislators to make these classes available throughout your state, just as they are in Minnesota.

Together we can make sure that parents of spirited children will *never* feel alone! Together we can insure that *every* place is one where spirit thrives.

1

WHO IS THE SPIRITED CHILD?

WHAT YOU'LL NEED

A comfortable chair, a beverage, popcorn or other munchies (chocolates are nice), a pen or pencil, and at least one spirited child. In case you need a refresher, let me give you my formal definition. Spirited kids are normal kids who are *more*! More intense, persistent, sensitive, perceptive, and uncomfortable with change than the average child. They are not children experiencing attention deficit disorder (ADHD); however, the information in this workbook will be extremely helpful to you if your child does have ADHD. In fact, the information in this book will be helpful to every parent.

Now let me give you my informal definition. Spirited kids are the exception to the rule "Ignore them and they'll stop." Spirited kids can cry for hours, and if by chance they do fall asleep, they'll wake up and start in again on the same issue. They are the kids who can be triggered by seemingly insignificant things such as a change in the weather, lint in a sock, the red cup instead of the expected yellow one, or a friend who looks at them the "wrong way." Relatives freely offer unsolicited advice as to how you should discipline them.

On good days spirited kids prove to be more delightful than you ever imagined. They make you laugh, pull your attention to the bugs and bees you would have missed without them, give you an excuse to play, and encourage you to take naps. On bad days they refuse to do anything you ask—usually in a loud and angry voice; they spit at you, kick you, and rob you of your sleep with their demands and the worries they arouse. Often they make you cry. They may also leave you feeling a little crazy, even stunned, wondering how, if it's like this now, you will ever survive adolescence.

So if you've got your munchies, writing tools, and at least one spirited child, you're ready to go. If by chance you can find a partner in parenting who will complete the exercises with you, the experience will be even more fun. And if you have the opportunity to set your chair among many and fill each with a parent of a spirited child, it can be even better.

WHY SPIRITED?

If you've read *Raising Your Spirited Child*, you know that *spirited child* is a term I coined. In 1979 when my son, Joshua, was born, there weren't any spirited-child classes or books. In fact, the only information I could find that described a kid like him used terms such as *difficult, strong-willed, stubborn, mother killer,* or *Dennis the Menace.* It was the good days that made me seek a better way to describe him, and as I searched, I began to realize that on those good days Joshua was just like his father, whom I love dearly. In fact, spirited children possess traits "in the raw" that are truly valued in adults but challenging to live with in a young child. It was this realization that brought me to the word *spirited,* which means lively, creative, keen, eager, full of energy and courage, and having a strong, assertive personality. So life with spirited children is really a love story, as we recognize their potential and help them to develop the skills they need to manage their temperament well and be successful. The designation "spirited child" is used as a tool for understanding. It is never an excuse for poor behavior.

WHAT'S NEW?

I suspect you'd like to know how *Raising Your Spirited Child Workbook* is different from *Raising Your Spirited Child.* I've listened to what parents have told me they needed, and as a result, you'll get *more*

- **help actually applying the strategies to your own everyday situations**
- **examples and stories about all age groups, infants to adolescents, to allow your skills to grow with your child**
- **insights and tips for working together as a family**
- **new and revised parent-tested strategies for those times you get stuck**
- **help managing your own intensity**
- **support and encouragement for the things you're already doing well**

HOW THE CHAPTERS WORK

I've developed a variety of techniques and strategies that I hope will offer something for just about everyone. In each chapter you will find the following features:

1. IN PREPARATION

I'll ask that you read *Raising Your Spirited Child* along with completing this companion book. That way you'll have the information we're going to focus on applying to your specific situation. I'll also update this information, especially for your older children, adding more stories and strategies gleaned over the last few years. If reading two books at the same time seems overwhelming, don't panic! I'll give you enough information in this workbook so you'll be able to do all the exercises. You'll just have more data if you're able to complete the additional reading.

I'll also ask you to gather materials for the various exercises in the chapter. You should be able to find all of the supplies in your cupboards. These exercises are not just gimmicks. They are specifically planned to help you gain new insights—and they're fun too. Every exercise and strategy in this book is parent-tested.

2. CHAPTER HIGHLIGHTS

For those of you who like to cut to the chase, I'll let you know the key points of each chapter.

3. THINGS TO OBSERVE

Children never tell us that they're intense or that change is difficult for them. They simply act it out. Learning to read your spirited child's behavior cues is an essential skill for parents. If you are unaware of the signals your child is sending you, you can't respond appropriately or prevent potential problems. In this section I'll include hints to enhance your observation skills. Success depends upon a keen eye and ear and a sensitive heart.

4. A NEW POINT OF VIEW

Each spirited child is unique, yet there are similarities among them. Compared with the "average" child, most are more

intense	They feel every emotion deeply and powerfully.
persistent	They are committed to their goals.
sensitive	They are keenly aware of sights, sounds, tastes, smells, textures, and sometimes emotions; they feel what others do not.
perceptive	They are visually attuned to the world around them; they may not "hear" directions.
slow to adapt	They hate surprises and find it challenging to shift from one thing to another.

Many but not all spirited kids are also

irregular	Figuring out when they will need to sleep, eat, or eliminate is a daily puzzle.

energetic	They're on the move. If they're not climbing or running, they're pacing, fidgeting, or taking things apart.
cautious in new situations	A quick withdrawal from anything new is very typical.
serious	They're analytical, they tend to see what needs to be fixed, and they're reserved with their smiles.

This section is filled with exercises that enable you to picture and experience each of these temperament traits. This new point of view will allow you to see your child's behavior (and maybe even your own) in a more helpful way. My hope is that ultimately you'll see a child struggling with a scratchy sweater and automatically recognize that the reaction is a result of his sensitivity. Or you'll hear a child say "Just two more minutes" and know this is a persistent child who has a goal to accomplish, not a child just out to "get you" or to make your life miserable.

I'll also help you identify the triggers that tend to set up a negative reaction for each trait. Once you understand each of the temperament traits, you won't feel like a victim waiting for the next bomb to explode. You'll know what will set off your child and be able to avoid those triggers whenever possible.

5. EFFECTIVE STRATEGIES

In order to help your child be successful you need to know what strategies work with each temperament trait. If your child is intense, a sticker system won't help him learn to manage his intensity. He needs to know how to soothe himself. If your child refuses to get dressed because his clothes don't "feel right," a time-out won't help a bit. This child needs to understand his sensitivity and learn strategies that help him avoid the triggers or at least minimize them. If your child won't take no for an answer, ignoring her won't be effective. A persistent child needs to learn how to work with others and solve problems. This section is chock-full of parent-tested strategies that *really* work because they meet the needs of each temperamental style.

Nancy Melvin, Ph.D., of the College of Nursing at Arizona

State University, writes, "Healthy development occurs when there is a goodness of fit between the temperament traits of the child and the demands and expectations of the environment." Finding strategies that fit your child is essential for her success.

6. PRACTICE, PRACTICE, PRACTICE

Learning new skills takes practice. I'll offer you scenarios and suggest possible responses with which you can compare your answers. (There isn't one "right" answer, but at least you can find out if you're in the ballpark.) There are activities to help you try out the techniques, hone your skills, and actually apply the strategies to your own situations. There will also be reinforcement to assist you when you're haunted by doubts or worries or surrounded by naysayers. I'll even offer suggestions for how to retool techniques if they don't work quite as expected. I'll do my best to address your "yes, buts" and "it worked, but" kind of questions.

7. SAVOR YOUR SUCCESSES

Building from success is the most effective way to learn new skills. It is important to take the time to recognize your accomplishments. This section is filled with stories from a variety of families who have put the information and strategies into practice. Since Progress, Not Perfection is our goal, I'll also let you hear about struggles these families experienced along the way.

8. CORNERSTONE

I suspect you don't have much time to linger over the lessons in this book. If your life is as busy and hectic as those of most parents I work with, you might find a few quick reminders of the key points from each lesson helpful. Whenever you need it, you can come back to the cornerstones for a review.

ONE MORE THING

When I was first asked to write a companion workbook for *Raising Your Spirited Child,* I balked. I often find workbooks boring and unclear. I did not wish to write a boring book. I also know that the spirited-child classes are *never* dull and that the opportunity to tell stories and ask questions is an essential part of the learning process. Having someone to share your woes and "ahas" with really makes a difference. It helps to know you are not alone in your struggles.

So I was challenged. How could I give you the exercises—and the discussion? My solution was to create a workbook filled with exercises *and* your very own spirited-child group to do them with.

You'll meet Phil, Brent, Sarah, John, Diane, Lynn, and Maggie. They're real parents, fictionalized a bit to cover the most common points and questions but nonetheless created from prototypes of real people trying to earn a living, maintain some adult relationships, and parent a spirited child or children. I'll take them through the same exercises you'll be doing. This way you can listen in as they respond and compare your thoughts and reactions with theirs. Always remember, *you* know your child better than anyone else, so take what works for you and leave the rest.

INTRODUCTIONS

The family center is just off Johnny Cake Ridge Road, around the curve. You turn at the Schwann ice cream distributorship. I always like to think sweet things begin to happen the minute you turn the corner. My group is scheduled to begin at 6:30 P.M., but I've been here since 5:45 setting up the room, reviewing the registration list, meeting with the early-childhood team to clarify our plans once more. Now everything is ready. The coffee is perking; hot water is steaming; clean cups, napkins, and spoons are laid out; the chairs are set around the table; pens, markers, and name tags are out. I stand at the door waiting for the parents and their kids to arrive. I fidget, always a little anxious the first night. I wonder if anyone will come, even though I know they will.

Finally the door swings open and the first family arrives. I can't help it: I smile, relieved and elated that another group is about to begin. You'd think after all these years another group would be just that—another group, but it never is to me. Excitement surges through my veins. "Welcome to 'Raising Your Spirited Child,'" I announce, thrilled to see Phil, his daughter Tara, and his son T.J. Watching them bounce into the room, I am reminded that there is a genetic aspect to being spirited.

Brent and his three kids slip in behind Phil. A Green Bay Packers cap is pulled low over his eyes. He has the sent-by-his-wife look. His response to my greeting is a narrow-eyed glare. I step toward him, offering my hand and a smile. "First group?" I ask. He nods. "There will be others who are coming for the first time too," I tell him and point out Phil, who is already engrossed in a construction project with his daughter.

Sarah, the mother of four, sighs deeply as she slides through the door with all four kids in tow. A yellow spit-up stain on her shoulder suggests a last-minute dash to get out the door. Her only makeup is a hint of pink lipstick, most of which has been chewed off her lower lip. I help her with the baby and her diaper bag and invite her to just sit down and play with her kids. "We'll clean up the mess," I promise as she looks tentatively at the paints.

Lynn arrives next. I'm pleased to see her again. She's been in other groups. "I need another fix," she remarks as she breezes by me. She's dressed in black stretch pants and a long black sweater to ward off the record-breaking April chill. It was 14 degrees Fahrenheit this morning, and even now the thermometer hovers at 27. On her the black is warm, not stark—perhaps it's her smile, which warms everything around her.

It's John's eyes that I notice when he enters. They are dark brown and deep. He doesn't smile but slowly glances around the room. I sense caution, yet there's warmth there too. He's alone. His kids are older and have stayed home to do their homework.

Diane is laughing as she sweeps into the room, tossing her hair and shepherding three boys in front of her. She's wearing purple. She greets me before I can say hello.

Maggie arrives last, not rushed. Her body is soft and round, the type that infants love to snuggle into and toddlers stroke contentedly when held on a sturdy hip. Her daughter immediately starts filling out a name tag. Her son stands quietly at her side.

We spend thirty minutes with the kids, playing games, building, painting, reading books, and singing songs. It's a great time for parents and kids to just enjoy one another's company without interruptions from telephones, doorbells, or televisions. It's a rich time for me as a teacher. I notice Brent's daughter Katie wants to stay right by him, visually taking in the room. His son heads for the climber, with two-year-old Sonja toddling behind him. That's fine, I reassure him. All three of Diane's sons need to touch and try every activity. That's all right too. Maggie's son finds a quiet corner where he can enjoy a new toy all by himself. During the hello song, he passes when it's his turn; he doesn't want his name sung.

The reactions are so typical of other spirited-child classes, and yet each is unique. The time together gives me an opportunity to begin discerning each child's style. Soon it will be our laboratory in which to demonstrate and practice the techniques we've discussed in class. The half hour whizzes by, and before I know it it's time for the parents to move to the discussion room, while the kids continue their class with the early-childhood team.

As they grab cups of coffee and sit, I remember that these parents who have come to circle my table are strangers to one another. Their children have brought them to this place, or, more accurately in some cases, driven them here—and not by car. I know from experience that some are at their wits' end. They are considering sending their child to Grandma's—with a one-way ticket. Others are doing fine but need a little refresher, a few more insights, a couple more strategies. Still others have read *Raising Your Spirited Child* four times. It sits on their bedside table for frequent reference, but they need a little help applying the information, especially when all of their kids start screaming at once.

The parents do not know yet if they are compatible. They have received the flyer from the community center advertising "Raising Your Spirited Child," Tuesdays 6:30–8:15 P.M., ten weeks April to June. The issues of life with "spirit" have brought them here.

Tonight our discussion focuses on two questions:

What do you enjoy most about your spirited child?

What do you find most challenging?

Over the years, I've tried other introductory exercises, but I always come back to these two questions. Somehow the responses to them build an immediate sense of comradeship that no others have done quite so well.

I ask the parents to write their answers. Lynn quickly creates a long list. She glances up, eager to share her thoughts. Others struggle, writing, stopping to reflect, writing again. Slowly, tediously, their answers evolve. Today it is Sarah whose eyes begin to glisten. The space under the question "What do you enjoy most about your spirited child?" is blank on her paper. She captures my gaze and holds on. I break into the silence.

"You might be finding it difficult to think of things you enjoy," I tell the group. "It's all right. You're here among people who understand." Sarah settles back into her chair.

After a few minutes of writing it's time to report. We begin "popcorn" fashion: anyone can jump in and speak. Anyone can take his time to warm up. It's all right to be a listener. It's all right to be passionate about the topic.

Lynn, the veteran, takes a sip of her coffee and volunteers to start.

"I have an eleven-year-old son, Aaron, and a nine-year-old daughter, Jenna. My daughter is the spirited one. I appreciate how determined she is—but I'm back for my second spirited-child class because she gets frustrated so easily." Lynn shakes her head. "Like yesterday. Jenna was working on a math sheet, and all of a sudden—blowup." She stops, grabs a piece of paper, crumples it into a wad, and throws it on the floor to demonstrate. "One little mistake, and she loses it! I thought I'd have to push my kids about getting good grades, but with Jenna, if she gets a B, it's instant despair."

John and Maggie both perk up, head shakes and soft murmurs signaling their common experience, but it's Phil who volunteers to speak next. Folding his paper and sticking it into his pocket, he begins, "I've got two kids, T.J., two, and Tara, four. Tara's enthusiasm and energy are great," he says, smiling broadly. "Tara's enthusiasm and energy drive me nuts." He stops with the grin frozen on his face.

Diane slaps her leg and whoops. "Isn't that true! What you love the most drives you crazy."

Chuckles float around the room as I make a chart on the board and start listing the responses on it.

Brent watches me write and plays with a paper clip left lying on the table. Slowly taking a deep breath, he begins. "I've got three kids, Sonja, two, Kate, who's four, and Danny, who's six. Getting Sonja dressed is like wrestling a steer. That girl is so stubborn. You have to chase her down to get her pants on, and then she kicks and hits you. My wife can hardly dress her."

Diane laughs again, her hair bouncing on her shoulders as she shakes with delight. "This is so great," she exclaims, urging Brent on.

"Danny is always busy," Brent continues, casting a glance to see if Diane will respond again, but she lets him continue. "You never know what he's going to break next. When he was little you couldn't let him out of your sight for a minute. We had to duct-tape the toilet tank lid because he kept taking it off."

"Don't let him tell my boys that one!" Diane giggles. "That's actually one idea they've missed."

Brent gives her a sideways glance, continuing with a little grin twitching the corners of his mouth. He seems to enjoy being center stage and triggering Diane's reactions. "Now that Danny's older, he still climbs on things—fell out of a tree yesterday—and if he's bored, he pokes the dog, his sisters, whatever is near."

"What do you enjoy about Danny?" I ask, wanting to make sure I have responses for both sides of the chart.

He twists the clip as he thinks for a moment. "Well, when he's not breaking things, Danny can throw a mean ball."

I added *athletic* to the chart. "Is Danny more like you or your wife?" I ask.

Brent glances at the clip, now mangled in his hand. He snorts. "Well, I'd say there are some similarities between us."

Diane puts down her coffee cup. "That's the trouble," she says seriously. "I know my son's like me, but I don't want him to be like me! I've got three boys: Andy, three, Brandon, five, and Justin, eight. I know Justin is sensitive, and that's supposed to be good. It's true he's kind and affectionate, but he cries over anything. He takes everything personally. If another kid tells him to hurry up on the slide, his feelings are hurt. Even if the kid is yelling at someone else, he's still upset. I know how he feels, and I also know it's not easy to live this way."

Maggie reaches over and pats Diane's arm.

Diane pauses for a moment, pleasantly surprised by Maggie's support, then continues. "Brandon is a magnet for people. They love him. He's outgoing and vivacious. But it is impossible to take him shopping or to feed him. Nothing tastes right. His milk has to be cold, or he won't drink it. He's always complaining that the television is too loud, the lights hurt his eyes, the people make him crazy, or Grandpa smacks when he chews."

I write as quickly as I can trying to keep up with her. She slows, realizing my struggle.

I add her last responses to the chart as Maggie turns to face Diane. "My son has really deep feelings too," she says, "but right now most of them are angry feelings. His reactions have always been tough to deal with, but since the divorce they're worse." She looks down for a moment, carefully running a finger around the rim of her cup. "He just doesn't get over things easily. It takes a long time for him to come back to center." Then, catching herself, she says, "He isn't a bad kid. He can be funny." Her voice grows lighter. "And I think he's bright." But her chin drops as she admits, "Right now he's just wearing me out."

Diane leans toward Maggie, whispering something I can't quite discern. Maggie's eyes soften as she listens. Their side conversation seems like a good thing for the moment, and I leave them alone.

Only John and Sarah have yet to introduce themselves. John looks around, and catching a nod from me, begins speaking. His voice is as soft as his eyes and so earnest that suddenly everyone is quiet. "My son, Todd, is twelve. I enjoy his creativity and his persistence for the things he really cares about, and the drama in which he lives life—the ups and downs. I find most challenging"—he pauses to look at Phil—"the ups and downs of his life, and his lack of persistence for things he's not interested in." Phil gives him a thumbs-up.

John quietly continues. "My thirteen-year-old daughter, Kelly, is smart. The teachers love her. I just wish she would be more open to trying things. She's so talented in everything and anything, but getting her going is a major endeavor."

I add his comments to the chart. Only Sarah is left to speak. Her body is rigid, her fingers tightly gripping her pen. The paper lying in front of her is still blank. "It's okay to pass," I tell her.

She chews her lip. "I'm sitting here trying to think of something I enjoy," she says softly. "But right now I'm faced with four kids and so many challenges I can't find any joys. I'm at a point that I feel desperate. I just find myself having less and less emotional and physical energy. I'm not sure I can keep doing this."

She looks away as she falls silent. The others stir, not sure how to respond. To my surprise, Brent saves the moment by joking, "Yeah, if this was a paid job, I'd quit!"

Sarah almost cracks a grin. Collecting herself, she says, "I guess I could say David doesn't follow the crowd. That's a good thing," she almost whispers, reassuring herself. "Except on family outings. He turns them into a nightmare. He refuses to do what everyone else wants to do."

"He's independent?" I ask.

She looks puzzled. "Yeah. I guess. I never thought of it that way."

"And what about Cara?" I ask.

"She's always been horrible about clothes," Sarah replies. "It's better now that she's ten—unless she has to dress up. She hates anything with a tight collar or cuffs. Sadie, our four-year-old, takes so long to get out the door. Either she doesn't want to go, or she has to stop and look at everything as she walks out to the car. With four kids, someone is always upset."

"You've come to the right place," I assure Sarah. "And with four kids you are working harder. You've taken a very important step. You've come to a place where other people understand and there's information available that can help you make it better. Welcome."

The frustration that pushed many of the parents to attend this session seems to creep back to the corners of the room. They seem to realize that there are people who truly understand the emotional roller-coaster of parenting a spirited child.

You are not alone either! As the parent of a spirited child you are one of ten to fifteen million people in this country parenting a spirited child. You too are working harder to parent this child who is normal but more. Take a few minutes to add your joys and challenges to the chart.

Exercise

1. The top of the chart lists the characteristics mentioned by the parents in the group. Review these joys and challenges, and check off those that fit your experience.
2. Add your own joys and challenges in the spaces below. Don't be surprised if at this point the challenges outnumber the joys.

What do you enjoy most about your spirited child?	*What do you find most challenging about your spirited child?*
determination	quick frustration
creativity	high expectations
enthusiasm	enthusiasm
energy	energy
sensitivity	fidgeting, poking
vivaciousness	won't quit
charisma	easily upset
strength	taking him shopping
athletic ability and coordination	anger and tantrums
humor	demands
intelligence	never takes no for an answer
focus	mercurial moods
drama	won't try new things
caution	doesn't listen
doesn't follow crowd	the time it takes to shift
notices everything	doesn't work with others
	getting dressed
	notices everything
	eating

What do you enjoy most about your spirited child?	***What do you find most challenging about your spirited child?***

Compare your responses to those of the parents in the group. Do your answers surprise you?

If you're feeling a little overwhelmed, like Sarah, pat yourself on the back. By picking up this book, you've already taken the first step to making things better. There are strategies that can make filling out the enjoyment column one of the quickest and easiest exercises you've ever done. Just wait and see!

CORNERSTONE

- ✔ **You are not alone.**
- ✔ **It does take more knowledge, skill, and patience to parent a spirited child.**
- ✔ **There is information in this book that can help you.**

2

A DIFFERENT POINT OF VIEW

Building on Strengths

IN PREPARATION

- Read Chapters 1 and 2 of *Raising Your Spirited Child.*
- Grab a stack of index cards or a writing tablet and a pen.

CHAPTER HIGHLIGHTS

- Facts explaining why it is so important to hold a positive vision of your child.
- Practice creating positive labels.
- Examples of how to hold that vision even during the tough times.

THINGS TO OBSERVE

- What words do you use to describe your child?
- How does your child respond when you say something positive about him?
- How do you feel when someone says something positive about your child?

Can your expectations of your child's behavior unwittingly cause this behavior? The answer is YES!

In a famous study conducted by A. S. King, a welding instructor was told that five men in his class had the potential to be outstanding welders. In truth the men had been randomly selected and were no more or less capable than the other class members. The instructor was advised that the information about the five men's high aptitude was simply for his awareness and that he was not to do anything special for them.

At the end of the class, records showed that the five randomly selected men

- **scored ten points higher than their peers on the final test**
- **learned the tasks in half the time it took the other students**
- **were selected by their peers as the most desirable work partners**
- **had a higher attendance rate**

What happened? Why did these men excel when they were really no different from their peers? While the instructor firmly believed he had not done anything differently for these men, observations showed that in fact he had. Thanks to this study and others like it, we now know that when you expect good things, *your* behavior changes. It's called the Pygmalion effect.

Holding that positive vision leads you to

- **smile more**
- **give more positive feedback and helpful hints**
- **give more information**
- **listen better**
- **be more expressive, warm, and encouraging**
- **offer more interesting and challenging opportunities**

As a result, the person on the receiving end of this positive vision experiences greater confidence and achieves a higher performance.

Your positive perspective is an essential ingredient for your spirited child's success. The formation of that vision begins with the words you use to describe your child.

Spirited kids seem to attract labels, unfortunately not always positive ones. That's why it is so important that you become aware of the labels you apply. Do those labels garner images of kids who are intelligent, creative, inquisitive, and strong leaders? Are they the kind of descriptors that would make others envy you the opportunity of raising a spirited child? Do they make you puff up with pride, smile in appreciation, chuckle with enjoyment, and expect success? Let's take a look.

A NEW POINT OF VIEW

The weather had warmed dramatically in the past week, and as Diane and her three boys swirled through the center's front door, a warm spring breeze ruffled their hair. Today Diane wore pink leggings with a long purple-and-pink sweatshirt. Andy, her youngest, clung to her leg. He wasn't sure he wanted to go into the children's classroom for family time. We showed him the discussion room where Diane would be sitting and let him pick a chair for her. Through the one-way mirror to the children's room, I pointed out the purple modeling dough he'd enjoyed the previous week. He also saw his brothers already making worms and snakes and decided maybe it wouldn't be too bad. We headed for the children's room, and when it was time for Diane to separate he gave her a kiss and a hug without any tears.

After we'd all gathered in the discussion room, I announced to the group that we would be starting with the nitty-gritty—the bad days.

"You know," I said, "those days when your child has already been in time-out three times before ten A.M. When nothing he does, or you do, is right. When you seriously wonder if you're going to be able to make it through another day with this child."

"Oh." Sarah sighed. "Those days!"

"I'm going to let you be honest," I said. "Squelch those censors, and let yourself go!"

"Great!" Diane exclaimed.

Brent rested his chin on his hand and looked at me from under the bill of his cap. I didn't think he felt exactly wild and free, so I pulled out a stack of index cards, ruffled the edges, and dealt them out, three cards to each person. "Write a word or a phrase that describes your child on the bad days," I directed, "then toss your completed cards into the center of the table to be randomly drawn and read."

The confidentiality led to some interesting labels.

Diane drew three cards and volunteered to read them: "'Rebellious,' 'demanding,' and 'little shit.'"

I cocked an eyebrow at Brent. He smirked and raised his hands in innocence. I didn't believe him. The others laughed, their voices rising as energy built around the table. Phil grabbed three cards to see what other treasures lay within. He read: "'emotional roller-coaster,' 'perfectionist,'" and—he coughed nervously before reading this one—"'anal-retentive brat.'"

The group wasn't quite sure how to respond. Some laughed; others groaned in recognition of both the harshness of the words and the anger lying behind them. There was silence before John selected his cards. "'Negative,' 'irrational,' 'whiny,'" he read.

Sarah reached for the pile. "'Disobedient,' 'manipulative,' 'always has to have his own way,'" she added.

I wrote each word or phrase on the board. The atmosphere of the room grew gloomy. Shoulders unconsciously began to droop as a seemingly overwhelming challenge formed on the board.

rebellious
demanding
little shit
emotional roller-coaster
perfectionist
anal-retentive brat
negative
irrational
whiny
disobedient
manipulative
always has to have his own way
obstinate
resistant
bossy

"What surprises you about the list?" I asked.

"It's really sobering when you see it up there," Phil replied, his voice soft. "I didn't realize I was being so negative."

"I feel the shame," Sarah whispered. "But my family tells me I have to tell him he's bad. They think he acts up because I don't tell him he's bad. Telling him he's bad is shaming, isn't it?"

"It is shaming," I agreed. "And studies show that an expectation of disaster can become a self-fulfilling prophecy."

"Yeah," Phil chimed in, grabbing a pen and jabbing it at the board. "And I hate it when people use words like 'little shit' to describe Tara because people used to describe me that way."

Diane's voice rose. "I see words that were used to describe me too—still are—like *obstinate*. Justin always has to have his own way. That's like me, and it's gotten me into a lot of trouble." She snapped her pencil in half, dropping the pieces on the table in front of her.

Maggie looked at Diane, waiting to see if she wanted to say more. Diane glanced away. "My experience is so different," Maggie said quietly. "Looking at those words, I realize my son and I aren't alike at all. I was the easygoing kid. No wonder it's so hard for me to understand him."

"I just feel tired," Sarah replied.

"I'm worried," Lynn remarked.

Sometimes when we're dealing with our spirited kids we're so different from them that it is difficult not only to understand them, but to appreciate them. Other times our spirited kids are so much like us that it scares us, especially when we see what we consider our greatest weaknesses being repeated. But whether we are similar or different, the negative labels sap our energy, often leaving us feeling overwhelmed and angry.

EFFECTIVE STRATEGIES

It is essential to examine the negative labels we use to describe our kids and change them. The reality is that in every single one of those behaviors is a potential strength. Our task is to identify those strengths and help our children maximize them by learning how to manage their behavior.

Take another look at the list. Are there any words that described you when you were little? Is this trait an asset for you today?

"They used to call me bossy," Lynn said. "But now I'm a manager and quite successful at it."

"Demanding," Phil said, "and perfectionist. Today I'm in charge of an airplane-mechanics crew—being demanding and perfectionist is real important. My boss prizes my high expectations and the way I strive for excellence."

I realized I wanted to fly on this man's planes. It's true, many of the traits we find challenging in children are valued in adults. Somehow along the way those adults have realized their potential strengths and have learned to manage them well. We can help our children to develop those strengths too. It begins by simply changing the words we use to describe them and promising ourselves to drop the negative labels and replace them with words that identify the potential strength.

Changing Negative Labels into Positive Ones

1. **Review the list of negative labels already created.**
2. **Add your own negative labels.**
3. **Transform those negative labels to positive ones.**
4. **Check the "Suggested Positive Labels" list for potential answers. There isn't one right answer, but these are some examples of good ones.**
5. **If you get stuck or find yourself truly unable to think of anything positive about your child, ask a friend who knows and loves your child to do it with you. Another possibility is to review Chapter 2 in *Raising Your Spirited Child* or to grab a dictionary or thesaurus.**

Old, Negative Label	*New, Positive Label*
rebellious	
demanding	
little shit	
emotional roller-coaster	
perfectionist	
anal-retentive brat	
negative	
irrational	
whiny	
disobedient	
manipulative	
always has to have her own way	
obstinate	
resistant	
bossy	
temperamental	
mouthy	

SUGGESTED POSITIVE LABELS

Old, Negative Labels	*New, Positive Label*
rebellious	independent
demanding	persistent
little shit	future leader
emotional roller-coaster	sensitive
perfectionist	holds high standards
anal-retentive brat	organized
negative	analytical
irrational	creative
whiny	expressive
disobedient	strong
manipulative	charismatic
always has to have her own way	committed to her goals
obstinate	not easily swayed, confident
resistant	focused
bossy	future manager
temperamental	whimsical
mouthy	honest

How did you do?

If you were able to come up with a positive label for each negative one on this list, you are on your way to becoming a real visionary! If you were able to develop ten or more positive labels, you're doing great. If after three days of working on this you're still on number five, I suspect you're a little stressed. Stress hinders your imagination. Get some exercise, take a hot bath, walk with a friend, go out on a date, decide you really don't have to do something that's on your calendar, and then try again. This next exercise may help you get started if you're still having trouble.

Describe a Favorite Photograph

1. Select a favorite photograph of your child. Place it in front of you.

2. Describe the photograph for someone (like me) who cannot see it but would like to enjoy it:

Describe your child's expression.
Tell us how he or she is dressed.
How is her body positioned?
What's in the background?

3. Why does this photograph delight you?

Hear Those Words

Once your new, positive label list is complete, read it out loud. Start by saying, "I am the parent of a spirited child." Go on to add the words from our list: "Spirited children are independent, persistent, future leaders, sensitive, hold high standards, organized,

analytical, creative, expressive, strong, committed to their goals, not easily swayed, and confident."

Hear those words! Feel those words!
What happens inside when you hear them?
Write down your feelings and thoughts here.

When my child is described positively I feel

____

____

____

____

____

In class I read the list of positive labels slowly, emphatically, then paused.

Lynn laughed. "Wow! I never knew I had it so good!"

Phil grinned broadly. "It is pretty amazing."

Diane blew her bangs off her forehead. "Whew, they really are qualities we admire in adults."

PRACTICE, PRACTICE, PRACTICE

Brent leaned forward, perusing the completed chart. "Yeah, sure," he muttered. "Danny's tearing apart his room, and I'm supposed to say, 'Danny, you really are energetic.' Give me a break!"

I had to agree. "It would be awkward. That's why the vision the words create is so important. You want to stop Danny from destroying his room; it isn't all right for him to be destructive. But as you approach him, you can either be thinking, 'There's Danny, the destructive brat going at it again,' or be telling yourself, 'Danny is a kid with very strong feelings. He must be extremely upset about something.' This vision of Danny will help you stay calmer and allow you to feel more compassionate rather than victimized as you curtail the destructive behavior and help him find words or appropriate actions to express those feelings."

Brent looked doubtful.

My mind raced. How could I help him understand?

"What do you see in this room?" I asked.

"Is this a trick?" Brent questioned.

"No. There isn't a right answer. Anyone, what do you see?"

Quickly we brainstormed: people, posters, papers, blue/gray walls, people listening.

"What red things do you see in the room?"

They looked at me quizzically, then began brainstorming again: three red coats, a chair, the wall border, the bow on the stuffed bear, red letters on the bulletin board, the minute hand on the clock, and flowers. Suddenly minute details that we hadn't noticed earlier stood out.

I pointed out to the group that we see what we're looking for. "Let's apply that thought to everyday situations," I said. "Give me examples of things your kids did this week."

"I asked Kristen to take her plate from the table to the cupboard," Maggie began. "She looked right at me and said, 'No!'"

"Andy, my three-year-old, took all of my pots and pans out of the cupboards and created a percussion ensemble," Diane offered.

Phil added, "When we left class last week, Tara took off running in the parking lot."

"All right," I said. "Let's take each one of these scenarios and come up with a negative response and then a positive one."

Situation	***Negative Response***	***Positive Response***
Kristen refusing to clear plate	Kristin, you are so defiant! I don't know how I ever got such a stubborn kid!	Kristen, you do like to be independent. But remember, in our family everyone helps.
Andy creating a percussion ensemble from pots and pans	Andy, you are so destructive. How dare you use my pots and pans for drums!	Andy, you are creative and quite the musician too. But I'm worried about my pots and pans getting scratched. What else could you use for drums?

Situation	*Negative Response*	*Positive Response*
Tara running in the parking lot	Tara, *no*! I don't know what I'm going to do with you. You're so wild. You're out of control!	Stop, Tara! Running in a parking lot is not safe. I can tell your body is full of energy right now, but you must hold my hand. When we get home you can run in the yard. Now you can hop, you can gallop, but you must stay with me.

You can see from these examples that positive responses do *not* excuse bad behavior. They simply help us create a positive image of the child and remind us of the child's value as an individual with potential strengths.

Remember that when you see your child in a positive light, you respond more warmly. You listen better, and you react in ways that are more effective. It isn't easy to keep that positive vision in negative situations, but you can start using the positive words on the good days, when it's easy. The image created will gradually grow and direct you even during the tough times.

Maggie pressed her back against her chair. "But what do you say to other people? Yesterday I picked up Brian from his first day at a new school. He's only six, a first grader. His teacher shook her head and huffed. 'He was very defiant today.' What could I say? I was shocked, embarrassed, hurt! I just grabbed him and ran out the door."

"Have you considered another school?" Phil questioned.

Part of me felt as Phil did, but I knew all the facts weren't in and it was too early to make that kind of a decision.

"It's very difficult to respond when other adults, especially those in authority positions like teachers, physicians, grandparents, or child care providers, speak ungraciously about your child," I said. "It's fine to go back later and talk with your child's teacher after you've had time to think about your response and she's not quite so frustrated. You don't have to have an immediate answer.

But it is important to let her know that you are aware that your child is strong and independent. You'll also want to let her know that Brian may have been frightened on the first day at his new school. He might have needed more time, or a warning that something needed to be done. It's very likely that your perspective will help her to see your child's potential strengths. Allow her time to get to know your son better. If she doesn't respond positively over time, you may have to consider another classroom. Remember the Pygmalion effect—her vision will affect your son's performance."

Our time was up. "Keep the vision," I called out as they left the room. "Think positively and notice what happens." I noted Brent still didn't look convinced as he left.

SAVOR YOUR SUCCESSES

"Those labels are contagious!" Phil exclaimed the next week. "Tara, our four-year-old, was really being difficult. She was stomping her feet and being very demanding. My wife and I have gotten very tired of this behavior, but I decided I'd try the vision." He exaggerated *vision,* raising his arms to the ceiling as though looking to the heavens.

"I looked at my wife and wisecracked, 'My, isn't Tara feeling assertive today.' I was joking, but I just kept it up. She really is committed to her goals. I don't think Tara totally understood what I was saying, but she liked the tone and started to smile. She couldn't smile and stomp at the same time. Suddenly we were all laughing."

"I wasn't that successful," Maggie reported, "but I did find myself more tolerant and understanding."

"I'm so stressed," Sarah murmured. "I realized I haven't been able to see anything positive. That's my problem. I guess I have to start with me."

I reached across the table to touch her arm. "That's what's interesting about being a parent," I said. "We get to learn about ourselves too—things like recognizing you got yourself and four kids to class tonight. And you came up with some great positive labels."

She looked at me and vowed, "I am going to try to be more positive. I really am."

Gathering my papers after the group had left, I realized I was feeling great about Sarah's last comment. But I was also a bit frustrated. I'd hoped a fresh point of view might help Brent see things more positively. But it didn't seem to have had much impact. Maybe, I thought, if I had used another exercise, if I had somehow just been a better teacher, but then I reminded myself that every individual learns at his own pace. I didn't know what Brent's experience had been. I didn't know how many hurdles had been thrown in his path. My job was to give information, ask questions, offer experiences. Patience, I reminded myself. But I didn't want to be patient. I'm really not a very patient person, especially when I have a goal in mind. I reviewed the lesson of the day in my mind once again: focus on strengths. I thought about Brent. What were his strengths? He was funny. He'd made all of us laugh several times during the group. And even though he really had been "sent by his wife" to class, he was getting there on his own—she worked nights. So I walked out thinking about the dad with a great sense of humor. The one who obviously cared.

Record Your Successes

1. Imagine that your child has been asked to write an essay entitled "Who Am I?" How would she describe herself? (Even if she's only two years old, someday she'll be asked this question, and her answer is forming now.)

2. What positive labels did you use today to describe your child?

3. How did you feel when you heard those positive words?

4. Who can encourage you if you're struggling to create that positive vision?

CORNERSTONE

A positive vision of your child begins with the words you use. Circle your favorites, and add a few.

affectionate	innovative	confident
alert	more!	independent
bright	creative	persistent
buoyant	a leader	organized
capable	articulate	analytical
competent	perceptive	expressive
caring	athletic	strong
determined	coordinated	charismatic
exciting	passionate	honest
energetic	sensitive	playful
imaginative	deeply caring	funny
sparkly	committed to goals	

Add your own.

Hang this list on your refrigerator so it's there for you on the bad days.

3

WHAT MAKES KIDS SPIRITED?

Identifying the Triggers

IN PREPARATION

- Read Chapters 3 and 4 in *Raising Your Spirited Child.*
- Grab a pen.

CHAPTER HIGHLIGHTS

- A definition of *temperament.*
- A profile of your child's temperament.
- A profile of your own temperament.
- Identification of the key temperament triggers for you and your child.

THINGS TO OBSERVE

- What is your child's first reaction to new things?
- How is your child's reaction similar to or different from your own?
- What is your child's reaction to surprises?
- What is yours?

People are different. Recognizing and understanding these differences is essential to building healthy relationships. So today when the parents and children arrived they found huge rolls of paper spread across the floor of the early-childhood classroom. Next to the paper was a dishpan full of purple tempera paint, a dishpan filled with warm water, and a big brush. The theme was animal tracks, and each child was invited to make his own tracks.

Brent's six-year-old, Danny, immediately tore off his shoes and socks and demanded to be first. He giggled as the paintbrush tickled his toes. Quickly he jumped from the chair to the paper and stomped across it. Sarah's four-year-old daughter, Sadie, watched. Only her eyes gave away her interest. Intently focused, she observed Danny's every move. Diane's five-year-old son, Brandon, cut in line ahead of Sadie. She backed away, content to be a spectator as she slid her thumb into her mouth. Brandon requested that only his toes be painted, then tiptoed across the sheet. Sadie watched. Brandon washed up, and five other children made their prints, some hopping, others sliding, one very precisely forming "perfect" tracks. Sadie waited. Finally, when no other child was in line, her thumb dropped from her mouth. "I want to try," she told the teacher softly.

Carefully she removed her shoes. Refusing the teacher's help, she chose to paint her own feet. Starting with her toes, she tiptoed across the sheet like Brandon, then, sitting down again, she painted her soles and heels before prancing across the floor. Then she stopped, added more paint, stomped and laughed. She continued making tracks for the next twenty minutes, walking on her heels, the sides of her feet, in small steps and huge leaps. Each child had made tracks, but their methods were very different. These differences reflect their temperament.

Research has demonstrated that children are born with a tendency to act and react to people and events in their lives in specific ways that can be identified and predicted. The reactions are relatively consistent for each child in different situations and at different times. This preferred style of responding, a child's first and most natural way of reacting to the world around him, is called his temperament.

Temperament describes a range of different characteristics that include our energy level, the intensity of our emotions, and how quickly we adjust to new situations. Danny and Brandon jumped right into making animal tracks. Sadie waited and watched before participating. Their temperamental styles are different. A child like Sadie, who is temperamentally cautious in new situations, not only prefers to watch and listen first, but *needs* time to warm up in order to feel comfortable and participate fully.

Until the 1950s temperament wasn't given much credence in the child-development field. Up to this point, the "experts" told us that a child's personality was determined by the parenting he received. Nurture was everything. Parents' protests that their children had arrived with their own style of reacting were ignored or minimized.

Fortunately, a husband-wife team of psychiatrists, Alexander Thomas and Stella Chess, realized that parenting alone did not explain the differences in children. So they began observing infants in hospital nurseries and then followed them in their families until adulthood. Through their studies they identified distinct differences in how children respond to the world around them. As a result of their work and many studies since then, we now know that nature *and* nurture together determine children's personalities. For example, the temperamentally intense child will always have strong feelings, but it is not appropriate for him to throw lengthy tantrums or hurt others. He can learn to avoid the tantrums, communicate his strong feelings respectfully, and focus his intensity on worthwhile endeavors.

You cannot choose your child's temperament, but you are her guide, helping her to understand her temperament, emphasizing her strengths, and teaching her the skills she needs to express herself appropriately.

I hope the following exercise will demonstrate how important it is to identify and work with your child's preferred style of interacting with the world.

Write your name right here in this space.

____

How does that feel? A strange question, you might think, but go ahead and answer it.

When I write my name with my preferred hand, it feels

1. ______________________________

2. ______________________________

3. ______________________________

If I asked you to write me a letter with this hand, would you say yes or no?

____

Now, write your name in the space below with your nonpreferred hand.

____

How does that feel?

When I write my name with my nonpreferred hand it feels

1. ______________________________

2. ______________________________

3. ______________________________

If I asked you to write me a letter with this hand, would you say yes or no?

____

Did I hear a resounding "No"? That's typically the response I receive.

This exercise demonstrates that when you use your preferred style, in this case your dominant hand, you write easily, comfortably, naturally, and quickly. It's very likely, therefore, that when I ask you to do something more complicated or challenging, like write me a letter, you're willing to try.

If, however, I push you to use your nonpreferred hand, you feel awkward, frustrated, and maybe even embarrassed. As a result, if I ask you to try something more difficult, like writing a letter, your response is probably a flat-out refusal.

Spirited children—because they are more—are often pushed to use their nonpreferred style. In the classroom a high-energy child may be forced to be quiet too long. Or the child who finds transitions daunting may be faced with one surprise after another. Unprepared and pushed to "not be" who he is, the child may become exhausted and frustrated. He may even refuse to cooperate or simply quit trying.

Once you recognize and understand temperament traits, you'll be better able to work with your spirited kids in their preferred style as much as possible. I know the world is not perfect. Children can't always use their preferred style, but if they live in a family that respects their preferred style the majority of the time, they will have the energy to use their nonpreferred style when a situation requires it.

We'll start by getting a picture of your child's temperament and your own.

There are nine different temperament traits. Each of these traits can be placed on a continuum from a mild reaction to a strong reaction, or from low to high. Think about your child's first and most natural reaction in each category. Where would her typical response fall on the continuum? Remember, there isn't a right or wrong answer. Each style has its strengths and weaknesses. Your task is to get a picture of your child's temperament so that you can work with her to plan for success.

Once you've selected a response for your child, think about your own.

In class we review each trait together. I read the written examples, and the group members give me a few of their own. I'll share their responses with you, and you can add your own.

THE TEMPERAMENT TRAITS

1. INTENSITY

"'Intensity' describes the power of our emotional reactions. Kids who experience mild reactions rarely fuss, and if they do, it's only for a short period of time."

Before I could continue, Brent interrupted. "And those quiet kids belong to your sister-in-law," he joked, "the one you don't like."

Diane hooted and pointed at Brent, adding, "And she thinks she's doing something right and you're doing something wrong, because your child throws a fit over anything and hers doesn't!"

I smiled with them. "Spirited children do experience every emotion strongly and powerfully. Many are loud and expressive, but some are not loud at all. Their intensity is directed inward—until they surprise you with a blowup that seems to come out of nowhere, leaving you wondering what you're doing wrong. The reality is you're not doing anything wrong. Spirited kids tend to be more reactive. When they're stressed, their brain immediately tells them to be ready for fight or flight, so they get upset more easily and they stay upset longer."

Sarah pushed her hair behind her ear and sighed. "That's David. He isn't loud, but the intensity seeps through his pores like invisible waves of energy. You can feel it coming—it crawls up your neck."

Think about your child. Can you expect strong emotional reactions? What about your own reaction? Circle your responses. Feel free to add your own examples.

INTENSITY

How deeply and powerfully are emotions experienced? Is every emotional reaction mild or intense?

MILD REACTIONS	INTENSE REACTIONS
squeaks when upset	every reaction is strong and powerful
is not easily riled	a scrape or fall can be a blood-curdling experience
easily stops crying	is certain she'll flunk or things will never be better
	turns purple when upset is easily frustrated

YOUR CHILD'S REACTION

1	2	3	4	5
mild				intense

YOUR REACTION

1	2	3	4	5
mild				intense

2. PERSISTENCE

Spirited children stick to their guns. They stay committed to their goals even when faced with obstacles. Kids who are not persistent will often let go of an activity or idea when faced with an obstacle, making it easier to redirect them. Spirited kids are not easily redirected, and it is impossible to ignore them. They don't take no for an answer, and they won't quit.

Diane threw down her pen. "Yesterday Andy wanted a Coke. I told him no Coke before dinner. 'Coke, Coke, Coke,'" she mimicked. "I offered him juice, milk, water—no good. I wasn't about to give him a Coke. I started to get real ticked, so I walked out of the kitchen. The minute I turned my back on him he was opening the refrigerator. I ran back in and slammed the door shut. He screamed for the next forty-five minutes!"

"That's a child committed to his goals," I remarked.

"I guess," Diane admitted, "but he really can make my steam engines roll."

"It can be very challenging to live with a persistent child," I agreed. "At the peak of a conflict you both want to *win*!"

Diane smiled.

Think about your child. Is she committed to her goals or easy to redirect?

How persistent are you?

PERSISTENCE

If you tell your child to stop doing something that interests him or he wants to finish, does he stop or fight to continue? Now ask the same question of yourself.

EASILY STOPS	**PUSHES TO CONTINUE**
can be redirected quite easily	continues despite obstacles or difficulties
asks to try something but may lose interest after the first try	wakes up with plans for things he wants to accomplish that day
accepts no for an answer	insists on doing things herself
	needs to finish tasks
	never takes no for an answer
	locks in
	likes to negotiate
	is certain he's right

YOUR CHILD'S REACTION

1	2	3	4	5
easily stops				pushes to continue

YOUR REACTION

1	2	3	4	5
easily stops				pushes to continue

---

3. SENSITIVITY

Some people are very aware of sights, sounds, textures, smells, tastes, and noises. Others are not.

Maggie pointed at her temperament chart. "I swear this story is true. The kids were eating all of the junk food, so I hid it. Brian went through the house sniffing like a drug dog until he found the fruit snacks in my dresser drawer!"

Diane looked puzzled. "Brandon is sensitive to sights, smells, and sounds, but Justin isn't. He reacts to emotions."

"You're both very observant," I responded.

Over the years I have learned that some people are sensitive to smells but not textures. Others notice emotions but are not sensitive to sensorial stimulation, like odors or colors. Clothing may trigger reactions in some children, but foods may not bother them. When selecting your response to this question, think about the intensity of your child's response. For example, if your child is extremely sensitive to emotions but not to other things, select a 5 because that one area is very important to her and you will want to take note of it. We'll talk more about the different aspects of sensitivity in Chapter 7.

SENSITIVITY

Think about your child's reaction to slight noises, emotions, changes in temperature, tastes, and textures. Does he react to certain foods, tags in clothing, irritating noises, or other people's stress?

LOW SENSITIVITY	HIGH SENSITIVITY
sleeps through noisy routines	is bothered by lint, strings, or tags in clothing
isn't affected by scratchy textures	complains about smells or bright lights
eats most foods—isn't concerned about textures, smells, or temperatures	finds shopping centers, amusement parks, and other loud, bright places overwhelming

experiences more pain and requires more pain medication

is keenly aware of and responsive to other people's emotions

YOUR CHILD'S REACTION

1	2	3	4	5
low sensitivity				high sensitivity

YOUR REACTION

1	2	3	4	5
low sensitivity				high sensitivity

4. PERCEPTIVENESS

Perceptive kids notice the four-leaf clover in the grass; the color, make, and model of the car that just passed; the Christmas tree hung on the construction crane; and the ant crawling on the window glass. It seems as though perceptive individuals have antennas out, picking up all of the extraneous information and stimulation around them. As a result it can be very challenging for them to sort out the most important information or to remain focused on their original goal.

Sarah touched her hand to her chest. "That must be why I have to put a light blanket over Kim when I nurse her. Otherwise she turns at every sound and takes the nipple with her!"

"Ouch!" Lynn responded. "Isn't that a killer? Aaron did that too. Now when we're driving he always notices the hawks on the electrical poles, and last week, when we were at a friend's cabin, he was the first to spot deer feeding. But it's a problem for him at school because he complains about all the distracting noises and movement. How do you know if they're perceptive or have attention deficit?"

I am frequently asked this question. There isn't a simple answer. Both perceptive individuals and children experiencing attention deficit hyperactivity disorder (ADHD) tend to be very visual. Verbal directions alone may not capture their attention. In order to help them hear you, you have to add visual cues to your words. For example, in the early-childhood room, the teacher tells the kids that it's almost time for circle *and* turns the traffic light that is mounted in the corner to yellow. When it's time to stop, she says, "Stop," *and* turns the light to red. The same is true at home. You can tell your child to put on his shoes *and* place them in front of him as you speak. Or you can tell him to start the dishwasher *and* write a note.

When you give both verbal and visual directions, perceptive kids are able to follow them and stay focused. Visual instructions are also very helpful to children experiencing attention deficit, but even with the visual cues these children are not able to stay focused. One child with attention deficit told me, "It's as though there's a hundred radio stations in my head and I can't tune in to any one of them." Distinguishing a perceptive child from one who is also experiencing attention deficit requires a complete medical analysis. In Chapter 8 we'll talk more about attention deficit.

Right now, think about how perceptive your child is. How easily does outside stimuli pull her away from what she's doing? If she is perceptive but *not* easily distracted, circle a 3. If she is very perceptive *and* easily distracted, circle a 5. How perceptive and distractible are you?

PERCEPTIVENESS

How easily do outside stimuli interfere with or change the direction of your child's behavior? How aware is she of people, colors, noises, and objects around her? Does she frequently forget to do what is asked because something else catches her attention? How about you?

LOW PERCEPTIVENESS/ NOT EASILY DISTRACTED	**VERY PERCEPTIVE/ EASILY DISTRACTED**
may not notice your new haircut	needs visual cues in order to hear you

remains focused despite outside stimulation/can read an entire book while riding on the school bus	goes to get dressed, notices a toy, and stops to play
remembers multiple directions	easily forgets what he was about to do when something else catches his attention
	finds multiple directions difficult to follow
	stops sucking if someone passes by while he's nursing

YOUR CHILD'S REACTION

1	2	3	4	5
low perceptiveness				high perceptiveness

YOUR REACTION

1	2	3	4	5
low perceptiveness				high perceptiveness

5. ADAPTABILITY

I think of adaptability as the sneaky trait because the triggers often seem to come out of nowhere. Your child has been playing beautifully—until you ask her to come to dinner. Then she bursts into tears. Or you ask her if she'd like something to drink. She tells you yes, but when you hand her the glass she gets upset because the glass is the wrong color. Or your child protests going to swimming lessons, but once you get him there he's fine—until you try to get him out of the pool. The common factor in all of these situations is a shift from one thing, place, or expectation to another. These transitions are often hard to recognize. Adaptability describes our ability to cope with these "little" things that can make or break our day.

Sarah shifted in her chair and exhaled. "Maybe Sadie is slow to adapt. Yesterday I was grocery shopping, and she was in the cart. I told her I had to go to the bathroom, but she wouldn't get out of the cart. I had to go! So there I was, one hand holding the infant seat with the baby in it, the other grabbing Sadie to drag her into the bathroom with me. I was surprised someone didn't call security, she was screaming so loudly!" Tears of frustration filled Sarah's eyes as she realized how the simple act of moving from the cart to the bathroom could so upset Sadie.

ADAPTABILITY

How quickly does your child adapt to changes in his schedule or routine? How does he cope with surprises? How easy is it for him to shift from one activity to another? How about you?

ADAPTS QUICKLY	ADAPTS SLOWLY
goes with the flow	does not like change
	falls apart at the end of an activity
	is upset by surprises
is able to shift gears quickly	hates changing into different clothing as seasons change
is not easily upset by surprises	insists on wearing shorts even though the temperature has dropped to 40 degrees Fahrenheit
easily shifts from one activity to another	prefers same foods
	has taken a peanut-butter-and-jelly sandwich for lunch every day for years
	experiences difficulty falling asleep or getting back to sleep if wakes during the night
	needs lots of time to wake up

YOUR CHILD'S REACTION

1	2	3	4	5
adapts quickly				slow to adapt

YOUR REACTION

1	2	3	4	5
adapts quickly				slow to adapt

---

6. REGULARITY

How predictable are your eating, sleeping, and eliminating patterns? In their studies Chess and Thomas found that some individuals are very regular and predictable about their schedules. You know they will always be hungry at noon or ready for bed at ten. Other people are very unpredictable. One day they may want lunch at noon, the next day not until one o'clock or maybe not at all.

"That's Tara and me," Phil remarked. "And it drives my wife crazy. You never know when Tara will be tired or if this is an eating day or not. It doesn't bother me, but my wife, who is very regular in her schedule, finds it extremely irritating. She can't imagine why or how anyone could skip a meal. She gets a headache if dinner is fifteen minutes late."

Where on the continuum does your child fall? Are her body rhythms regular or irregular? How about yours?

REGULARITY

Is your child quite regular about eating, sleeping, and other bodily functions? How about you?

REGULAR	**IRREGULAR**
needs to eat, sleep, and eliminate at very specific times	naps and bowel movements occur irregularly
falls asleep at a predictable time each day	may have eating days and noneating days
needs to eat at specific times throughout the day	may "graze," wanting to snack
	is not always tired at bedtime

YOUR CHILD'S REACTION

1	2	3	4	5
regular				irregular

YOUR REACTION

1	2	3	4	5
regular				irregular

7. ENERGY

Stop what you're doing right now and take note. Are you sitting quietly? Are you fidgeting and moving about? Is your foot wiggling? Are your nails getting shorter? Are you tapping your pen or chewing on it? Have you been twisting and stretching or sitting quietly?

Some of us have a very high energy level and need to move around, while others can sit quietly for an extended period.

Diane jokingly tapped on the table with her pen to get our attention. "How do you survive when you've got three boys under eight and they all score fives on the energy scale? I swear, between the hours of five and seven every night I'd like to move out of my house. That's when Andy and Justin really rev up. They wrestle, chase the dog, climb on the couch, and dart through the house. Andy has always been really athletic. He was riding a bike at three. Justin, the eight-year-old, is also very coordinated, but what amazes me is that he is constantly falling off his chair at dinner or spilling his juice."

Diane's kids are very energetic. What are yours like? How energetic are you?

ENERGY

Is your child always on the move and busy or quiet and quiescent? Does he need to run, jump, and use his whole body in order to feel good?

LOW ACTIVITY	HIGH ACTIVITY
may sit quietly for extended periods	gets irritable if there hasn't been time for exercise
will sit through religious service or dinner at a restaurant	fidgets
will play quietly in one place for extended periods	doesn't like being restrained in the car seat, stroller, or high chair
	loves to climb
	frequently spills things or falls out of his chair at meal times

YOUR CHILD'S REACTION

1	2	3	4	5
low activity				high activity

YOUR REACTION

1	2	3	4	5
low activity				high activity

8. FIRST REACTION

What is your child's first reaction when she's asked to meet new people or try new activities, ideas, or places? The key word here is *new.* First reaction is often confused with adaptability. The two traits are quite similar, but first reaction describes how we react to things that are new.

This time it was quiet, reflective John who had the example. "Kelly plays eighth-grade basketball. It was her turn to sit on the bench with the varsity team. The coach uses this as a ploy to encourage the eighth-grade girls to dream of playing varsity ball. Every game two eighth-grade girls sit on the bench. That's it. They don't go out on the court. They don't have to say or do anything—just sit there. But Kelly was upset. Three days before the game her stomach hurt. She was worried. She didn't know what to expect. She didn't want to go. Ultimately she did go and was fine, but it wasn't easy for her. I hate to see it, because I know she reacts like me—it's my genes, and I really wish she didn't have to deal with this discomfort." Clearly John was distressed.

"I bet you don't get into trouble for doing things without thinking," I said, offering another perspective.

He shrugged. "That's true, and neither does Kelly."

"Why do some spirited kids have a cautious first reaction?" Brent asked. "I'd think they'd be likely to jump into things."

Brent's question is a common one. Many people think it's more challenging to have the child who jumps right into things and often ends up in the emergency room. But gung-ho kids are frequently considered "all-American" or funny. Children who react with caution, who cling to their parents or refuse to participate, are often chastised for their wariness. Their parents are often told to push them and are criticized for coddling their children. This can make it very stressful to raise the child who experiences a cautious first reaction.

FIRST REACTION

What is your child's first reaction when she is asked to meet new people, try a new activity or idea, or go someplace new? What's yours?

JUMPS RIGHT IN	REJECTS AT FIRST
doesn't hesitate in new situations	initially says no when asked to try something new
leaps before looking	needs time to warm up to new things
is attracted to new people and things	experiences difficulty with anything new
frequently experiences "accidents"	says he wants to try something, then gets there and wants to go home
	frequently experiences a stomachache when trying something new

YOUR CHILD'S REACTION

1	2	3	4	5
jumps right in				rejects at first

YOUR REACTION

1	2	3	4	5
jumps right in				rejects at first

9. DISPOSITION

Is your child's prevailing disposition more serious or sunny? Some people are by their very nature more serious. They are not necessarily unhappy, they simply see life from a more sober point of view. Others are usually lighthearted. They tend to smile and laugh more. They may feel emotions intensely, but somehow they come up on the sunny side.

"Kristen is the serious kid," Maggie replied when I explained this trait. "She isn't grumpy, but she approaches things very factually. Yesterday I said the sun is out. She responded, 'Oh, yes, Mommy, the sun is out and there isn't a tornado or a flood.' She covered all of her bases. Even as a baby she was very selective about who received her smiles."

Brent whistled under his breath. "Danny's smiles save him. He's this wild, I mean, energetic, enthusiastic kid," he exaggerated, catching himself and looking at me. "But he's got a smile for everyone."

Is your child more serious or sunny? What about you?

9. DISPOSITION

Is your child more sunny or serious? What about you?

SUNNY	SERIOUS
sees the cup half full	notices what needs to be fixed
is usually in a good mood	is usually more staid
	may need to be reminded of what is good or nice
	tells you you've spent enough money shopping and it's time to go home
	may focus on the mistake he made in the soccer game rather than his two goals

YOUR CHILD'S REACTION

1	2	3	4	5
sunny				serious

YOUR REACTION

1	2	3	4	5
sunny				serious

Now you have a profile of your child's temperament and your own. Go back and tally your responses, then circle your total score.

SCORE:

My child is:

9–18	19–28	29–45
cool	**spunky**	**spirited**

I am:

9–18	19–28	29–45
cool	**spunky**	**spirited**

Diane leaned over and glanced at Sarah's profiles. "Hey, they aren't the same! Her spirited kids are different from mine. Could that be right, or did I do something wrong—again!"

I patted her arm. "Diane, you're doing just fine. You've just discovered that not all spirited children are alike. Each child is unique. Most spirited kids are more intense, persistent, sensitive, perceptive, and slow to adapt—but not all. The way we perceive our child's temperament may be influenced by our own temperament. For example, if you are temperamentally very energetic and your child is also, you may simply see his activity level as average and circle 3 for both of you. However, if you are temperamentally not energetic, you may perceive that same child's activity level as a 5+ because his style is so different from your own. That's why if you do this exercise with your partner, you may each come up with a different score for your child. That's fine. What's most important is that you get a picture of your child's temperament so that you can predict her typical reactions and your own. Then you can identify the triggers and plan for success together."

"Diane," I asked, "are you a four or five on intensity?"

She glanced down on her sheet. "How did you know?"

I just smiled, rather pleased with myself—temperament really can help us predict people's reactions.

EFFECTIVE STRATEGIES

"As you look at your profiles, what did you learn about your child and yourself?" I asked the group.

Phil sat back in his chair and tossed his pen into the middle of the table. "I've been wondering where these kids came from. I knew T.J. was just like my dad. He never sits down. He's really intense—but I didn't think I was spirited. I thought I was pretty mellow, but according to the profile I am very spirited."

We laughed, having noticed Phil get up for coffee and water three times during the hourlong discussion.

"Me too," Diane added. "I guess I knew I was spirited, but I didn't think I was off the chart."

Lynn leaned forward. "I'm not spirited, but I didn't realize how regular I am. No wonder it was so hard for me when the kids were little and waking me at night. Now I know why I don't want them to stay up on weekends—it's because *I* can't."

"I think it's easier when you're alike," Phil commented. "Because neither Tara nor I want, need, or like regular eating schedules. I understand her. It doesn't scare me or bother me when she isn't hungry."

John shook his head. "Todd and I are both very intense."

"You're intense?" Brent asked.

"Yeah." He laughed. "I know, quiet John. That's what you see here. My intensity doesn't show in public, but it's there, especially at home or when I reach the end of my rope. Todd is so much like me. How do I teach him the difference between being assertive and aggressive when I can't figure it out myself? I'm either passive or bellowing. There is no in-between for me." He stopped abruptly, frustrated with himself. I could feel his tension.

"Intensity is passion," I replied. "It's drive and determination. And in the weeks ahead we'll spend a great deal of time talking about how to manage it and use it in those very positive ways."

John sighed and got up to get a glass of water.

Diane squirmed in her chair. "I can feel all of this emotion." She laughed, rotating her shoulders and neck to shake it off. "And Justin is sensitive like me—we're two peas in a pod. I actually experience his feelings. If he's sad, I'm crying too. Then I'm not his mother, I'm his soul mate. But my reaction doesn't help either one of us." She shook herself all over.

Sarah waited for Diane to finish, then glanced down at her worksheet. "This isn't the child I expected at all. I don't know what I expected, but this wasn't it. The nurses even told me, the day he was born—good luck with this one. I remember those words, and I've just kept thinking, why me?" Her eyes glistened, and she put her hand up to her mouth, choking back the tears. We waited. "But with this exercise," she continued, sniffing, "I can see that he's really cautious in new situations. I guess that's an aha for me. Maybe that's why he didn't want to go to the circus last week. He's never been to one before. Maybe he wasn't just trying to make the rest of us miserable."

Letting go of the dream child we imagined having and discovering the strengths and joys of the one who actually lives with us can sometimes be a very a tough task. You might find yourself grieving, wondering if there is anything you can do to fix it. While you do not get to choose your child's temperament, you do have control of *your* responses. You can learn strategies that help your child to be successful, no matter what his temperament. You really can believe that he does have tremendous strengths and potential, and you can learn strategies to help you enjoy your time together.

"You're in the right place," I assured her.

And so are you.

Review the temperament profiles.

What did you learn about your child and yourself? Record your thoughts here.

____

____

____

____

____

PRACTICE, PRACTICE, PRACTICE

It doesn't matter if your child is similar to or different from you in temperament. What is important is getting a picture of the real child who has come into your life, not the fantasy child you might have imagined before birth.

Review your temperament chart again. This time select the traits that you realize are the most challenging for you to handle. These are your "trigger traits." For example, if your child rates 4 on sensitivity and you realize you are constantly battling over clothing, food, lighting, or smells, list sensitivity as one of your top three triggers. If your child scores 5 on energy but this trait rarely causes difficulties for either you or your child, don't list it here.

The top three trigger traits for my child and me are

1. ______________________________

2. ______________________________

3. ______________________________

These three temperament trigger traits for you and your child are a starting point for your plan for success. Now you can establish your priorities and focus your efforts.

"Who wants to publicly commit to working on one specific trait?" I asked the group.

"No commitments!" they complained. But I turned to my left, and Phil was willing to give it a shot. Leaning back in his chair until he almost toppled over, he said, "I'm choosing energy. My kids and I are always on the move, and I just don't know why." We laughed with him.

"How about you, Brent?" I asked.

"Persistence," he grumbled.

I couldn't help it. "Good choice!" I exclaimed. He didn't think I was funny.

John selected intensity. "I've got to get a handle on my own before I can help Todd with his," he said.

"Sensitivity," Diane stated. "I have to feel comfortable with it."

Lynn and Maggie both selected intensity because their kids were more intense than they. Trying to understand their strong reactions was very difficult for them. John agreed to offer an "insider's" point of view.

Finally we came to Sarah. My glance was met with silence. She shrank in her chair. Finally she said softly, "I'm not sure. Can you pick nine? They're all a problem for us."

"You can see the whole picture," I acknowledged, "but sometimes when you're learning new skills the whole picture can be overwhelming. Which one is the most challenging to cope with?" Again she shook her head.

"Do you need to think about it? It's all right to take your time. Use this week to reflect. Which temperament trigger sets you and your child off most often? I'll check with you next week and ask if you've found your starting point or if you'd like help." Sarah nodded, tears welling.

"Everyone ready to take this information home and try it?" I asked.

Brent raised his hand. "One question. So the kid is persistent or sensitive—won't he just outgrow it?"

Thinking quickly, I asked, "Brent, are you right-handed or left-handed?"

"Right," he replied.

"Okay, imagine this," I said. "Your assignment is to use your left hand as your preferred hand all week. I don't want you to be right-handed anymore. I want you to write with your left hand, eat with it—everything. You need to grow out of being right-handed. You need to just stop it!" I paused breathlessly. "What do you think?"

He looked at me curiously—I suspect questioning my sanity—then shook his head and smiled. The group broke up. Catching Sarah's attention, I gave her a thumbs-up. She nodded ever so slightly.

What's your starting point? Which temperament trait would you like to focus on in the next few weeks? If you need to think about it, come back in a day or two and complete this exercise.

The temperament trait I will focus on is

SAVOR YOUR SUCCESSES

It is so important to savor our successes and build from them. For this reason I start every class discussion with a report. "Who has a success to share?" I asked the following week.

"I found out I'm a pretty good lefty," Brent joked.

I laughed. I liked this guy.

Sarah shyly raised her hand. My heart leapt. I was so pleased that she had a success to report. "With four kids, it seems like someone is always upset," she began. "I didn't notice any pattern. I guess I was just too busy and tired. I've always been waiting for the next explosion, never knowing what will hit me. But this week I realized David reacts every time there is a surprise or change."

"Yes!" I cheered. "And that information can help you to *prevent* the blowups because you now recognize the temperament trigger."

Sarah slid back, more relaxed than I'd ever seen her in group. "Do you take high fives?" I asked her.

"Yes," she said, so I gave her a great big, full-swing one. "You're doing it, Sarah. You're noticing the cues and tying them to temperament. You've got it!"

Savor your successes too.

Record your success:

I realized my child's reaction was tied to temperament when I saw

1. ______________________________

2. ______________________________

3. ______________________________

I am noticing that my child and I are easily triggered when

____

____

____

CORNERSTONE

- ✔ **People are different.**
- ✔ **Each of us is born with a preferred style of interacting with the world around us, called our temperament.**
- ✔ **There are nine different temperament traits, which describe how intense, persistent, sensitive, perceptive, adaptable, regular, and energetic we are; how we approach new situations; and our prevailing mood.**
- ✔ **Understanding our own temperament and our child's helps us to maximize our strengths and work together more effectively.**

4

EXTROVERT OR INTROVERT

Finding the Energy to Cope

IN PREPARATION

- Read Chapter 5 in *Raising Your Spirited Child.*

CHAPTER HIGHLIGHTS

- Cues to help you recognize the introverts and extroverts in your family.
- Clarification of what introverts and extroverts need to recharge.
- Strategies for those daily tough times.
- Strategies for working together as a family.

THINGS TO OBSERVE

- When your child is playing and other children come to join him, does he choose to move away, tell them or push them to move away, slide over to give himself more space, or continue to play?
- After being with a group, does your child seem to be drained or energized?

I am a writer. I spend hours working at my computer with only Sunny Autumn Frost, my yellow Labrador, to keep me company. I love writing, but it's exhausting work for me. I often write with my headset on—the one connected to my telephone. I have a lengthy list of willing listeners who give me feedback and keep me going.

I'm also a teacher. After each class for parents, I'm energized, challenged to find new exercises or to explore the research further, or elated that a lesson really seemed to work. I meet with families privately too, in what I call tutoring sessions. I like getting to know individual families and helping them with their concerns. In addition, I speak. The audiences range from fifty parents at a preschool to a thousand parents and professionals at a national convention. No matter what, I am always scared, really nervous before I begin. So I always talk to people in the crowd as they arrive. By focusing on them, instead of me, I feel better. After I speak I can't sleep—I'm too charged.

As you can see, my profession is multifaceted. Over time, I have learned the behaviors necessary for me to be able to spend time alone, work with a group, or to talk with individuals. Although I can learn these behaviors, I cannot control which of them recharge me and which ones drain me.

In 1942, spurred by the idea of bringing peace to the world by understanding individual differences, Katharine Briggs and her daughter, Isabel Briggs Myers, began developing the Myers-Briggs Type Indicator. Their work was based on the research of Swiss psychologist Carl Jung, who like Chess and Thomas believed that we are born with specific preferences. Two of those preferences Briggs and Myers described are introversion and extroversion, which explain how we get our emotional energy.

Extroverts recharge by seeking stimulation from the environment and others around them. They need to be with other people and actively "do" things in order to feel energetic.

Introverts recharge by going within. They need quiet and a break from stimulation in order to feel energized. Extroversion and introversion do not describe social skills or how much we talk. Those are learned behaviors.

Ultimately our personality styles reflect both these genetic preferences and early life experiences. That's why I can learn the behaviors I need for my profession but can't control which ones recharge me.

A NEW POINT OF VIEW

I am an extrovert, and while I have learned to spend time alone as a writer, it drains me. I have to admit, by the end of the day I get rather cranky. I *need* my husband to talk with me. My husband, however, is an introvert who spends most of his day in meetings. At night he *needs* some quiet, or he gets a bit irritable. Our differences could potentially lead to some nasty fights, but after more than twenty years of married life, we've learned to recognize our differences, empathize with each other's needs, and figure out how to work together.

As parents, we face the same challenge. It is our task to identify our children's preferred style of energizing, understand their point of view, and help them find ways to recharge without draining those around them. This is especially true for spirited children, who must keep their energy bank well stocked in order to manage their strong temperament.

So let's get down to business and figure out who in your family recharges as an extrovert and who prefers introversion. When you understand and recognize the differences between the introverts and extroverts in your family, instead of getting angry, you'll find solutions that work for everyone. Building healthy relationships requires recognizing the introverts and extroverts, appreciating the differences, empathizing with opposing needs, and finding ways to work together.

For our purposes a formal study in Psychological Type is not necessary. In order to discover your child's preference, we're just going to use information that your child gives to you each day. I've included a few examples from the group. I hope that their stories will help you link the concepts to behaviors you see every day. Once you've read the stories, complete the checklist which follows.

IF YOUR CHILD PREFERS EXTROVERSION, SHE PROBABLY . . .

1. THINKS BY TALKING

Extroverts need to hear their thoughts in order to figure out how they feel or what they want. It's important to recognize that what they say may not be their final decision. They're simply thinking out loud, sorting through emotions and ideas. They may not even need a response from you. Knowing you're listening may be enough.

Maggie laughed. "That's what Kristen must be doing!" she exclaimed. "She'll put her homework in the middle of the kitchen table and then proceed to say, 'Where are the scissors? Where's my pen?' I get really frustrated, because I'm thinking she wants me to get them for her. Maybe she's just thinking aloud."

"Don't you do that?" Diane asked. "I do. It drives my husband crazy. I'm always talking to myself, figuring out what I need to do or thinking something through. Yesterday he told me I was repeating myself, but I like to think of it as refining my thoughts." She laughed. Maggie looked at her blankly.

It was Lynn who acknowledged, "I do that too."

"Do little kids do this too?" Phil asked.

"Yes," I said. "You can see the preferences even in young children. Do you have an example?"

He nodded. "T.J. grabs our hands and drags us around the house pointing to things, saying, 'What that? What that?'"

Does your child think by talking?

2. BECOMES ENERGIZED IN A GROUP— EVEN ONE FILLED WITH STRANGERS

Extroverts are energized by groups of people. They are the individuals in your family who might reluctantly go to a party on a Friday night because they're tired, but once they're there they don't want to leave. They are the kids who come home from school or child care and complain, "I'm bored. Who can I invite over?" They are the people like me who love a kitchen that opens to the dining area so that they can talk with family or guests as they prepare a meal.

"Or they're kids like Tara, who even as a baby got so excited in a group that she'd coo and wave and start cycling her legs until she'd almost fall out of her infant seat," Phil added. "Now she's four and plans her life around her preschool days." The extroverts in the group all nodded.

Is your child energized by a group? Is she excited and talkative afterward? The key word is *energized.* Introverts may also be very social and work well in groups, but afterward they are quiet and drained rather than energized.

3. SEEKS ACTIVITY AND STIMULATION

Extroverts need activity and stimulation. If things are dull, your little extrovert may start picking on his siblings or the dog just to get some action going. They're the kids who come running home after school and yell, "I'm going to Katie's house be back by five o'clock!" as they run out the door. They're the babies who insist on being carried looking out at the world. They want to see the people, lights, colors, pets. Instead of being comforted by snuggling into your shoulder, they'll fuss and fume until you turn them around or take them out to do something.

"Oh, that reminds me of last Thanksgiving," Maggie said. "It was a wonderful, relaxing day. But on Friday Kristen was so grumpy. She wouldn't play by herself. Nothing would satisfy her. She kept asking, demanding to go do something. So I invited some friends over. The kids played like crazy. Kristen was ecstatic."

Does your child seek stimulation and activity? Does she get a bit grumpy if things are too mellow?

4. IS DRAINED BY SPENDING TOO MUCH TIME ALONE

Because extroverts are energized by being with people, they are drained by being alone too much. Little extroverts tend to hate time out. Send them to their room, and they're liable to sneak back out. If the only way you can get your child to take a break is to go with him, you probably have an extrovert. They are the kids who can't fathom why you would want to be alone in a room and join you to "cheer you up." Trying to get them to play alone is a major endeavor. They might play a few minutes, then start asking questions. Before you know what's happening, you'll find yourself either helping them or taking part in the game.

"I'm an extrovert," Diane interjected. "But after being with the kids all day I am not energized!"

Diane is right. If you are an extroverted parent who is at home full time with small children, you may find yourself exhausted by the end of the day. Interacting with small children does *not* energize the extroverted adult. That's why you need to get out with the kids, see other people, and do things.

Is your child drained by spending too much time alone?

5. LIKES AND NEEDS FEEDBACK

Extroverts like immediate feedback. They're the kids who finish a worksheet and bring it to you for your approval. They want to know what you're thinking and if you like what they're doing. You might worry about their self-esteem. You probably don't need to fret. It's likely that you have an extrovert who's simply seeking feedback. Does your child need lots of feedback?

6. IS ENERGIZED WORKING WITH OTHERS

Working with others and bouncing ideas off other people recharges the extrovert. If you can't get your extrovert to clean his room, go in and start working with him. It's amazing how hard he can work when he's got a companion. Create a quiet, comfortable study space for this child in his room, and you might be disappointed. It's likely that he prefers to do his homework at the kitchen table, where he can talk to you, ask questions, and be part of the action as he works. And if you can't get your little extrovert to dress himself, bring his clothes to the kitchen and let him dress while you make breakfast.

Does your child work most efficiently and energetically when he can work with others?

7. WANTS TO SHARE IDEAS AND EXPERIENCES IMMEDIATELY

Just try walking away from a little extrovert who's trying to tell you about her day. Lock yourself in the bathroom, and she'll stand outside the door and continue the conversation. Extroverts like to share their ideas immediately. They're the ones who give you a complete description of the day's experiences the minute you walk in the door. They're the kids who may actually put their hand on your face, turn your head to them, and demand, "Watch!" "Look!" Or "How about if we . . ." If you're an introvert, they can wear you out.

Does your child need to share ideas and experiences immediately?

Now review the following statements. Check each one that "fits" your child. As you complete the checklist remember both introversion and extroversion are on a continuum. Some people have a very strong preference, others only a mild one. Your child may demonstrate both extroverted and introverted behaviors. You simply need to know which one he *prefers* to use in order to keep his energy high.

If your child prefers extroversion she probably:

____ thinks by talking
____ is energized by a group
____ seeks stimulation and activity
____ is drained by being alone
____ likes and needs feedback
____ is energized by working with others
____ shares ideas and experiences immediately

Remember, this exercise is not a scientific instrument. If you are not certain of your answers, watch and listen more closely to your child. Try to pick up the cues, the words and actions that tell you how she is recharging.

Now let's take a look at the behaviors common to introverts.

IF YOUR CHILD PREFERS INTROVERSION, SHE PROBABLY . . .

1. THINKS BEFORE ANSWERING

Introverts need time to think before answering a question. They're not ready to talk about raw feelings. Ask them how they feel, and they may not answer, not because they're angry or are trying to be difficult—they simply need time to think in order to figure out how they feel. That's why many little introverts become talkative at bedtime. They've had time to reflect on their day and are now ready to converse. They're not just stalling.

"My husband," Diane declared, before I explained further. "I'll ask him, 'What do you want for dinner?' No answer. So I'll just start fixing something. Then he'll say, 'I thought we'd grill hamburgers!' But"—she flipped her hair back over her shoulder—"that's why we're still married. I talk and he listens."

John laughed. "That's my wife and me too. But it took me a while to convince her to give me some space and time."

"Doesn't she think you're mad at her?" Lynn asked.

Diane didn't wait for John to answer. She blurted out, "I still think my husband's mad at me!"

John shrugged. "I doubt he is. I know I'm not. I just haven't decided what my answer is yet."

Does your child need to think before answering?

2. BECOMES DRAINED WHEN AROUND GROUPS OF PEOPLE FOR TOO LONG

Introverts may enjoy being in groups but are drained by them. That's why your child may be a bear after school but an angel in the classroom. Introverts need their space and quiet time. Even teenagers, who love to be with their friends, may ask if the family could go away together for a quiet weekend retreat, to escape from all the demands of peer activities.

Little introverts may be fine in a family gathering, then suddenly fall apart. If they're playing with a friend, they may abruptly stop, sit down to watch television, or ask the friend to go home. If you're an extrovert, you may worry that they're being rude.

Is your child drained after spending too much time in a group?

3. NEEDS TO REDUCE STIMULATION AND ACTIVITY

Send your introvert to her room for time out, and you may have to go and get her because she doesn't want to come out. She isn't angry; she's playing all by herself and having a great time. Introverts need a break from stimulation and activity. They're the toddlers who will crawl under the table and sit there with their blanket, shielded from the activity around them. They're the kids who get into trouble for "escaping" from their classroom, especially around 11:00 A.M., when they need a break from the group.

Does your child need to reduce stimulation and activity in order to recharge?

4. HAS A STRONG DESIRE FOR PERSONAL SPACE

Introverts do need their space, not only their physical space but also their visual and auditory space. They are drained by crowding. They're the kids who move away from an activity when other kids start to play. At circle time, they may pull away from the group. They aren't being unsociable. They simply prefer to have more space and quiet.

John pointed to his chart. "That's my daughter, Kelly. On Wednesdays my wife picks up our kids and two neighbor kids after school. Getting in the car with the all the others really irritates Kelly. She constantly complains that the other kids are talking too much. If my wife brings a snack and lets them eat in the car, Kelly complains that they're chewing too loudly!"

"I believe it," Maggie replied. "Our family room is open to the kitchen. Brian complains if people walk by him when he's watching television or if I'm making noise in the kitchen. He's even complained when Kristen "looked at him!"

Brent adjusted his cap—his signal that he was about to speak. "Is that why my four-year-old will put her hands over her ears and shout, 'Everybody be quiet!'"

Maggie let out a long breath. "That's what Brian must have been doing the other day. He'd been playing in his room when his cousins came over. Everyone piled into his room. The next thing I knew he was running out. I thought he had to go to the bathroom, but he came back with a squirt gun and squirted them. It certainly did clear out his room."

Does your child have a strong desire for personal space?

5. IS SELECTIVE ABOUT WHICH FRIENDS SHE BRINGS HOME

Introverts may be elected class president. They can be very social and popular, but they may rarely invite friends over. I asked my introverted son one day why I had never met some of his friends. "I see them at school," he told me. "Why should I bring them home?" Introverts need less interaction than extroverts and thus tend to be more selective about their friends. Some need only a few close friends. If you're an extrovert, you may worry that your child isn't popular. But this may not be the case. As John said, "I like people, but enough is enough!"

Does your child tend to be more selective about which friends he brings home?

6. TALKS A LOT WITH FAMILY MEMBERS BUT IS QUIETER AROUND OUTSIDERS

The noisiest members of your family may be the introverts. When they are comfortable, introverts may sing loudly, be superb joke tellers, and talk your ear off—but they like to have control of the noise and choose when to converse. Around others, especially strangers, the introverts may be quiet until they feel comfortable. A teacher's request that your child participate more may be a tip-off that she prefers introversion.

Is your child more talkative with family members than with outsiders?

7. WATCHES OR LISTENS BEFORE JOINING IN AN ACTIVITY

Introverts need to process information internally. They prefer to watch or listen before joining in. If your child is an introvert, she may refuse to sing at school but will perform the entire song at home for you. You may worry that she'll never perform, but with practice and an opportunity to watch or listen first, introverts can be outstanding performers.

Does your child need to watch or listen before joining in an activity?

Now review the following statements. Check each one that "fits" your child.

If your child prefers introversion she probably:

- ____ thinks before talking
- ____ is drained after being in a group
- ____ needs to reduce stimulation and activity
- ____ has a strong desire for space
- ____ is selective about which friends are brought home
- ____ talks more with family members than with outsiders
- ____ watches or listens before joining an activity

How did you do? If you feel like you still need more information or would like to try a formal Myers-Briggs Indicator, you can contact the Center for Applications of Psychological Type, (800) 777-CAPT. I hope, though, you've gotten enough information to clarify your child's preference.

Your child doesn't live alone. He lives with you and the other members of your family—that's what makes this all so interesting. Identifying how each member of your family prefers to

recharge allows you to find ways for each individual to get his or her needs met without draining others.

1. In the first row write the name of each family member.
2. Check each statement that fits that individual.
3. Review your picture of each family member's preference.

Here's a sample from Sarah's family.

EXTROVERT TRAITS

Name	*Tom*	*Sarah*	*Cara*	*David*	*Sadie*	*Kim*
1. thinks by talking	x		x		x	
2. is energized by a group—even strangers	x		x			
3. seeks stimulation and activity	x		x	x	x	
4. is drained by being alone	x		x		x	
5. likes and needs feedback	x		x		x	x
6. is energized by working with others	x		x		x	
7. shares ideas and experiences immediately	x		x			
TOTAL	7	0	7	1	5	1

INTROVERT TRAITS

Names	*Tom*	*Sarah*	*Cara*	*David*	*Sadie*	*Kim*
1. thinks before answering		x		x		
2. is drained after being in a group		x		x		x

Names	Tom	Sarah	Cara	David	Sadie	Kim
3. needs to reduce stimulation and activity		x		x		x
4. has a strong desire for space		x	x	x		x
5. is selective about which friends are brought home		x	x	x		
6. talks more with family members than with outsiders		x		x		
7. watches or listens before joining an activity		x		x		x
TOTAL	0	7	2	7	0	4

You can see from Sarah's example that she and David both have a very strong preference for introversion. Cara, who demonstrated strong extrovert tendencies, shares some introverted qualities with her mother and brother. While she often recharges by being with others, her personal space needs to be respected. She doesn't like to be pushed into activities. Kim seems to be showing a preference for introversion, but because she is an infant, we are unable at this point to answer some of the questions for her. She'll show us her preferences as she grows and matures.

Your turn. A picture of your family:

EXTROVERT TRAITS

Name						
1. thinks by talking						
2. is energized by a group—even strangers						
3. seeks stimulation and activity						

Name						
4. is drained by being alone						
5. likes and needs feedback						
6. is energized by working with others						
7. shares ideas and experiences immediately						
TOTAL						

INTROVERT TRAITS

Name						
1. thinks before answering						
2. is drained after being in a group						
3. needs to reduce stimulation and activity						
4. has a strong desire for space						
5. is selective about which friends are brought home						
6. talks more with family members than with outsiders						
7. watches or listens before joining an activity						
TOTAL						

Here's an opportunity to test your new skill. Read the following scenario, and see if you can identify the introverts and extroverts.

A mom says, "I can predict that every day after school my kids will fight. My son will come home and just want to play video

games. My daughter wants him to play with her. She also wants me to talk with her, but I really get drained from her constant chatter. I tend to put her off, and they end up fighting."

From the information gained in the story, what do you think each person's preference is?

MOM

introvert or extrovert? Circle one

SON

introvert or extrovert? Circle one

DAUGHTER

introvert or extrovert? Circle one

My initial guess would be that the mom prefers introversion. She needs quiet and is "drained" by the "chatter." The son also prefers introversion; after being in school he seeks space and time alone. The daughter prefers extroversion. She needs to recharge by being with people and doing something.

This scenario may seem a bit obvious, but when your kids start to hassle one another or drive you nuts, it's easy to get caught in the moment and not stop to think What's really going on here? Recognizing the extroverts and introverts in your family allows you to understand what's happening. Instead of feeling like a victim, exhausted and hassled by your kids, you can use your new understanding to help your children plan for recharge without irritating one another or you. The next step is to understand what each individual needs to recharge most effectively and efficiently.

EFFECTIVE STRATEGIES

Spirited kids have to work harder to manage their strong temperaments. It is essential that each day include time and activities for them to recharge. How do you do it with all of the other demands facing you and your child? One important thing to remember is that you don't have to spend all day recharging. A mere fifteen minutes at the right point in the day can be enough.

I looked around the room. Brent was stringing paper clips together. Phil was up getting another glass of water, and Diane, who'd chosen to sit in the rocking chair, was pitching back and forth. We needed to move.

"To the lobby," I announced. "It's time for a human continuum." Brent eyed me suspiciously. Diane playfully jabbed at his shoulder. "Aww, come on," she said. "It can't hurt."

Pushing aside the jungle gym and the four-foot replicas of Bert and Ernie, I created enough space for all of us to stand in a line. On the board I drew a continuum, like this:

Extroverts   Introverts

"Imagine this line is on the floor, and place yourself on it," I directed the group. "Strong extroverts, please move to the left." Diane leaped to the far end. Lynn and Phil followed her.

"Strong introverts to the right," I directed, pointing in that direction. "And if you are uncertain, place yourself in the middle wherever it feels right." John, Brent, Sarah, and Maggie filled up the continuum on the introverts' end. (You can mark your spot with an X.)

"Now I want you to complete this statement," I said. "When I am feeling drained, I need . . . "

"Chocolate," Diane proclaimed.

I had to laugh. I snitch chocolate every afternoon.

"I was thinking more in terms of what you need as an extrovert or introvert," I explained.

The introverts groaned and rolled their eyes at me. They did not appreciate that I had disrupted their space and asked them to now publicly talk about their feelings and needs.

"I apologize for pushing you out of your preferred style. This is an extroverted activity," I admitted. "But I've got two reasons for doing it. One, even introverts tell me they like hearing that others experience similar feelings, and two, the extroverts usually listen better when the introverts' responses are supported by *many* individuals." (Extroverts like to "hear" things more than once.)

"So it's your fault we're here," Brent joked, pointing at the extroverts.

Before I share with you their responses, write your own right here:

When I'm feeling drained I need . . .

____

____

____

____

Now, if you're an extrovert and you like to think by talking, find an introvert in your family to interview and ask him to complete this statement. Remember to give him time to think about his answers.

If you're an introvert, find an extrovert and do the same.

I suspect you might turn me down. So I've included responses from both types. Place a check mark next to those that are right for you.

The extroverts are always willing to start first. Here's what they had to say:

As an extrovert I need . . .

____ ***1. people to help me think***

- ____ **to ask questions and share ideas**
- ____ **to talk in order to figure out how I'm feeling (I've got to hear it to know I feel it)**
- ____ **to discuss an issue more than once**
- ____ **to immediately be able to talk about my day or an event**
- ____ **time on the telephone**
- ____ **to be able to change my decision as I talk about it**
- ____ **to be able to voice my opinion**

____ ***2. feedback***

- ____ **an acknowledgment that I have been heard**
- ____ **an answer, even if it is simply that you want to think about it**
- ____ **a warm greeting**

_____ to know what you're thinking

_____ attention

_____ *3. time with people, activities, and stimulation*

_____ to get out and do things!

_____ to work or play around other people (I don't like to be alone too long)

_____ hands-on activities

And after they'd had time to think about it, the introverts also had a great deal to say.

As an introvert I need . . .

_____ *1. time alone*

_____ time with just my immediate family

_____ quiet music that blocks out other noise

_____ you to know that I am not rejecting you when I take time to be by myself

_____ control over when I leave a group

_____ quiet

_____ *2. physical space*

_____ personal space

_____ a walk by myself or with a very close friend

_____ to be alone in my room with the door closed—not for hours but for fifteen or twenty minutes

_____ to be able to sit or stand with space around me

_____ *3. time for reflection*

_____ a chance to sit and think (I'm not wasting time)

_____ quiet when I'm reading

_____ to be asked one question at a time

_____ a chance to think about my answer before I commit

_____ for you to know that when I am quiet, I'm thinking. I am not angry

_____ for you to be patient and listen, so I can talk more

_____ an opportunity to vegetate on the couch

____ *4. uninterrupted work time*

____ a chance to ask questions privately

____ a chance to practice new skills alone or with one other trusted person

____ a chance to play or work alone or with a partner I choose

____ to work on one thing at a time

Now let's match your family members with their needs.

1. Go back and look at the introvert and extrovert charts. Total the number of points each person received. Select the preference that was checked at least four times. (If necessary, start with your best guess.)
2. Review the "I need" statements above, and feel free to add your own. Select two that are especially important for each family member.

Here is a copy of Sarah's chart.

Names	*Tom*	*Sarah*	*Cara*	*David*	*Sadie*	*Kim*
Extrovert	x		x		x	
Introvert		x		x		x
As an extrovert or introvert I need...	to talk about my day	space	to *do* things	quiet after school	atten-tion	quiet
As an extrovert or introvert I need...	people to work with	time to think	a warm hello	to tell you about my day day later	to ask ques-tions	hugs from Mom

Now do your family's chart.

Names						
Extrovert						
Introvert						
As an extrovert or introvert I need...						
As an extrovert or introvert I need...						

If these "I need" statements are new to you, write the ones that are most important to you on Post-its. Have them ready wherever or whenever you could use a reminder. Carry them in your pocket; put them on your refrigerator, the dashboard of your car, or your nightstand. These are the statements you can teach your child.

When you see your little extrovert starting to get irritable, teach him to say, "I need people!" or "I need to *do* something!" instead of picking on others to recharge.

When your introvert begins to complain that people are sitting too close or talking too much, teach her to say, "I need quiet" or "I need space" instead of pushing or screaming to drive others away. When kids have the words to describe what they are feeling and needing, they don't have to act up in order to be heard.

PRACTICE, PRACTICE, PRACTICE

Diane was thoughtful as she looked down the continuum. "My husband, Bob, would be standing right there," she said, pointing to John and Brent on the introverts' side. "No wonder we get into fights when he comes home from work. I want him to talk to me when he comes in the door, and the boys want him to play, but he refuses or starts yelling at them to be quiet. What are we supposed to do?"

"Do you want to develop a plan?" I asked.

She nodded.

"Bob's an introvert?" I confirmed.

"Oh, yes," Diane stated, "a real *strong* introvert."

"And you're a *strong* extrovert?"

"That's me!" she proclaimed, throwing her arms out and taking a bow. "And so are all three boys."

"What needs did you select?" I asked.

"I need to talk about the day, a warm greeting, attention, and just to be with another adult."

"And Bob?"

"I think he needs quiet," she said. "And time to think about his day before he talks. He also wants space and a break. But he does like to be with us."

"The boys?" I continued.

"They definitely need to talk," she replied. "They really want to tell Bob about their day. And they want his attention. Most of all, they just want to be with him."

As Diane answered, I completed the following chart on the board.

Diane	**Bob**	**Boys**
EXTROVERT	INTROVERT	EXTROVERTS
to talk	quiet to think	to talk
to review the day's events	a chance to think about the day	to review the day's events
	uncrowded space	hands-on contact
warm greeting	break from stimulation	warm greeting
attention	time with immediate family	attention
to be with people	a break without guilt	to *do* something

It's pretty obvious that what the extroverts need in this situation is the direct opposite of what the introvert needs. So how can they have a harmonious dinnertime?

I turned the question over to the group. "How can they work together, respecting the needs of both introverts and extroverts?"

It was John who offered the first potential solution. "I'm an introvert," he said. "I can identify with Bob. My wife and son are extroverts, and even though my daughter is an introvert, with two adolescents our evenings are full of extracurricular activities. What I've come to realize is that my extroverting can't end when I leave the office. I have to have a few more hours left in me. I can't expect to recharge when I come home. When I walk in the door, we've usually got to eat and run."

Brent snorted. "But if you're drained, you're drained."

"You're right," John replied, "so I have to fill up somewhere during the day. I always take my lunch. Then I'll close the door to my office and just eat it at my desk, or I'll go out for a drive, maybe run one errand. Somehow I get some space and quiet, then I'm not totally drained at six P.M."

"Do your kids jump on you like ours do on Bob?" Diane wanted to know.

"Todd would," John admitted, "but if I call home after school and talk with him about his day, he doesn't jump me at the door. I also try to talk with my wife during the day so we've had time to connect without the kids interrupting."

"Does this solution meet the needs of both introverts and extroverts?" I asked.

Brent slouched in his chair, arms crossed. "Sort of, but John really is giving a lot."

"I am getting what I need, though," John replied. "I just have to get it before I go home. And if I haven't gotten it, I let my wife know and she tries to give me a few minutes if I need it."

"So you really are working together," I pointed out.

John agreed. "It works for us. "

"But what if you can't recharge during the day?" Sarah asked. "Sometimes that's just not possible."

"We had that problem," Lynn said. "Or, I should say, we used to. Our dinnertime was not fun. Everyone was crabby and complaining. What we decided is that I would pick up the kids. My partner, who is an introvert, gets to drive home alone, but we both arrive at the house at the same time. Before changing clothes or anything else, we pull out carrots, celery, cheese, crackers, yogurt, whatever, and stand around the kitchen snacking and eating. The foods are all nutritious, so I don't worry that we're eating junk. It's just our first course."

"But aren't the kids whiny?" Sarah asked.

"They like the attention. They're getting something to eat, so they aren't complaining about being hungry, and because they're just snacking, no one is yelling about manners. We can actually talk. It's peaceful enough that it's nice for the introvert too. After snacking, everyone changes clothes, I help the kids if they need it, and my partner makes dinner *alone* in the kitchen. A lot of times the kids have gotten enough attention, so if we want to, we can cook together."

"Let's review this strategy," I interjected.

"In this scenario are the extroverts getting to talk?" I asked. Heads nodded.

"Is the introvert getting peace?" Again everyone agreed.

"There's give and take. That's why it works," I confirmed.

Just for fun, we continued our brainstorming for Diane. I like to be sure there are several options so that everyone can see that there isn't one right or magical answer. Phil suggested, "Bob could go out for a walk or a run before dinner."

Diane nixed that idea. "I need another adult by that time of the day. I don't want him to leave again. I'd probably stand at the door and cry the entire time he was gone!"

Lynn interrupted. "You could make sure you get out with people during the day even though you're home with kids. I know that was really important to me when I was home, and then when my partner came home, I wasn't so needy."

The ideas continued to flow.

- Set a timer for fifteen minutes of playtime with the kids, then fifteen minutes of quiet for Dad.
- Make sure the kids have played with friends during the day so that they are energized and don't need Dad so much.
- Write notes to Dad in the afternoon so the kids are able to let go of their thoughts and not jump on him the minute he walks in.

The possible solutions multiplied, and Diane was free to choose the one or two that she thought might work best for her family. It didn't matter if someone else would have chosen the same solutions. Diane just needed to think about her family.

When we recognize the cues of introverts and extroverts and understand their needs, we stop telling ourselves things like, "This person is intentionally trying to irritate me!" Instead we realize that this is an introvert who needs space or an extrovert who needs to talk, and we find solutions that work.

Now it's your turn.

1. Select a tough time of the day that you think may be tied to differing needs of introverts and extroverts.

The problem: ______________________________

2. Using your family picture, including each member's preference and needs, think about potential solutions that respect the needs of both types.

Possible solutions:

1. ______________________________

2. ______________________________

3. ______________________________

3. Choose a solution that best matches the needs of everyone involved.

____

4. A few days from now, sit down together and talk about how the strategy is working. Make adjustments as needed.

It's important to concentrate on your successes. Keep your journal sheets to review by yourself or with a friend. Feel free to boast about your effective strategies and share them with others. If something isn't working, make changes and try again.

SAVOR YOUR SUCCESSES

I saw red-winged blackbirds perched on reeds as I drove to class. Their shiny black feathers and the splash of red on their wings created a sharp contrast with the falling snowflakes. Spring plays with you in Minnesota. One day you think winter is done, then it smacks you again. I was looking forward to being in the cozy discussion room and hearing some great success stories.

Lynn was willing to oblige. "It was Sunday afternoon," she said. "We'd had a really quiet, restful weekend. But at about two o'clock Aaron started to get irritable. Nothing suited him. He started poking his sister and picking on the dog." She demonstrated by jabbing the air around her. "There was no doubt he was seeking activity, but he had fifty pages to read for homework. He reads well, but for whatever reason he finds it more draining than enjoyable. He was crabby just thinking about it. That's when the phone rang. It was his friend Kellen asking him to go Roller-blading. My first reaction was absolutely not! But I thought about what we had talked about in class. He is an extrovert, who needed to recharge after our quiet weekend. Reading is draining work for him, and to get through it he needs energy. That means he needs people, stimulation, and activity.

"One potential solution was that I work with him, which I didn't want to do. Or I could have let him go with his friend and recharge. I wrestled with myself"—Lynn pretended to tussle with herself, wrapping both arms around her body—"and then I forced myself to say yes." She laughed. "But the old part of me couldn't let him off too easily. I pointed my finger right at him and admonished, 'Set your watch for thirty minutes, and don't be late! Then it's time to read and no excuses!'

"He agreed and headed out. Promptly thirty minutes later he returned, hair flying, skates flashing as he and Kellen raced the last block. Bursting through the door, he pointed to his watch, verifying the time. Laughter resounded as he said good-bye to his friend. Recharged, he hit the books and finished his work, no fussing, no complaining, no problem!"

Lynn's spine straightened, her chin lifted, and a general feeling of pride seemed to wash across her face. The others erupted in spontaneous applause. Embarrassed, Lynn diverted the attention by turning to Diane. "And what about you? Did any of the plans work?"

Diane gave a thumbs-up. "I showed Bob the chart," she said. "And told him about some of the ideas, and then"—she sat taller in her chair—"I gave him time to think about it. He's still thinking. I'll let you know what happens next week!"

Record your successes here.

How did you help your child recharge today?

What did you do to allow yourself to recharge?

How did you work together as a family to recharge without draining one another?

CORNERSTONE

Extroverts need

A chance to talk about what they are thinking . . .

✔ to ask questions

✔ to share their ideas

✔ to change a decision as they hear themselves think

✔ to talk about an issue over and over again

Feedback . . .

✔ an immediate *wow*

✔ a warm greeting

✔ a *hmmmm* that indicates they've been heard

✔ to know what others are thinking

Time with people and lots of activities and stimulation . . .

✔ to talk on the telephone

✔ someone to do chores with

✔ to *do* something on the weekend

✔ to be with friends

Introverts need

Time alone or with selected companions . . .

✔ to just be with family

✔ quiet music

✔ to take a walk around the block

✔ to play alone

Physical space . . .

✔ to sit on the couch alone

✔ to be in a room alone

✔ to not be crowded

Time for reflection . . .

✔ **to daydream**

✔ **to think before making a decision**

Uninterrupted work time . . .

✔ **to ask questions privately**

✔ **to practice new skills alone**

✔ **to choose to work alone or with a selected partner**

5

INTENSITY

Diffusing Strong Reactions

IN PREPARATION

- Read Chapters 6 and 12 in *Raising Your Spirited Child.*
- You'll need a bottle of vinegar, a box of baking soda, a teaspoon, a tablespoon, two glasses (wineglasses work well), cotton balls, and a tray with sides.
- You'll also need a highlighter.

CHAPTER HIGHLIGHTS

- Cues to help you know when your child is about to "lose it."
- Tips for managing your child's intensity and your own.
- Strategies for those high-intensity times of the day.
- Tips for dealing with blowups.

THINGS TO OBSERVE

- What do you see, hear, sense that tells you that your child's intensity level is rising?
- What activities or experiences seem to soothe and calm your child?

I can't help thinking that volcanoes are the earth's temper tantrums. Fueled by hot molten rock, they rumble and grumble, spit and fume. They're really rather harmless until the pressure builds to the bursting point and they explode. Then they aren't harmless at all. Scientists can tell us which ones are active by the sounds they make and the things they spew. But they still can't tell us exactly when they're going to erupt.

Geologists studying volcanoes and parents of spirited children have something in common. They both need to know the cues that signal increasing pressure, and they need to take precautionary measures as soon as possible because the blowups can be rather nasty. It's preferable to avoid them altogether.

Intensity is the driving force behind your child's strong reactions. Cool kids may simply whimper when they're hungry or hurt, but spirited children are likely to scream. People often mistakenly think that cool kids react less intensely because their parents are more effective. In reality their physiological stress systems are not as easily activated.

As the parent of a spirited child you need to know that intense children react more vehemently, not because they want to embarrass you, but because their bodies physiologically react more than those of cool children. Or, as University of Minnesota professor Megan Gunnar, Ph.D., says, "Spirited kids experience more physical stress; they aren't just doing it to make you stressed. When spirited kids experience an emotion, their bodies surge with hormones, which tell the brain to be on alert for 'fight or flight.' Intense people do not choose to produce more stress hormones. Their bodies automatically do it."

Intensity is difficult to talk about. It's hard to put your arms around and touch, yet it's there, a real entity that needs to be addressed. So I've created an exercise to make intensity more concrete. (I really want you to do this. You've got to see it! The image it creates is very important.) You'll need a box of baking soda; vinegar, to which you can add a few drops of red food coloring for a dramatic effect; two glasses (wineglasses are a perfect

size); a tray with sides; a tablespoon; and a teaspoon. Set the tray on the table in front of you, and place the two glasses on it. Imagine that one of these goblets is a cool kid and the other is an intensely spirited child. Now I'm going to tell you a story about these two children.

It's breakfast time, and both children come to the kitchen to eat. The dishwasher holds dirty dishes, and their favorite bowls and spoons are in it. You pour cereal into two clean bowls and set them on the table. Your cool kid looks at that bowl and asks, "Where's my favorite bowl?" When you explain it's dirty and in the dishwasher, he says, "Oh," and proceeds to eat. Now pour a teaspoon of vinegar into his glass—this represents the stress hormones his body produces when he's surprised.

Your spirited child arrives, takes one look at the bowl of cereal, and starts screaming. You explain that his favorite dish is dirty, but he can't hear you above his wails. He demands the bowl, and ten minutes later he's still shrieking. Finally, just to get him to eat, you take his favorite bowl out of the dishwasher, wash it by hand, and put his cereal in it. He settles down and eats. Pour two tablespoons of vinegar into his glass. This represents the stress hormones that rushed into his system.

Now it's time to get dressed. It was 70 degrees yesterday and the kids wore shorts, but this morning the temperature has dropped to 50. You tell the kids they need to wear pants.

"But, Mom," protests your cool kid, "I want to wear shorts."

"Maybe tomorrow," you say.

He puts on his pants. Add another teaspoon of vinegar to his glass.

Your spirited child ignores your direction and pulls on his shorts. You tell him it's too cold, but he insists he needs to wear shorts. You tell him to step outside on the stoop, which he does. But he doesn't care that goose bumps rise on his skin. He wants to wear shorts. It takes thirty minutes to get him to throw on wind pants over the shorts. Pour three tablespoons of vinegar into his glass, which nearly fills it to the top. (If it doesn't, add a little more until it does.)

Now it's time to leave the house. Usually you drive the car pool, but today you have a meeting on the other side of town, so

your neighbor is taking the kids to school. Your announcement of this change in plans doesn't faze your cool kid. He gets in the car. Toss a half teaspoon of baking soda into his glass. Watch it fizz as little bubbles evolve into bigger ones, which quickly dissipate. The mixture never comes near the top of the glass.

Your spirited child doesn't moan or groan when you announce the change in plans; he shouts. "*No!* I'm not riding with her!" he screams as he darts away. You grab him and he bursts into tears. You drag him to the car and hand him over to the neighbor, along with a box of tissues. Dump a teaspoon of baking soda into his glass. Bubbling and boiling, the mixture spills over the top, flowing like lava onto the tray. Add another teaspoon of soda. Watch the eruption continue, the escaping gases hiss, fueling the explosion.

This is the spirited child on overload. The reason is physiological. It is not a plot to frustrate his parents. His body produces more stress hormones, and as a result his stress reaction is harder to turn off. He gets upset more easily, and he stays upset longer. He doesn't choose this response; it is part of who he is.

Intensity reflects a physiological reaction within the body. By their very nature, spirited kids are intense. But this doesn't mean that because your child drew the high-intensity card from the gene pool you have to be a victim waiting for the next blowup. You can help him learn to understand his intensity, manage it, and still enjoy the depth of emotion available to him.

A NEW POINT OF VIEW

Geologists know there are warning signs of an impending volcanic eruption. The water temperature in nearby springs rises. Light quake tremors reverberate through the earth. Later comes the big blow, a violent explosion with great clouds of boiling steam and molten lava.

Kids' outbursts follow a similar pattern. Their rising intensity may be preceded by complaints about being hot. This may be followed by hitting, biting, or whining. Finally you end up with a full-fledged meltdown. Of course, just as no two volcanic eruptions are alike, so tantrums are different for each child. The key is to catch the intensity before the glass fills up. In order to do this you have to become aware of the nuances of behavior that indicate rising stress levels.

Let's take a close look at what you can see, hear, or sense that will tell you your child's intensity is rising—his glass is filling up. I'll let the group help you get started. Here's what they had to say when I asked, "What behaviors do you see *before* your child loses it?"

The chatter was rowdier than usual. The energy in the room reflected the topic of the night—intensity. Sarah and Maggie sat straight in their chairs, focused. They'd been waiting weeks for this topic and were ready to talk.

"Brian starts demanding things," Maggie began. "For instance, lets say he wants a snack. So I give him a snack, but he'll get mad because it's not the right snack."

"Does he get more sensitive?" Diane wanted to know. "Justin starts crying about things that happened years ago, like his goldfish that died when he was three!"

"It's amazing how sensitive they can be," Lynn replied softly. "Jenna complains about noise. She doesn't want us to talk or even walk by her. Everything frustrates her. Sometimes she ends up in tears; other times she gets belligerent."

Brent had moved to the back of the room and was standing there watching me as I listed the responses. I wasn't even sure he was listening, but then he pointed at the board and said, "Sonja and Danny go crazy. Sonja jumps all over and starts running around the house. Danny tries to tackle her. They scream; I yell." He shrugged. "That's what happens."

Sarah looked at Brent, then at me, and asked, "Do spirited kids always get loud and wild?"

"No," I explained. "Some kids, especially introverts, get quiet, which is why their blowups surprise you."

"Yeah," she said thoughtfully. "David becomes quiet. When I'm sitting next to him I can feel his intensity. Sometimes I feel like the mother of the little glowworm—I know he's upset, but he's like me. He doesn't want to talk about it."

John listened intently, and I noticed he leaned forward as Sarah and Brent spoke. Something they had said struck him, but he didn't comment.

Now it's your turn.

Review the chart created by the group. Think about your child. What do you see, hear, or sense that tells you your child's intensity is rising? How do you know his glass is filling up? No two individuals will signal in the same way. Introverts may become quieter—until the big explosion. Extroverts may "get in your face." Individuals who are sensitive sometimes become more so. Infants and toddlers may cling.

1. **Highlight the responses that fit your child, then add your own.**
2. **If your child is four or older, let him help you identify the behaviors. You can ask him, "What happens when there's a volcano inside of you?"**
3. **Mark your child's three most common cues with a big red X.**

CUES THAT INDICATE INTENSITY IS RISING

- won't share
- gets louder
- makes jerky movements
- complains about noise
- stomps
- can't get dressed
- whines
- runs away
- flops on floor
- growls
- prowls
- breathes faster
- doesn't listen
- becomes impatient
- swears
- slams doors
- uses nasty tone of voice
- becomes belligerent
- grows irritable
- wants to be held
- becomes confrontational
- name-calls
- becomes grumpy
- gets "in your face"
- clings
- is easily frustrated
- becomes sarcastic
- throws things
- becomes wild or silly
- becomes quiet
- bites
- hits
- grits teeth
- face flushes
- becomes indecisive
- gets more sensitive
- becomes bossy

Some cues may be consistent for your child over time; others may change as your child grows and matures. For instance, while an infant may cry, a school-age child may insult you. Remember to take note of the changes so that you and your child are up to date on what behaviors signal rising intensity. When you learn to identify the cues, you'll have time to move in and redirect your child *before* he loses it. The earlier you notice the glass starting to fill, the easier it is to take preventive actions.

Here's your opportunity to test your skills.

Read the following real-life scenario and see if you can identify the cues that indicate rising intensity.

When eight-year-old Sean arrives home from school, he yanks open the door and drops his book bag inside. Ignoring his mother's request to put the book bag in the closet, he walks into the kitchen and demands a snack. "You can make your own," she reminds him.

"Make me a snack," he whines. His mother offers him crackers and cheese, which he rejects.

"What do you want?" she asks.

He doesn't know. He rummages through the cupboards but can't make a decision. His sister asks a question. "Shut up!" he yells at her.

"Sean," his mother snaps, growing frustrated with him. Two minutes later he pushes his sister as she walks by him.

In this scenario the initial cues are subtle:

- **yanks the door**
- **drops the book bag**
- **ignores the request**

If the cues are not identified, the glass starts to fill and the reactions grow stronger.

- **demands snack**

- **whines**
- **prowls**
- **can't make a decision**

The pressure builds to a near blowup:

- **tells his sister to shut up**

Finally he lets loose:

- **pushes his sister**

It's easy to think that your child has hit, bitten, or blown up for no apparent reason, but with this very typical scenario you can see that the glass gradually fills over time. Sometimes, especially if you haven't been with your child for a few hours, you may not be aware of what's already in his glass. In other situations stress can fill the glass. That's why it is so important to monitor cues.

How did you do reading the cues in the scenario? Did you catch them at stage one—that first yank of the door? Or maybe you noticed when he started whining. Did it take a punch to catch your attention? If it did, try to observe your child more closely. The earlier you can catch the cues, the easier it is to manage the intensity.

Your child has to learn to read his own cues.

You will play a key role in helping your child to identify his intensity cues, but ultimately your child has to take over this task. Infants and toddlers won't be able to do it themselves, but you'll want to describe with words the cues you see. For example, you might say, "You're breathing faster," or "Your voice is getting louder." It will probably amaze you how quickly your child starts to notice these behaviors and is able to tell you, "Mommy, I breathe fast! Help me!"

Kids really do want to learn how to manage their intensity. The eruptions frighten them and make them feel out of control. That's why if I'm working with kids who are four or older, we make volcanoes together. As the soda and vinegar erupt, I ask them if their body ever feels that way inside. "Oh, yes," they've told me.

"There's a lion inside of me, and sometimes he gets out of his cage!" Or "There's a tornado inside of me."

Kids know the feeling of intensity; they just don't have the words to describe it. Once you've made volcanoes together they have a concrete image of intensity and you have a way to talk about that mounting pressure. So if your kids are four or older, do this exercise with them. Then when you notice the cues, you can ask them, "Is your glass getting full?" Or, if your child has created a wonderful metaphor, like the lion or tornado, you can ask, "Is your lion starting to roar?" Or "Is your tornado escaping?" The images are fun and nonthreatening, making it easier to talk about the rush of strong feelings.

Your child's intensity doesn't exist in a vacuum. It's there right in front of you, potentially fueling your intensity. That's why it is just as important to know your own behavioral cues that indicate *your* glass is filling up.

Think about yourself. What do you find yourself doing, saying, or feeling when your intensity is rising?

1. **Review the cues chart.**
2. **Circle those that fit you.**
3. **Add your own.**
4. **Mark your three most common cues with a big red X.**
5. **If your kids are four or older, ask them what your cues are. You might find it quite an interesting exercise. I did.**

I asked my daughter how she knows when my intensity is rising. She immediately scrunched up her face, pointed at my chest, and demanded, "I want you to do it NOW!" It was a bit embarrassing. She pegged me perfectly! I do get very impatient when my intensity rises. Now she actually recognizes it and often playfully says, "A little intense today, Mother?" She knows the correct tone to use. It doesn't add to my intensity, and while I hate to admit it, her teasing usually does make me laugh or at least stop and take notice. So what are your cues? Are you aware of them? Do your kids know them?

When I asked the group, "What are the cues that your intensity is rising?" Phil glanced at the chart and quipped, "All of them." The others laughed in agreement.

"Do any of them stand out for you?" I asked.

"I get quiet," Sarah said.

"My blood pressure goes up, my muscles get tight, and I get rigid," Lynn replied. "That's when I hear my father's voice coming out of my mouth!"

"I try to ignore my intensity," John admitted. "I guess I'm like Sarah, I get quiet, but then I start to feel crazy. I can feel the blood rushing through my veins. Then I'm like Brent, I start yelling. I hate it when I yell at the kids. I promise myself I'm not going to do it again, but then I do. I never hurt them, thank God, but I don't want to be yelling."

I listened thoughtfully, noting the struggle in John's eyes. This man who was very gentle and loving with his children and supportive in the group wrestled daily with his own intensity.

"It is a struggle when you have strong feelings," I affirmed. "It's difficult for the kids too, when they are hit with a surge of stress hormones like adrenaline moving through their body. We can learn to catch the feelings early and develop daily habits that create natural soothing agents. Then you can enjoy the passion of intensity but not feel overwhelmed by it."

"Well, hurry up and tell us how," Diane demanded as she shook herself all over. "Just talking about this stuff is making me intense!"

"Hey, you're noticing cues," I pointed out. "That's the first step in pulling the plug on those volcanoes. The second step is finding the most effective strategies for reducing the pressure.

EFFECTIVE STRATEGIES

Learning how to turn off or reduce the magnitude of a stress reaction is an essential skill for high-intensity children. Your job is to teach them how.

For this exercise you'll need all of the volcano ingredients and some cotton balls. Ask your child to make another volcano with you, but this time fill the glass halfway with vinegar. Then pull out the cotton balls. Let your child hold one and rub it against her cheek. Talk about how soft it feels against her skin. Then ask her to tell you things that make her feel better when she's upset, things that make her feel all soft inside like the cotton balls. If she can't think of any answers, you can give them to her. You might say, "If Mommy holds you or scratches your back, does that make you feel better?" If she says yes, let her drop the cotton ball into the glass. Continue dropping a cotton ball in the glass for each soothing activity you can think of until the glass is full of cotton. Then throw in a half teaspoon of soda. The volcano will fizz, but it won't go over the top, and it definitely will not blow up like the first one. That's because the cotton balls absorb the vinegar and diffuse the explosion, just like calming activities reduce the stress reaction in the body. The result is fewer and smaller explosions. Explain to your child that the cotton balls soothe the volcano, and when she does things like ask for a hug, or reads a book, she creates "cotton balls" that can soothe her and stop the volcanoes from erupting inside of her.

Now you have a concrete image of stopping or reducing the stress reaction. You just have to know which activities will do it. Here are some suggestions:

1. exercise
2. repetitive motion—especially of the jaw
3. deep breathing
4. humor
5. changing the scene or activity, especially activities that engage the senses, like a back rub, warm bath, or pounding modeling dough

EXERCISE

Daily exercise is a great tool for managing intensity. It lowers blood pressure and resting heart rate. The exercise can be anything you and your child enjoy, as long as it makes you feel good. If you're jogging for twenty minutes and spending the entire time ruminating about how miserable you are or who you're going to tell off when you get back, it will not soothe you. Think about your child. What physical activities does she enjoy? Plan those activities into your child's day just as you plan her meals.

"But that's pretty hard to do when it's raining out or there's six inches of snow on the ground," Diane reminded us.

"Well, there are lots of things you can do when it's too lousy to go outside," I suggested to the group.

"We went ice-skating at the community rink all winter," Lynn offered.

"I let the kids make obstacle courses in the house," Maggie admitted. "I let them tip over the chairs and move them next to each other so that they can go over and under them. Just climbing around seems to help."

The group continued, creating a long list of physical activities for indoors and out that were not only fun, but very effective ways to manage intensity for both parents and children. The list included dancing, exercising to an aerobics tape, chasing foil balloons, rollerblading, bouncing a ball, playing on a jungle gym, and going for a bike ride.

John rubbed his hand across his chin as he perused the list. "It's true I do feel so much better on the days I lift weights or go for a run," he said. "I just don't get around to it very often."

"Exercise," I reiterated, "is a great tool to have in our coping toolbox. John, if you will plan exercise into your day at least five or six times a week, I bet you'll find it much easier to manage your intensity. It's one of the best preventive measures you can take."

As he rubbed his chin, I couldn't help thinking the idea excited him. There really was something he could do to help him manage his intensity. He didn't have to feel like a victim of his own adrenal system.

REPETITIVE MOTION

Repetitive motion, especially of the jaw, soothes and calms. This is why babies like to suck on pacifiers or nurse when they're starting to get upset. Other kids suck their thumbs. When they stop these activities you have to help them find other things that soothe. If your older kids start to get cranky, you can calm them by giving them a straw to drink their juice with. Sucking a beverage through a straw is a socially acceptable repetitive motion that brings down intensity.

"Not if you're making that dreadful noise when the liquid is nearly gone," Lynn retorted.

"Right," I said. "When you *properly* drink through a straw"—Lynn nodded to let me know she appreciated the correction—"the motion actually makes you *feel* better. And if you don't have a straw, you can chew gum like John is, or have a piece of licorice."

John flicked his gum from one side of his mouth to the other. "Yeah, I'm mellow," he joked.

"Chewing gum is a very effective way of managing intensity," I continued. "I've even suggested that kids who experience test anxiety get permission to chew gum or licorice or to suck on hard candies during tests. It helps them manage their stress reaction, reduce anxiety, and stay focused. Try it. Next time the intensity levels start mounting in your home, give everyone a stick of gum."

Phil eyed me cautiously. "Are you kidding?"

I raised my hands in innocence. "It works. We don't know why for sure, but it does. Any other suggestions of repetitive motion? They don't all have to include the jaw."

"I built a trapeze in the garage," John said.

"A trapeze?" we all asked.

"Yes, a trapeze. When Todd was about eight, I realized that he really needed exercise and that he missed swinging. He plays sports but he wasn't practicing every day, so I built a trapeze in the garage. He'd go out there, put a Beatles tape in his boom box—he especially liked *A Hard Day's Night*—and swing from one side to the other for an hour. When he came back in he was a different kid. Now I know why."

Swinging, rocking, walking, jumping rope, playing Ping-Pong, and hitting a tennis ball against a wall are all activities that can calm your child.

DEEP BREATHING

Sit up straight. Put your hand on your belly button. Inhale, drawing your breath from your abdomen. Feel your hand rise as it lies on your belly, then blow out slowly. Focus on the breath itself. It might feel strange, since most adults are shallow breathers, but don't give up. Continue for several minutes. Feel the change in your neck muscles? Deep breathing calms us. When intensity rises, we tend to hyperventilate or hold our breath. Catch yourself, and move into deep, slow breathing.

In order to teach children how to breathe deeply, get a bottle of bubbles, the kind that comes with a wand. The toddler tumbler bubble bottle is best because it doesn't spill. Hold the wand, and let your child blow. When children blow bubbles they are doing the same breathing that women learn in childbirth classes. If you don't have a bottle of bubbles, simply hold up three fingers and let your child blow out each "candle" on your birthday cake. Encourage older kids, who might think bubbles and birthday candles are not cool, to watch professional basketball players at the free-throw line. Hands on hips, they breathe deeply before taking that shot. They know it helps them to center themselves. Deep breathing is literally a lifeline for intense individuals.

HUMOR

Laughing changes our perspective, our breathing, and the circulation in our facial muscles. It helps us manage our intensity. Smile, tell a joke, chuckle, and you'll stay calmer.

"But what do you do when you're really not feeling very funny?" Sarah asked.

"I've got an answer," Maggie volunteered. "I'm not too good at humor either, but the other day we were in a restaurant. The kids started to get impatient. I knew the glass was filling up. I was too tired to think of any creative response, so I just asked, 'Who's got a joke?' The kids looked at me like I'd lost my mind, but then Brian had a knock-knock joke. Kristen had one too, and before we knew it our food arrived."

A good belly laugh, an unexpected silly response, a different voice, a funny mask or puppet are all ways to diffuse intensity. It's okay to have fun as a parent and to be playful with your children. Developing a good sense of humor is an essential life skill—especially in families where spirit lives.

CHANGING THE SCENE OR ACTIVITY

Merely walking outside, taking a break, finding a quiet space, pulling out the Legos, jumping into the bathtub, getting a hug, playing a musical instrument, petting the dog, working on a collection, or reading a good book can help you and your child manage intensity. You'll notice I didn't say turn on the television. While watching a funny movie can lower intensity, simply diverting the kids by turning on the television doesn't work in the long run. Spirited kids tend to absorb the stimulation of television and become wilder the longer they watch.

The key to changing the scene is to momentarily distract and disconnect from the source of the intensity. It's pretty hard to think about what made you angry when you're focused on Legos.

"Wait a minute," Brent demanded. "The kid is stomping and pouting, and you want me to say, 'Go play with your Legos'? Get real."

I realized this advice was a bit unusual. But then I asked, "Brent, when you get angry with your boss, what do you need to do?"

He thought for a moment, then grinned. "If I'm smart, I walk away for a minute."

"Right," I replied, "to bring down your intensity so that you can think. That's all you're doing with the kids. You're bringing down the intensity. Later, when everyone is calm, you'll go back and talk with the kids—just like you'd talk with your boss."

"But what if they're like Andy?" Diane asked. "If I give him crayons or Legos, he'll just throw them at me. Then what am I supposed to do?"

"Setting limits is essential," I advised. "If he throws things, you'll need to stop him and clearly say, 'You may not throw or break things.' Then remove the crayons. If he hits you, hold his hands and stop him. Later, when you're both calmer, tell him, 'No matter how angry you are, you can't throw things.' Teach him that he *can* say, 'I don't want to color. I need to run.' But make it very clear that violence is unacceptable."

Diane looked uncertain. "I try," she said. "But when he's totally lost it, it's nearly impossible to bring him back."

"Timing is important," I agreed. "If you catch the glass when it's just starting to fill, coloring or playing with Legos will probably work very well. But if the glass is full or boiling over, these activities may not provide enough of a physical outlet. Remember, when the stress reaction occurs in the body, hormones like adrenaline stream into the brain telling it to be ready for flight or fight. Bev Boss, an early-childhood professional in California, advises taking the child by his hand and walking around the room, up and down stairs, or even outside, as briskly as you can. The idea is to move, to let that adrenaline diffuse. Afterward you can deal with the real issue."

"Wait," Maggie said, holding up her hands. "That's it—timing! When Brian starts getting irritable, I just want to get away. All I can think is, God help me, here it comes again. I don't deal with it until it's overflowing!"

Sarah hugged herself. "Me too. I can feel my chest tighten and my heart pound. I don't want it to happen. Sometimes I think if I don't do anything, maybe it'll just go away—but it doesn't."

I nodded in agreement. "Frequently when your child's intensity rises, so does yours. The cues don't have to scare you. When you become aware of your child's cues and your own, you can tell yourself, 'This is about intensity. I do not have to panic. This doesn't have to result in a blowup. There are strategies I can use to empty that glass!'"

It's easier to keep your cool when you're prepared.

1. Review the following chart of calming activities.
2. Add your own.
3. Highlight the most effective strategies for your child.
4. Circle the most effective strategies for you.

Suggested Calming Activities

EXERCISE

Younger Children	*Older Children and Adults*
crawling	Roller-blading
riding a tricycle	weight lifting
chasing a ball	aerobics
climbing	walking
obstacle course	flying on a trapeze
dancing	dancing
tumbling	ice-skating
running	running
	sports

REPETITIVE MOTION

Younger Children	*Older Children and Adults*
sucking: nursing, bottles, pacifiers, thumb	drinking from a straw
	chewing gum or licorice
swinging	swinging
rocking	rocking
riding a rocking horse	jumping rope
riding a tricycle	jumping on a trampoline
riding in a baby carrier	going for a walk
	riding a bike
	talking to a friend
	going for a walk

DEEP BREATHING

Younger Children	*Older Children and Adults*
blowing bubbles	counting to ten
blowing out pretend birthday candles	placing a hand on your belly and breathing from there
	taking three deep breaths before responding

HUMOR

Younger Children	*Older Children and Adults*
being silly	being silly
creating imaginative characters	making funny comments
doing funny voices	giving unexpected reactions
making silly noises	telling jokes
playing with puppets	being playful

CHANGE OF SCENE OR ACTIVITY

Younger Children	*Older Children and Adults*
going outside	going outside
hugging	hugging
singing	singing or whistling
listening to music	playing an instrument
playing with modeling dough	watching a funny movie
dancing	dancing
taking a bath	taking a bath or shower
getting a massage	working on a card collection or other hobbies
taking a break in a quiet space	taking a break
playing with water in the sink or a dishpan	cooking or baking
playing in sand or a dishpan of rice	talking to a friend
holding a blanket or favorite "lovie"	cleaning
playing with puppets, stuffed animals	knitting
	woodworking
	reading
	drawing or painting

playing with Legos or Duplos
reading
coloring or drawing
being held
stroking pets
going for a walk
getting a massage
stroking pets
walking
gardening

If you really want to be prepared, complete a chart for your entire family.

1. **Fill in the name of each family member.**
2. **Review the chart of calming activities.**
3. **Select the most effective strategies for each family member.**

Here's an example from Sarah's family.

Name	*Bob*	*Sarah*	*Cara, 10*	*David, 8*	*Sadie, 4*	*Kim, 6 months*
REPETITIVE MOTION	chewing gum	chewing gum	swinging	chewing gum or licorice	sucking thumb	sucking pacifier
	talking	walking	talking	jumping on trampoline	using rocking horse	being in baby carrier
			drinking with a straw	biking	talking	rocking
			chewing gum			
DEEP BREATHING	taking three deep breaths	counting to ten	taking three deep breaths	taking three deep breaths	blowing bubbles	
EXERCISE	running	walking	sports	sports	riding tricycle	crawling
	weight lifting	dancing	dancing	skating	dancing	
		weight lifting	skating	running	tumbling	

Name	*Bob*	*Sarah*	*Cara, 10*	*David, 8*	*Sadie, 4*	*Kim, 6 months*
HUMOR	joking	joking	joking	joking	creating imaginative characters	using silly voices
				giving unexpected responses	using silly voices	making funny sounds
CHANGE OF SCENE OR ACTIVITY	using the computer	playing piano	being with a friend	going outside	holding blanket	being massaged
	reading	watching a movie	drawing	taking a break	reading	being held
	wood working	taking a break	doing projects	reading	playing with modeling dough	going outside

MY FAMILY'S FAVORITE CALMING ACTIVITIES

Name						
REPETITIVE MOTION						
DEEP BREATHING						
EXERCISE						
HUMOR						

Name					
Change of Scene or Activity					

PRACTICE, PRACTICE, PRACTICE

If you are spirited, it is as essential to "fill your glass" with cotton balls of soothing activities as it is to fill your stomach with food. Living with intensity doesn't mean our lives have to be filled with volcanoes waiting to erupt. We can take preventive measures and enjoy the depth of feeling tied to intensity without constantly experiencing the hazards of it. I asked the group to think about those times of the day when volcanoes are most likely to erupt in their families, so we could plan for success.

Lynn immediately volunteered. "All right, help me deal with practicing a duet for a piano recital. Aaron and Jenna are performing a duet together, but every practice session turns into a war. I'm ready to say forget it."

I groaned. As an adult piano student myself, I could really empathize with the kids. Duets are not easy!

"I think you'd better start by filling up with soothing activities *before* the practice," I advised. "When are they practicing?"

"After school," Lynn replied.

"When they come home from school," I asked, "are their glasses full?"

"Very. They're both tired and cranky. That's why I want them to get it done."

"Think about what we said," I replied. "When the glass is full or close to it, we've either got to diffuse the tension or somehow get rid of the excess. If you try to practice the duet at this point, you're adding to the intensity. It's like throwing the soda into a glass of vinegar. Participating in calming activities first will help reduce the intensity of a stress reaction. Check your list, and see what it tells you."

She perused it carefully.

"Exercise," she replied.

"And if the intensity levels start to rise in the middle of practice?" I asked.

"Let them take a few breaks," she answered.

"Anything else you want to add to your plan?"

"I think I need to tell Aaron that he can't yell at Jenna. He needs to say what he really means, not 'I hate you!'"

Maggie had been chewing on her fingernail, listening intently. "This is nice—if you know an explosion is coming. But what do you do if there isn't any warning?"

"Do you have an example?" I asked.

"Well, Saturday Brian was playing with a friend. He was standing on the ground, and the friend was in our tree house. The friend jumped out and landed on Brian. Neither one of them was injured, but Brian was livid. He totally lost it for at least ten minutes."

"Look at the summary of calming activities," I said. "Which ones could you use in the middle of a volcano?"

She read through the chart. We waited.

"I guess I could have said, 'Breathe with me.'" I nodded. "Or perhaps I could have asked him to walk with me, or I could have tried humor." She looked up to see the group was agreeing with her. "Maybe refocus—I could have said, 'Let's go get a drink of water or a Band-Aid.' And if I couldn't move him, I could have taken the other child away to give Brian space," she added, completing her list of options.

"And later, when he's calm," I said, "you can talk with him about better ways to deal with being startled."

"But what do you do when you've run through your bag of tricks to no avail?" Sarah asked.

"You take a break, ask for help, figure out how to reduce your own stress reaction, and start again," I replied. "Remember, the only behavior we really can change is our own."

John listened intently. He made a few notes on his handout but said nothing. I couldn't tell what he was thinking. I wanted to ask, but I knew from last week's discussion that he preferred introversion. As hard as it was, I chose to respect his space and reflection time, and wait.

Think about the high-intensity times of your day. For example, mealtimes, after school, bedtime, riding in the car during rush hour, et cetera.

1. **Select one or two high-intensity times in your day. (You can deal with the others later.)**
2. **Plan soothing activities you can do *before* each situation.**
3. **Plan steps you can take if the intensity starts to rise and you get caught in the middle of it.**

High-Intensity Time	***Soothing Strategies to Use Beforehand***	***Soothing Strategies to Use When Your Child Is Already Upset***

SAVOR YOUR SUCCESSES

A week later the sun was shining and the thermometer had hit 70 degrees Fahrenheit for the first time this year. Rose-breasted grosbeaks had returned to my feeder. I found myself humming "Oh Happy Day" as I arrived at the center. The others were obviously enjoying the sunshine too. Brent's daughter Kate held up her leg so that I could admire her new red sandals. Brian wore a T-shirt and flexed to demonstrate his really strong muscles. After interaction time, the kids headed outside to the playground while we went to the discussion room.

As everyone settled in, the focus moved to Lynn. We were all eager to find out how the duet practices had gone. She was beaming. It was obvious she was ready to share a success story with us.

"It worked!" she exclaimed. "I went home and wrote down: 'Exercise, take frequent breaks, teach Aaron to say what he really means instead of 'I hate you.' This last note was for me. I wanted to talk to Aaron privately about the 'I hate you's.' I didn't think Jenna needed to hear that part of the discussion. I wanted Aaron to know it wasn't all right to tell his sister he hated her, when he really was just frustrated with her. The 'I hate you's' hurt Jenna a lot. What her older brother thinks of her really matters to her, and I wanted him to know that."

She paused for a sip of water before continuing. "When they came home, I told them that playing the piano was supposed to be fun. Their battles were awful for everyone. They immediately started pointing fingers at each other, but I stopped them. I explained that I understood practicing was very hard for them. I showed them the volcano. They're eleven and nine, so they thought it was stupid, but I couldn't think of any other way to describe the rising intensity. We turned it into a joke, telling each other, 'Oh, the glass is filling.'

"Anyway, I told them to each go exercise for forty-five minutes, then come back and practice. I didn't want any more fighting. If they started to feel their glass fill up, they were to take a break. Forty-five minutes later they sat down to practice. I couldn't believe it. They didn't fight. They did take a couple of breaks, but Aaron never screamed at Jenna. They did great at the recital on Sunday!"

There was a round of high fives for Lynn.

I waited, looking around the room. Brent started to chuckle, then burst into laughter. "The floor is yours," I invited him.

"My wife got ticked at Danny," he said, choking on his words. "He came running to me crying that Mom was mad at him. I told him to hang out with me and explained, 'Your mom's bubbles are up—wait until she fizzes out.' We'd done that volcano stuff, so he knew what I meant. Anyway, later that night"—and he started to laugh again—"my wife asked, 'What is this stuff about bubbles?'

Danny had sneaked back into the kitchen and whispered, 'Mom, are your bubbles done now?'" Brent was bent over laughing. "I guess you had to be there," he said wiping a tear from his eye.

I was thrilled. That's the neat thing about the volcanoes. They give kids a way to talk about intensity.

I felt like my day was on a roll. I decided to take a shot. "John," I asked, "anything to report?"

"Well," he said, drawing it out, then picking up a handout and shaking it in front of him. "I decided you're right. I can't get rid of my intensity." He raised his eyebrows. "It's there with me all the time. So"—he paused—"I started exercising again, every day. I also stopped watching so much television. I thought I was relaxing when I watched, but I wasn't. I didn't realize how much of the intensity I was absorbing.

"Saturday I put it to the test. Kelly had a softball game. My wife will tell you her games are very tough on me. I see her hesitate, and I think she gets that from me. I get upset. The people around me are yelling and—" He stopped.

"Not a pretty sight?" Diane asked.

"That's probably an understatement," he answered, hanging his head. "I wanted this game to be different. I got up early to exercise. I stopped and bought gum, and when I sat down, I took a seat down on the end, slightly away from the other parents. I wanted my space, and I didn't need their intensity fueling mine. I can't say I was exactly calm, but it was dramatically better."

John's story was worth the wait. I was still humming "Oh Happy Day" on the way home.

Take this opportunity to record your successes.
What high-intensity situations have you predicted lately?

How did you help your child and yourself manage the intensity?

____

____

____

What did you do today to calm your child? Yourself?

____

____

____

CORNERSTONE

Children who are intense need to hear

Statements that help them feel good about their intensity:

- ✔ You have very strong feelings.
- ✔ You do everything with zest.
- ✔ You feel passionately about things that are important to you.
- ✔ You can channel your intensity into music, athletics, art, and more.

Statements that help them recognize intensity is rising:

- ✔ Listen to your body.
- ✔ Is the lion inside of you roaring?
- ✔ Is the volcano inside of you ready to erupt?
- ✔ Do you feel wild inside?
- ✔ Do your muscles feel tight?

Statements that help them manage their intensity:

- ✔ Do you need to exercise?
- ✔ Breathe with me.
- ✔ You can take a break.
- ✔ Remember, a smile can help you feel better.
- ✔ Would you like a stick of gum?

6

PERSISTENCE

Choosing Your Battles

IN PREPARATION

- Read Chapter 7 in *Raising Your Spirited Child.*

CHAPTER HIGHLIGHTS

- Reasons why persistence is a real asset for your child.
- Identifying the triggers that can set off persistent kids.
- Knowing when to say no.
- Strategies for getting persistent kids to "unlock" and solve problems with you, even when you're both "locked in."

THINGS TO OBSERVE

- What tends to make your persistent child lock in?
- What words or actions help your child to unlock and work with you?
- How do you feel when you are solving problems with your child?

It was to be a fun family outing, the first time the whole family was attending a professional baseball game together. Dad had taken the kids to a game before, but Mom had never come. They grabbed sodas and hot dogs on the way in to their seats. Dad and the oldest child ended up on one side of the aisle, eight-year-old Seth, two siblings, and Mom on the other.

Between bites, Seth asked, "When can we go to the baseball store and get a pennant?"

Mom hushed him by saying, "The game is just starting."

Seth watched the batters for five minutes, then tried again. "Dad always takes us to the store. When can we go, Mom?"

"Did you bring your own money?" Mom asked.

"No, Dad always buys," Seth responded.

That didn't set well with Mom, and she hushed Seth again. But Seth wasn't to be deterred. Every ten minutes he begged again. The fun family outing was quickly turning into a nightmare of badgering for Mom. Finally she said, "You'll have to wait until after the game. Then we'll talk to your dad."

At the end of the game, as she walked out, Mom ran into friends. Seth pranced in front of her. "Now can we go to the baseball store?" he pleaded.

"Wait," Mom said firmly. "We need to talk to Dad." She turned back to her friends.

Seth took matters into his own hands. He took off for the store. Ten minutes later his terrified mother found him there trying to negotiate with the salesperson.

Living with the raw gem of a persistent child is not easy. These kids are incredibly strong and determined. Even when they're infants their demands are loud and clear. Telling persistent kids no is to risk their wrath. Advice to ignore them is useless. They are prepared to go to battle when their plans are thwarted or their wishes stymied. They don't give up, and they don't forget. They also love to negotiate. If you give them an extra thirty minutes at bedtime, they push for fifteen more.

A NEW POINT OF VIEW

Persistence is the temperamental trait that plays a major role in power struggles. But we don't have to fight every day. We can teach our persistent kids to respectfully channel their persistence and to work with us rather than against us. The challenge is to overcome our fear. Power struggles scare us. We worry: "What is this persistent child going to be like at sixteen?" When we're scared we don't think quite as well, which puts us at a real disadvantage with goal-oriented, focused, committed, persistent kids. In order to keep our cool, we have to create a positive vision. We have to believe that persistent children were not simply sent to this earth to irritate us. (I realize you may find this a little challenging to accept at the moment, but bear with me!)

Persistence really is a valuable trait. Research completed by Barbara Keogh at the University of California, Los Angeles, has determined that high persistence is a key factor in a child's academic success. Look around you, and you'll find hundreds of examples of friends and relatives who have focused their persistence to overcome obstacles and achieve goals. People like Bill Gates, the founder of Microsoft, whose "little idea" was scoffed at by many.

In the discussion room Lynn cocked an eyebrow and looked at me suspiciously. Stroking her chin, she said, "I'm finding it a rather large leap from Bill Gates to persistent kids."

I laughed. My colleagues will tell you, I'm known for my leaps. "You're right," I admitted. "Fine, I won't ask you to think of anything positive—yet. Let's describe what your persistent kids do that can drive you nuts. You can write your answers on cards and toss them in the middle. The anonymity will allow you to be totally honest."

Lynn grabbed a card. "This exercise I'll do!" She laughed.

Cards were quickly completed and tossed into the center of the table.

Brent grabbed three cards and read them.

"'Throws a fit any time you tell her no.' 'Has to do it her way!' 'Won't quit.' That's Danny," he remarked as he passed the cards to Phil.

"'Always has an idea.' 'Goes nuts if we tell him he's wrong.'

'Wants to negotiate everything.' I'm exhausted just thinking about it," Phil remarked as he handed the stack to Maggie, who finished off the pile.

"'Freaks out if she thinks someone isn't listening to her.' 'Won't give up.' 'Argues.' 'Badgers me.'" Maggie shuddered as she laid the cards down on the table. "I can't wait for adolescence."

"Thank you, Maggie," I exclaimed. "You just gave me the perfect segue to the rest of our exercise."

Life with a persistent child can be very taxing. That's why it is essential, when your persistent child is driving you crazy, to recognize that behind that raw persistence lies the potential for a strong, independent, and successful individual.

Recognizing Important Skills

1. **Review the following list of irritating, frustrating, challenging behaviors persistent kids may demonstrate—the raw resources of persistence. Add your own.**
2. **Review your list of positive labels from Chapter 2. With a little guidance and training, the raw resource of persistence can become a real asset. Think about the potential strength behind each "raw" behavior. Create a label that reflects that strength.**
3. **When in your child's life will this strength be an important trait? Record your answer.**
4. **Check the next chart of the group's responses for potential answers.**
5. **If you get stuck, ask a friend to help you.**

Persistence in the raw	*Positive label*	*Someday this skill will be important when my child needs to . . .*
Throws a fit when I tell her no	**committed to her goals**	**find a way to get things done**
Has to do it her way		
Won't quit		
Always has an idea		
Goes nuts if I tell him he's wrong		

Persistence in the raw	*Positive label*	*Someday this skill will be important when my child needs to . . .*
Wants to negotiate everything		
Won't give up		
Argues		
Badgers me		
Screams, "I won't. I won't."		

Remember, there is not one right answer. Your answers may be very different from those of the group. What's most important is recognizing the value of persistence.

Here are the group's responses:

Persistence in the raw	*Positive label*	*Someday this skill will be important when my child needs to . . .*
Throws a fit when I tell her no	**committed to her goals**	**find a way to get things done**
Has to do it her way	**independent**	**stand up to a peer group**
Won't quit	**focused**	**finish a degree**
Always has an idea	**creative**	**solve a problem**
Goes nuts if I tell him he's wrong	**holds high standards**	**set high personal standards and goals**
Wants to negotiate everything	**a negotiator**	**buy a car**
Won't give up	**tenacious**	**learn to play an instrument or play a sport**
Argues	**assertive**	**demand accountability in a business deal**
Badgers me	**perseveres**	**find the truth or get others to help**
Screams, "I won't. I won't."	**knows his own mind**	**tell his friends he's not interested in drugs**

Persistence in the raw	Positive label	Someday this skill will be important when my child needs to . . .

It is not uncommon to struggle with this exercise. It isn't easy, and it can be a bit of a stretch, especially if your persistent child has worn you out. However, if you wish to avoid the daily battles, it is essential that you are able to see the potential. To recognize that if your child is going to be able to say no, achieve her goals, or learn to effectively solve problems, she has to have somewhere to practice. If you recognize this need, it is much easier to take the time and garner the patience to help her refine her skills. So . . .

Read the following aloud: *I am raising a persistent child who will be able to*

- find a way to get things done
- stand up to the crowd
- get a degree
- solve a problem
- set high personal standards
- buy a car
- learn to play an instrument or sport
- demand accountability
- find the truth
- get people to help one another
- say no to drugs

Now when you're faced with those challenging behaviors, you'll have a vision of essential life skills that your persistent child is practicing. It's a beginning. The next step is to teach your child to work with you by getting to "yes."

EFFECTIVE STRATEGIES

The behaviors that get persistent kids into trouble reflect their triggers. They become upset when someone tells them no and when they feel their interests are not being listened to. Recognizing these triggers is essential to winning their cooperation.

Persistent kids have goals—things they want to accomplish. If their goals or interests are not considered, they can easily "lock in" to their position and refuse to work with you. A key to preventing battles with your persistent child is to be a resource for him, rather than a brick wall. If you can stop yourself from automatically saying, "No, you won't" and instead look for ways to say, "Yes, you may," you will teach him that you can work together.

Working together doesn't mean giving in. It requires considering what's important to all involved and coming up with creative solutions that work for *everyone.*

In *Getting to Yes: Negotiating Agreement Without Giving In,* authors Roger Fisher and William Ury write about "principled negotiation," a method that focuses on finding common interests and solutions. This method can help us to develop a relationship with our children that fosters a sense of teamwork: two individuals working together, listening to each other, and finding solutions that allow both a sense of dignity and personal power. It is a process in which everyone wins.

Ury and Fisher wrote for business managers, so I've adapted their work for the family. My adaptation uses an acronym, PIECE. When you use it, you'll get PEACE! There are five steps.

1. POSITION: WHAT DOES EACH PERSON WANT?

Whenever there is a disagreement, people, like boxers in a ring, tend to take positions. One says, "I won't." The other says, "You will." For example, you have decided it would be best for your child if she did her homework immediately after school. She refuses to do it. You are adamant. She is to do her homework. She is just as insistent that she won't. You are both locked in to your positions. Positions fuel conflict because they are solutions that do not consider the interests or needs of others. Positions push us into battles. The challenge is to move out of our positions and instead find solutions that are acceptable to all involved—to focus on our common interests rather than our positions.

2. Interests: Why does each person want this?

When you find your child and yourself locked in to positions, it is important to remember that there is an interest or a need you are trying to meet. In order to resolve your differences and work together, you have to clarify those interests. You can try using phrases like

"Stop. I'm listening. I'm trying to understand."
"What do you need?"
"What is most important to you?"
"What do you want to do?"

If your child is five or older, you can also ask, "Why is this important to you?" Children under five years of age often have difficulty answering "why" questions. If your child is too young to answer you or unable to communicate her interests, start guessing.

"Do you need . . . ?"
"Were you trying to . . . ?"
"Is this important to you?"

For example, if your child refuses to do her homework after school, as you have asked, take a deep breath to calm yourself, then say, "I'm listening. I'm trying to understand. What do you want to do after school?" Or "When are you willing to do your homework?" Or simply, "Why don't you want to do your homework after school?" Do your best to find out what is important to your child. Perhaps her work is too difficult and she dreads sitting down to do it. Maybe she has been inside all day and needs to go outside. She might be an extrovert who needs to recharge before settling down to work alone. Her interests may surprise you.

Then think about your own interests. They are just as important as your child's. There is a reason you're locked in to a position. What is most important to you? Do you want to be available to help your child with homework and the only time you have is after school? Do you want your child to get good grades? Are you worried that she will forget to do her homework?

Identifying interests helps you to avoid feeling like you're giving in. When you clearly know what is most important to you, you can make sure that your interest is addressed in the final solution.

Identifying interests also allows you to be more creative. You can see from the example that if your child's fear of homework is her interest and your interest is good grades, the solution would be quite different from the solution if she is an extrovert who needs to recharge and you are afraid she will forget to do her homework at all. Once you identify the interests, the number of potential solutions expands exponentially.

3. Expectations/Rules: What Rules or Expectations Come into Play?

Every family has guiding principles or rules by which they live. When you're solving problems your rules or expectations help you to define the boundaries you and your child need to work within. For example, if your child wants to visit a friend on a school night and your rule for weeknights is homework or family time only, your rule will guide you. If the purpose of the visit is to finish a school project, you will be open to negotiating with your child. If, however, he wants to go to a movie with his friend, just for fun, you will know this is not something to negotiate. (If his homework is finished, you can consider his interest for fun and do something exciting as a family, but you can hold the line on going to a movie with a friend.)

4. Consensus: What potential solutions would meet the interests of everyone involved?

Persistent kids tend to have persistent parents. You both want to win! That's why it takes time for both of you to unlock and move out of your positions. Try saying to your child, "You're locked in, but you are creative. You're a good problem solver. What else could we do?" Let your child start to offer potential solutions. If she is too young to do that, offer suggestions yourself. Keep brainstorming until you find solutions that respect the interests of each person involved. There isn't a loser when everyone's interests are addressed. You will all feel like winners.

For example, if your child doesn't want to do her homework after school because she needs time to play outside, and you're worried that if she plays, she'll forget to do her homework, you might find consensus by agreeing that she can go outside for an hour and then must start her homework. This plan allows her to play while you're assured that enough time has been set aside for homework. Both of you win.

5. Evaluate: What adjustments need to be made?

Finally, you'll want to evaluate your solution. Does everyone feel comfortable with it? Are interests met? Is it working? Does it respect your family's rules and expectations? A scheduled evaluation time allows you to be more open and creative because you both know that you will have the opportunity to change your mind if necessary.

For example, once you and your child have established a homework time, set a date one week later to evaluate your solution. If it isn't working, review it, figure out why, and change it. If your child is "forgetting" to come home, maybe she needs an alarm watch to remind her it's time to quit playing with friends. Or maybe her friends aren't available during her playtime and the schedule needs to be adjusted. A planned evaluation time allows you to make those changes.

PRACTICE, PRACTICE, PRACTICE

Maggie sighed. "Will you go through an example with us? My mother is always telling me I spoil the kids. I'm too easy on them. I never know when I should hold the line or let go."

I reiterated, "Working together and getting to yes does *not* mean giving in. The solutions have to respect the interests and needs of both the child and the parent. If you feel like you're giving up something important to you, you probably haven't found the best solution yet."

I paused to think of an example. "All right. Here's one. A parent and child are leaving an auditorium after a performance. The exit ramps are very crowded. The mother wants the child to hold her hand and walk beside her. The child insists on walking behind her. The parent and child lock horns as hundreds of people look on."

Phil moaned. "A parent's worst nightmare." The others agreed.

1. POSITIONS

"Think first about positions," I said. "What is the solution the parent wants?"

"The child to hold her hand and walk beside her," Lynn replied.

And the child's?

"He wants to walk behind her."

I made a chart and filled in the responses.

Scenario	*Child Position*	*Parent Position*
stadium	walk behind	hold hand/walk beside

2. INTERESTS

"When we lock in to positions," I continued, "we end up with winners and losers—and big power struggles. To move ahead, we have to look at interests. You'll notice, however, that kids rarely come to us voicing their real interests. They come with demands that can push us into positions. Our challenge is to try and keep our cool while trying to figure out the interests. What do you think was the child's interest in this scenario?"

"Independence," Diane responded.

"Power," Brent added.

"Freedom?" Phil asked.

"It's difficult to know," I said. "And if an adult was refusing to walk next to someone, his interest probably would be independence or power. But when the mom stopped and said to the little boy, 'What do you need?' he told her the sun was in his eyes. She bent down next to him and realized that at his level the sun was practically blinding him. Kids don't think like adults. We have to remember that and take the time to discover their interests."

Murmurs and a few chuckles spread across the room as we all realized how frequently we'd been caught giving adult motivations to innocent kids.

I waited, then added, "The mom's interests are important too. What do you think was important to her?"

"Safety," Lynn confidently responded. I added it to the chart.

Scenario	***Child Interest***	***Parent Interest***
stadium	didn't want sun in his eyes	safety
		keeping track of child in the crowd

It is essential that you take the time to discover your child's interest and to clarify your own. You can see from this example that the child is not trying to be difficult. There's a legitimate reason for his behavior. His mother also has a valid reason for her actions. Understanding those reasons or interests is necessary in order to create a win/win solution—a resolution that allows both to have their needs addressed without feeling like they're giving in or losing.

3. EXPECTATIONS AND RULES

Looking at the rules helps us decide whether or not a given behavior fits the family's guidelines. For example, in this scenario I suspect the expectation would be for the parent and child to stay together while in a crowd. By clarifying the rules and expectations, you establish a standard for evaluating potential solutions. In this situation any solution that separates the child from the parent would not be acceptable.

Scenario	***Rules***
stadium	stay together in a crowd

4. CONSENSUS

"Having identified interests and clarified rules and expectations," I asked, "what are potential solutions?" Almost everyone in the room had a response. I scurried to keep up with them.

POTENTIAL SOLUTIONS

Let him hang on to the back of her jacket
Carry him
Let him walk on the other side of her
Find another exit
Let him wear sunglasses or a baseball cap if you have them
Show him how to shade his eyes

"This seems so easy," Maggie exclaimed as we finished.

I turned to Brent. He was shaking his head. "She told him to walk next to her. She's the boss. He needs to do it." He finished with his pen pointing directly at me.

A part of me agreed with Brent and I told him so. "A parent does need to be the boss, and there are times we do not negotiate," I said, "but we also have to choose our battles. If we constantly tell our children no and do not listen to their interests, they will soon stop coming to us and instead sneak around us. The issue is how to establish our authority *and* work together with our kids to solve problems." He looked at me thoughtfully. "Let's finish working this one through," I suggested. "We can evaluate the potential solutions for this mom and child and see what you think."

5. EVALUATE

"The mom's interest was safety. Do our proposed solutions meet her interest?" I asked.

"As long as he hangs on or stays next to her when he gets the glasses or ball cap," Brent answered.

"The child's interest was to get the sun out of his eyes. Does that happen?" Brent nodded.

"The expectation or rule was to stay together in a crowd. Was that honored?"

Again he agreed.

"This is a good example of choosing our battles," I said. "The mom may have slightly altered her first direction by giving him a cap or letting him hang on to her jacket, but she kept her child safe. That was her primary interest.

"And what do you think the child learned from this experience?" I continued.

"That his mom listens," Maggie replied.

"There's more than one solution," Phil offered.

"They can work together," John summarized.

I looked at Brent. "We teach different things at various points in time. Learning to respect authority is a very important lesson, one we teach by clearly setting and enforcing limits. Equally significant is learning that interests and feelings are important, that there is more than one solution to a problem, and that parents can be a helpful resource—lessons we teach by problem solving with kids."

He listened, his face unchanging. I couldn't even guess what he might have been thinking. Then he said, "I've got one for you. Sonja won't go to bed. She used to go down easily, but now she wants me to stay with her. I'm not sitting with her!"

The positions were clear. "What are the interests?" I asked.

"I want her to go to bed," Brent said. "My wife works nights. I've got all three kids to put to bed."

"What do you think Sonja wants?"

"You won't let me say she's just being a brat, will you?"

I smiled. "You can say whatever you want," I reassured him. "I'll just offer a few more possibilities."

"Give them to me," he said. "I'm listening."

"Two-year-olds go through a stage of separation anxiety," I said. "Sonja may be doing that and needing a little reassurance at night. You might find that if you lie down with her for a few minutes, she'll calm down and fall asleep quickly."

Unfortunately, our time was up and we had to stop. But as the group collected their kids and filed out I added one last remark. "This week, when you are faced with a struggle, try solving the problem using the PIECE model."

Now it's your turn.

Read the following real-life scenario, and see if you can identify the positions and interests. What solutions would you suggest?

Six-year-old Tad wanted to know what was inside his piggy bank. He'd had it since he was a baby and was certain there must be treasure inside. The only way to find out was to crack it open. But when he asked his mother if he could, she flatly refused. "But Mom," he protested. She didn't care. She'd just bought a new vacuum cleaner after destroying the last one catching little pieces of Tad's toys in the rotating brushes. She didn't want to lose another one, and she could just imagine chasing hundreds of coins across the floor if Tad busted open his bank. The mess would be bad enough, but the potential cost of another vacuum was the last straw. (You might wonder if she'd really break the vacuum, but it was a real concern for her. Our worries are not always logical, but they still need to be addressed.)

Positions: **What does each person want?**

____

Interests: **Why does each person want this?**

____

Expectations: What rules or expectations might come into play?

____

Consensus: What are possible win/win solutions?

____

Evaluations: What adjustments need to be made?

____

How did you do? Could you identify the positions and interests? Did you come up with solutions that met everyone's needs?

Here's what we thought. Tad wants to bust open his bank. His mother does not want him to do it. You can almost feel the tension rise as they voice their positions. They immediately begin to lock in.

That's why it's so critical to look at interests. Why does Tad want to open his bank? Why doesn't Mom want him to? What's important to both of them? From the information we have, it seems that Tad simply wants to know what's inside. He likes to explore. His mother doesn't want a mess, and she definitely doesn't want coins all over the floor, which might clog her new vacuum.

What rules come into play? I doubt any family has a rule specific to breaking open piggy banks, but there are probably expectations about cleaning up messes.

How can they come to consensus? What solutions allow both to feel that their interests are being considered?

This mom remembered the PIECE model when she realized that she and her son were locked in to positions. She thought about their interests, and when she recognized what was important to both of them, she suggested that he crack open his bank inside of a big cardboard box. This way Tad was able to find out what was inside his piggy bank, and she didn't have a mess to face or a worry about her vacuum. There were even unexpected rewards in their win/win solution. Tad was so elated with his cardboard "treasure box" filled with coins that he spent the remainder of the afternoon playing with it. Mom got to finish sponge-painting her bathroom.

Let's try another one. You might find this a bit more challenging.

Two-and-a-half-year-old Sam woke up delighted with life. He ran out of his room straight to the refrigerator, pulled open the door, and started taking out the mustard. "Mustard sandwich," he demanded. Then he reached for the mayonnaise and lettuce. Sam loved to explore all of the bottles and containers in the refrigerator and cupboards. He'd unscrew the lids, sniff and taste the ingredients, mix spoonfuls of one item with another.

His mother reminded him, as she did every morning, "The rule is, breakfast first, play later." He frowned at her through hooded eyes.

"Rule is play first," he retorted, stomping his foot. When Mom attempted to shut the refrigerator door, Sam fell to the floor in a flood of tears.

Positions: **What does each person want?**

Interests: **Why does each person want this?**

Expectations: **What rules or expectations might come into play?**

Consensus: **What are possible win/win solutions?**

Evaluations: **What adjustments need to be made?**

What are the positions? Sam wants mustard sandwiches. Mom says breakfast first. In her mind, mustard sandwiches are not breakfast food.

For some families this situation would not lead to a power struggle. Many parents would decide that mustard on bread was

really no different from toast and jelly. However, in this family mustard and bread was not acceptable to Mom, and she needed to work through the disagreement.

What's important to the mom? Her child? When you're dealing with a two-year-old, you often have to guess. Sam can tell his mom he wants a mustard sandwich (his position), but in order to figure out the underlying interest Mom will have to do some detective work. If I were Mom, I might guess that Sam wants to explore. He may want independence. He may want to do things himself. These are very common interests for two-year-olds. Or, if he is temperamentally irregular, he may not be hungry for breakfast. Because Sam wasn't refusing to eat, I'd begin with the assumption that his interest was to do things for himself.

Mom values routine. Making sure everyone eats breakfast is important to her. She wants to start out the day with a nutritious breakfast before anything else happens.

The rules in this family were clear. Mom told Sam the rule is breakfast first. The trouble is, Sam thought the rule should be play first. Mom can acknowledge Sam's feelings by saying something like, "You wish the rule was play first." But she can feel comfortable repeating and enforcing breakfast first. Setting limits doesn't mean ignoring interests and feelings. While Mom can remain firm about the timing of breakfast, she can also look at Sam's interests in order to win his cooperation.

Consensus means everyone's interests are addressed. Mom wants to begin the day with a nutritious breakfast. Sam wants to do things himself and explore. One win/win solution might be letting Sam help with getting out bowls, pouring cereal and juice (using a kid-size pitcher), and with Mom's supervision pushing down the toast and buttering it. Another more long-term solution might be making a breakfast box the night before and having it ready for Sam to pull out of the refrigerator and serve himself. This solution won't help at this moment, but it can prevent future hassles.

Both of these solutions meet Sam's interest in exploring and doing things himself. They also include Mom's interest in a nutritious breakfast first thing in the morning.

It is especially important to try these solutions and evaluate them, because if the guess that Sam's interest in doing things himself is incorrect, Mom will have to experiment with other possibilities.

Learning to get to yes is one discipline tool. It is by no means the only tool. You won't always want to problem solve with your child, but it is a very important skill that your persistent child needs to develop. In Chapters 8 and 9 you'll find more tips on how to get your child to work with you.

LOOKING FOR YES

Now it's time to practice your skills in one of your own situations. Try this exercise with your child.

Think of a struggle you have been experiencing with your child. Describe it here:

____

____

____

____

POSITION: What does each person want?

Parent:

Child:

INTEREST: Why does each person want this? What is the interest or motivation?

Parent:

Child:

EXPECTATIONS: What rules or expectations govern this situation?

1. ____

2. ____

Consensus: List three to five possible solutions.

1. ______________________________

2. ______________________________

3. ______________________________

4. ______________________________

5. ______________________________

Evaluate: Does the solution you selected meet the interests of all involved? Does it honor your rules and expectations?

____

____

____

SAVOR YOUR SUCCESSES

The next week when I asked who had a success to share, hands shot into the air. I was elated to see that one hand belonged to Maggie.

"Kristen, my eight-year-old, wanted to play tennis. She was adamant. It was rainy and windy outside. I told her she couldn't play in the house. She didn't care. She said she'd play in the garage. I countered that the car was in the garage and it was cold. She said she'd wear a jacket and I could pull the car out into the driveway. I tried another tack, pointing out that the garage floor was covered with gravel and sand. 'No problem,' she said, she'd shovel and sweep it out. I told her that by the time she finished, it would be eight-thirty and time for bed. She couldn't be deterred. She wanted to play tennis in the garage that night!

"I realized we were locked in to positions. I could hear my mother's voice in my head: 'Don't spoil her. Don't fold!' But another voice squeaked though—interests. Think about interests. Mine was for her to be in bed by eight-thirty. I wasn't sure what hers was, so I asked her. 'Why would you want to go to all that work when it's so cold out there?'

"'Because, Mom,' she said, 'I've been cooped up in school and in this house. I just want to play.'

"She was right. We hadn't been getting enough exercise. So to mentally defend myself from my mother's voice and to clarify my interest, I told her that I'd set the timer for eight o'clock. She agreed. I pulled out the car. She swept and shoveled. By the time she finished, she only had twenty minutes to play. She closed the garage door and started hitting the ball against it. *Whack, whack, whack,* nice even strokes. When the buzzer went off at eight o'clock, I called her in. 'Okay,' she called, and quit.

"She went to bed peacefully. I know if I'd just said no she'd still be screaming."

"How did you feel?" I asked.

"Great," Maggie replied. "It was nice. I felt successful. My goal was to get her in bed on time, and it worked. I didn't even feel guilty or like I was spoiling her. And Kristen felt good too. To her it didn't matter that she only had twenty minutes to play. She just wanted to do it."

"Why did it work?" I asked.

"The solutions met both interests," Diane offered.

"And the eight-thirty bedtime rule was honored," I confirmed. "That's problem solving."

The others had similar stories. Sadie wanted to change into a ballerina outfit minutes before they were to leave for our class. Sarah agreed to let her as long as Sadie limited herself to five twirls around the dining room table followed by a quick change back into her clothes. They'd arrived on time and in good spirits.

John's thirteen-year-old daughter, Kelly, wanted to go to an R-rated movie with friends. John told her she could be with her friends, but she could not go to an R-rated movie. Initially she protested, but when John pointed out that her real interest was to be with friends, which he was saying yes to, she got back on the phone and negotiated for a different movie.

When Brent raised his hand, I was beginning to feel a bit smug.

Wow! I couldn't help thinking, last week must have really been an effective class! Brent helped me contain my ego.

"I tried what you said," he told me. I think my chest puffed up just a bit. "I put Sonja down and lay with her for a few minutes."

"And?" I said.

"She went right to sleep," he continued.

"All right!" I cheered. It was then I noticed Brent was not cheering with me. Nor was he smiling. In fact, he looked a bit miffed.

"What's wrong?" I asked.

"It was ridiculous. I've got things to do at night. Lying there with her was like putting a straightjacket on me. By the time she went to sleep I was ready to blow."

"Ohh," I replied—a good extrovert filling the silence. I didn't know what to say.

And then Brent broke into a grin. "But I," he said, pointing to himself, "came up with a better idea. I realized that her interest was in seeing me. So I moved her bed so she could see out the door, and then I moved a chair into the doorway of my bedroom across the hall. I could sit there, watch television, read the paper, pay bills, whatever, and she could still see me. She went to sleep without my having to lie there!"

I gulped as I admitted, "A much better idea than mine." Then I asked the group, "Why didn't my solution work for Brent?"

"It met Sonja's interest but not Brent's," Lynn answered.

"And why was Brent's much better?"

"It met both of their interests. Sonja could see him, but he didn't have to lie still doing nothing."

"That's right, which is why evaluating is so important. Last week we were short on time and I goofed. I failed to check that the solutions offered really met both Brent and Sonja's interest. But Brent figured that out himself and adjusted as needed."

By now it was Brent who was feeling rather smug. His eyes twinkled as he sat back in his chair, arms crossed confidently across his chest.

"Great job!" I remarked.

He acknowledged my compliment with a tip of his cap.

Now it's your turn to savor your successes.

Savor Your Successes

Think of situations when you've been able to use PIECE to solve a problem for you and your child.

How did you feel afterward?

How did your child feel?

What did your child learn?

Why did it work?

If it didn't work quite as well as you had hoped, what will you do differently next time?

CORNERSTONE

Persistent children need to hear

Statements that help them feel good about their persistence:

- ✔ You are an independent thinker.
- ✔ You are creative.
- ✔ You are a good problem solver.

Statements that help them unlock and identify their interest:

- ✔ I'm listening.
- ✔ I'm trying to understand.
- ✔ What is important to you?

Statements that help them find solutions that will work for everyone:

- ✔ You can unlock.
- ✔ You can think of another solution.
- ✔ What else could we do?

7

SENSITIVITY

Understanding How Your Child Feels

IN PREPARATION

- Read Chapters 8 and 16 in *Raising Your Spirited Child.*

CHAPTER HIGHLIGHTS

- A detailed look at the triggers for sensitive individuals.
- Responses that help sensitive people manage their sensitivity.
- Successful strategies for those tough times, like dressing, going out, eating, and more.

THINGS TO OBSERVE

- When you are in a restaurant, shopping center, or place of worship, note what sensations bother you.
- When you enter a room, note whether you are aware of the emotions of the people present.

Six-year-old Steven was in trouble. His teacher called home after he continually refused to finish his assigned work sheets. His mother called me, seeking help. "The funny thing is," she said, "he does some of them but then absolutely refuses to try others."

"Have you asked him why he won't do them?" I asked.

"He won't say anything," she responded. "He just shrugs or says they're stupid."

With his teacher's approval, it was decided that his mother and I would visit his class on a Tuesday morning. Shortly after we arrived, each child was handed a packet of work sheets. Steven scrutinized each page, then settled down to work. He finished the first sheet, then the second, but when he turned to the third page he stopped.

"I'm not doing this one," he growled.

"Why not?" his mother asked.

"It's a cut-and-paste sheet," he answered.

"So?" his mother responded.

Steven reached into his desk and took out a film can filled with paste. He opened it and thrust it up to his mother's nose.

"Smell this!" he demanded. "Do you want to put your finger in there?"

Steven is sensitive. He is one of those individuals who feels emotions, sees sights, hears sounds, feels textures, tastes flavors, and smells odors to a greater degree than the average person. Like other sensitive people, he isn't kidding when he says he can't complete his work sheets because the paste stinks. He is dead serious when he says he can't wear a particular pair of socks or type of underwear because the seams drive him crazy. The commotion at the amusement park really does give him a headache. And even if the teacher isn't yelling at him, his stomach still hurts when there is conflict around him.

Some people are keenly aware of the sights, sounds, smells, and textures around them. Others are not. We don't get to choose how sensitive we are, but we can learn to manage our responses. It's our job as parents of spirited kids to help them identify their sensorial triggers. Is your child especially vulnerable to noises, lights, textures, smells, sounds, emotions? If so, she needs to know it and to know what to do about it.

A NEW POINT OF VIEW

The group was milling around the coffeepot. Maggie always brought tales of bargain shopping, and this evening she was advising John where to find cheap sporting goods. Brent and Phil, both wearing baseball caps turned backward, were eavesdropping. I had noticed earlier that Danny's cap matched his dad's. Diane was regaling Sarah with some tale. Her hands fluttered in front of her as her voice rose and fell. I couldn't help thinking that life bubbled inside her like a freshwater spring. It just didn't seem like a night to sit down and chat.

"Tour time!" I announced to the group.

"Hey, we get to leave the kids and take off?" Phil asked hopefully.

"The Mall of America—a night of shopping!" Lynn suggested, since it was just down the road.

"Nothing that exciting," I explained. "We're just going to tour the building. Tonight we're going to test your sensitivity. You can't fail this test. Just be yourself. Go ahead and walk around the building for five minutes. When you come back. I'll ask what you noticed."

As the group moved out, I called to Brent and Diane. "Would you two please go together?"

They looked at me curiously.

"I've got a hunch that your preferences are very different on the sensitivity continuum," I explained. "I'd like you to see and experience the same places."

"Hmmm," they responded, not quite sure if they really wanted to do this.

Maggie sensed their discomfort. "Okay if I join you?" she asked. They agreed and walked out together.

I invite you to take a kind of tour too. Right now, wherever you are sitting, spend a few moments taking in your environment. What do you notice? If other people are around you, ask them what they are seeing, feeling, hearing, smelling, or tasting.

Note your observations here.

___

___

___

When the group returned, I asked for their observations.

Diane opened the discussion as she munched on potato chips she'd picked up from the staff-room vending machine.

"They're remodeling on the other side of the building," she said between mouthfuls. "I can smell sawdust. And in the office down the hall, two people were working. One was getting very frustrated with the other. I also noticed"—she paused to wipe a crumb from the corner of her mouth—"that the wallpaper in the west hall must be a different dye lot from that in the east hall. They're just slightly off."

"What about you, Maggie?" I asked. "What did you notice?"

"The design along the hallways. I liked the colors, although I think I would have used a slightly different shade of green." She paused, eyeing the potato chips. Diane offered her one. She popped one in her mouth and continued. "The whirring of the fans in the staff room would drive me nuts. And there were pictures on the wall that had been put up unevenly. I also noticed someone must have had a tuna sandwich for lunch."

I noted their responses on a chart I had drawn on the board.

Smells	***Sights***	***Tastes***	***Tactile Sensations***	***Sounds***	***Emotions***
construction	pictures			fans running	frustration
tuna	wallpaper				
	wall design				

Brent turned to Diane and Maggie, his eyebrows raised in amazement. "We weren't in that office two minutes," he stated incredulously. "How do you know one of those women was frustrated with the other?"

Diane just smiled. "I know," she said, offering him a chip.

Brent took it, munching loudly. "I never even noticed there was wallpaper on the walls, much less that they were from different dye lots."

"How about the pictures?" I asked him.

"What pictures? I never saw them!"

The others in the group laughed, some easily identifying with Maggie and Diane's observations, others commiserating with Brent. Truly we were different.

"We're all normal," I affirmed, "but some people are much more sensitive than others. They experience sensations the rest of us might miss. It's important to realize that others may be reacting to sensations that we have not even perceived.

"Now think about your kids. What emotions, smells, tastes, sights, sounds, touches, or textures bother them?"

Sarah sat primly in her chair. "Oh, I know," she said excitedly. "When Cara bakes, she won't measure the sugar. She says that the smell of it makes her gag. Odors in the car bother her too. Heaven forbid if someone has left food wrappers in the car overnight. First she'll refuse to get in, then she'll want to ride with the windows down."

John nodded in agreement. "My daughter can't lick a stamp. She has to get one of us to lick it or use a sponge." Thank goodness for self-adhesive stamps, I thought.

Diane jumped into the conversation. "Brandon hates meat. He always complains about the texture and taste. Noises get him too, little things like whistling, tapping, chewing, even a knife scraping the plate will make him squeal."

Lynn laughed. "Yes, and the sound and vibration of the vacuum. When Jenna was little she used to scream; now she just complains that it gives her a headache. Sad movies get Justin," Diane continued. "He can finally watch *Bambi* without crying, but his older cousins have given him a ton of grief about being a crybaby, which only makes him cry more because he doesn't like teasing—even if he's not the one being teased."

"It's visual things that bother Tara," Phil said. "She complains about the sun. We even bought her sunglasses—expensive ones.

Otherwise she doesn't want to ride in the car or play outside in the summer. Even when she was a baby, she'd scream until she turned purple if the sun got in her eyes."

We started talking about our own pet peeves, and the list grew longer still.

"Oh, my gosh, look at that!" Diane exclaimed, reviewing the chart. "No wonder it's so hard. I never realized all the little things that could trigger my kids—and me."

With spirited kids, it is often the seemingly little things that can set them off. That's why it's important to teach yourself to notice the triggers for all the members of your family.

I made a chart and added each response.

Sensitivity Triggers

1. Think about your family. What sights, sounds, smells, tastes, touches, or emotions bother each individual?

2. Review the chart below and highlight the things that trigger each family member.

3. Add your own triggers.

4. If your kids are four or older, have them help you complete the chart. Together identify the seemingly little things—the situations, circumstances, and sensations—that can lead to trouble and misunderstandings.

5. Circle the most important ones for your family.

SENSITIVITY TRIGGERS

Smells	*Sights*	*Tastes*	*Tactile Sensations*	*Sounds*	*Emotions*
perfumed toilet paper	uneven pictures	meat	seams in sock	alarm clocks	sad movies
sugar	colors that don't match	lima beans	tags in clothing	sirens	others crying
food or wrappers left in car	things in motion	glue on stamps	wristbands and collars	vacuum cleaner	teasing

Smells	*Sights*	*Tastes*	*Tactile Sensations*	*Sounds*	*Emotions*
cigarettes	**the sun**	**foods mixing**	**playing in sand or finger-paint**	**people chewing or coughing**	
bad breath	**fluorescent lighting**	**spices**	**shots**	**whistling**	
coffee	**monotony —no color**	**tooth-paste**	**wool hats/ mittens**	**tapping**	
perfume	**hours of watching television**	**glue on envelopes**	**growing pains**	**knife cutting on plate**	
paint		**eating anything green**	**temperature changes**	**traffic noise**	
bathroom smells			**haircuts**	**chaos, lots of people talking, music**	
garbage			**stiff jeans**	**movies in the theater**	

Key Areas of Sensitivity for My Family

If you find it difficult to remember the specific triggers, think about categories. Which senses are most easily triggered for each family member?

1. **In the first row of the following chart, write the name of each family member.**
2. **Review the sensitivity-triggers chart.**
3. **Think about each member of your family. In which categories is that person most sensitive?**
4. **Complete the following chart to help you predict the most common types of triggers for each family member.**

Here's an example from Sarah's family.

Name	*Bob*	*Sarah*	*Cara*	*David*	*Sadie*	*Kim*
key areas of sensitivity	sights sounds	smells tastes emotions	smells textures touch	emotions sights sounds	sights	sights touch

Name						
key areas of sensitivity						

After completing her family's chart, Sarah let out a long breath. "No wonder Cara wouldn't go into the ape house at the zoo! I thought she was just being difficult. She's always complaining about how things smell—the school bus, her teacher's perfume, the dentist's breath. It all makes sense now, and I've been so embarrassed by her behavior. I really wasn't listening at all, and I'm sensitive too!"

It's very common for a sensitive child to scream and protest when her senses are being assaulted because she doesn't recognize or understand what's bothering her. The next time your child begins to protest that the lights are hurting her eyes or she can't eat the peas because they've touched the mashed potatoes, it's essential that you recognize that she is not just trying to get you. As you gain insight into her areas of sensitivity, you can help her find ways to cope.

Insights

Sarah realized that Cara is temperamentally sensitive. Cara wasn't just being difficult when she refused to go into the ape house. This awareness gave Sarah a new perspective and understanding of Cara's behavior. Take a moment to think about what insights your chart can offer you.

Looking at my chart, I realize . . .

EFFECTIVE STRATEGIES

Diane thought for a moment, then asked, "All right, even if you know your child is sensitive, what are you supposed to do? Like Steven in your story at the beginning. Even if the paste did stink, he still had to do his work sheets."

"Steven really wasn't doing some of his work sheets because of the smell and feel of the paste," I answered. "It wasn't that he wanted to be stubborn or difficult; the smell truly made him sick. Once his teacher realized that, she simply gave him a glue stick and he got down to work."

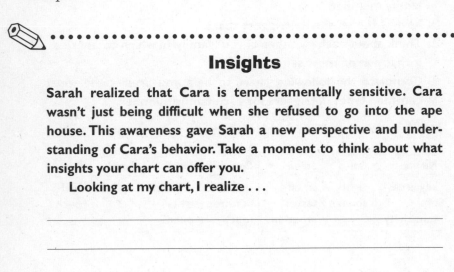

"Interesting," Lynn said.

"But what about the other kids?" Sarah asked. "Wouldn't they all want glue sticks? What do you do if you don't have enough for the class?"

"The teacher simply realized she needed to offer some choices," I said. "Most of the kids were perfectly happy with their cans of paste. Only a few wanted to try the glue stick, so it wasn't really a problem. I know adults often worry that if they give kids choices, every child will want to try every option. But that just doesn't seem to be the case. Kids tend to pick what they need and not bother with the other choices, or they'll try each option a few times, then settle on the best one for them. The most important factor is that the teacher provided a choice of paste or a glue stick. Anyone could have used the glue stick. Its use wasn't just limited to Steven. Everyone had the option."

"Come on," Brent demanded. "Why can't the kid just stick his finger in there and wash it afterward?"

"Because," Maggie stated very firmly, "I'm sensitive too, and I know that wouldn't be an easy thing to do. You can't just wash off that smell. It lingers."

Brent huffed. "That's what my wife and daughter would say. They're always complaining about stuff like that." Turning to Maggie, he demanded to know, "Why do you guys do that? Why can't you just ignore it? Why does it have to be such a big deal?"

Before she could respond, Lynn jumped in. "Brent, remember, why are you right-handed?"

Silence enveloped the room. Brent looked at Lynn, ready to respond, but then he stopped. Her point had hit home.

I waited another moment, monitoring the quiet for tension, but there wasn't any. They'd felt safe enough to ask each other tough questions, and they found answers that satisfied them—at least for the moment. We were still working together.

"Brent, you raise a very important point," I said. He looked at me surprised. "Steven's refusal could be frustrating to deal with. And many of you have remarked about how tough it is to be sensitive. That's why it's so important to have a positive vision. We need to ask ourselves, 'What's good about being sensitive?'" I looked at Diane. She waved her hands toward my face.

"Remember," she said, "I'm the one trying to figure that out."

Quiet, empathetic John came to the rescue. "Sensitive people are caring," he said. "And they make good arbitrators."

"Discerning," Lynn added. "You notice things other people don't."

"Selective," Maggie offered.

Phil lifted the cap off his head. "I've got it," he exclaimed. "I just heard on the radio that sound producers have to figure out how to make the right sounds for their movies. One guy used boiling spaghetti sauce for a volcano about to erupt!"

Lynn snickered. "What does that have to do with sensitivity?"

"You can get a job as a sound producer," Phil explained.

Diane hooted. "My next career! Wow! I really like all of these neat things about being sensitive. I never knew I was so special." She hugged herself. Brent shook his head at Diane and laughed. Tipping his thumb toward her, he said, "My wife would love her."

The world needs individuals who are tenderhearted, loving, selective, and discerning. That's why it's so important to help your sensitive child understand his sensitivity and learn how to manage it.

The Five Best Things About Being Sensitive

Think about sensitive individuals you know. List the five best things about being sensitive.

1. ____________________

2. ____________________

3. ____________________

4. ____________________

5. ____________________

Hold that vision!

"Ready to move on to more specific strategies?" I asked. They nodded.

Identifying your child's triggers and *believing* him when he tells you what bothers him are the first steps to helping your sensitive child be successful. The next step is to teach your child the strategies he needs to manage his sensitivity. You need to help him

1. Name the sensations and affirm the feelings
2. Eliminate or avoid the triggers if possible
3. Reduce or make adjustments for triggers that can't be avoided
4. Know when to take a break

1. NAME THE SENSATIONS AND AFFIRM THE FEELINGS

The smell of certain foods may make your sensitive child gag. Likewise tags, scratchy fabrics, bulky seams, and tight necklines can make certain clothing unwearable. Yelling, conflict, or prevailing negativism and sarcasm can make a classroom unbearable for emotionally sensitive children. But kids often don't have the vocabulary to tell us what is really bothering them.

When your child is calm, maybe when you're driving together in the car or saying good night, talk about sensitivity. For example, if the strings on her shirt irritated her that day and made dressing difficult, talk to her about it. You might say, "I think the strings on your shirt *tickled* you today. It frustrated you. Next time you can tell me that it tickles and that you're frustrated, rather than screaming."

It may be six months before your child ever uses the words *tickle* or *frustrated,* but if you keep using words that describe feelings and sensations, ultimately she will.

"That's true," Maggie confirmed. "Yesterday I took Kristen to a fast-food restaurant that had an indoor playground. After we were there twenty minutes she said, 'It's too noisy in here, and the air inside the tunnels stinks. Let's go!' A year ago she would have just thrown a fit. She even thanked me when we left."

It's also important to let your child know that other people experience similar sensations. If she complains about things that smell, you might say, "You're like Grandpa. He is really sensitive to smells too." This is especially important for the emotionally sensitive child, who needs to have his feelings confirmed and to know he is not alone.

When you name and affirm feelings, describe what you see that helps you figure out what the feeling might be. If your child is a toddler, keep it simple. For example, if your toddler sees another child struggling with a puzzle and then throwing it, you might say, "I saw that child try to do the puzzle, but he couldn't. Then he threw it. I think he was frustrated."

If your child is a preschooler, you could say, "That child must be frustrated. He tried and tried, but he couldn't get the pieces in, then he threw the puzzle. Remember last week when you couldn't get the blocks to fit together? You were frustrated too."

If your child is school age, you could say, "That child tried and tried to do the puzzle before he threw it. He must be very frustrated. Remember when you couldn't get your bike back together again? You were frustrated too. What do you think would help him? What could he do instead of throwing the puzzle?"

By helping your child name the feelings and sensations and understand that they are tied to her senses, you begin to give her the power to respond appropriately. The challenge, of course, is to trust your child and to believe her when she describes a sensation—especially if you are not as sensitive and are not experiencing it. Try your best to empathize rather than negate or ignore her complaints. When a child is ignored or told not to feel that way, her intensity rises. Inevitably, the sensitive child will make sure she is heard. The question is, will she be heard when she uses the words you have taught her, or will she need to escalate her requests to screaming fits before she is acknowledged? Listen carefully, and believe your child. Then the two of you can work together to figure out how to manage the stimulation.

Name the Sensations and Affirm the Feelings

Review the following situations. Write your answers in the space provided:

1. **Describe what you see that helps you figure out what the feeling might be.**
2. **Choose words to name the feeling or sensation.**
3. **Affirm that feeling with examples from the child's own experiences or those of others.**
4. **Check your answers with those from the group.**

Your child is watching *Bambi*. Suddenly he starts to cry.

Describe what you see:

____

Name the feeling or sensation:

____

Affirm the feeling:

____

The phone rings. It's your father, calling to tell you that your mother is very ill. You start to cry.

Describe what you see:

____

Name the feeling or sensation:

____

Affirm the feeling:

____

You are shopping in the mall. You can smell the coffee shop to your right and the caramel corn on your left. Nearby there's a shop selling incense. It's crowded. Your child starts to whine. She complains of a headache and stomachache.

Describe what you see:

____

Name the feeling or sensation:

____

Affirm the feeling:

____

Here are responses from the group—a few of many possible responses.

Your child is watching *Bambi*. Suddenly he starts to cry.

Describe what you see:

I see big tears rolling down your cheeks, and I hear you crying. Bambi can't find his mother.

Name the feeling or sensation:

I think that movie is making you feel very sad.

Affirm the feeling:

Sometimes movies make me feel sad too.

The phone rings. It's your father, calling to tell you that your mother is very ill. You start to cry.

Describe what you see:

Yes, Mommy is crying. Grandpa just told Mom that Grandma is very sick.

Name the feeling or sensation:

Mom is feeling sad and scared. You are very sensitive. When Mommy is upset you worry.

Affirm the feeling:

Right now we're both worried.

You are shopping in the mall. You can smell the coffee shop to your right and the caramel corn on your left. Nearby there's a shop selling incense. It's crowded. Your child starts to whine. She complains of a headache and stomachache.

Describe what you see:

The mall is really crowded today. The lights are bright, the noise is loud. People are jostling one another. I can smell coffee, caramel corn, and incense.

Name the feeling or sensation:

I'm wondering if the lights are hurting your eyes and making your head hurt. The smells may be making you feel nauseous.

Affirm the feeling:

Too many sensations at one time really bother Dad too.

Once your child is able to name the triggers, you can help her figure out how to manage them.

2. ELIMINATE OR AVOID THE TRIGGERS IF POSSIBLE

The most important question to ask when faced with a trigger is: Can it be eliminated or avoided? For example, if your child is triggered by itchy sweaters, consider a cotton sweatshirt or sweater instead. Your child will still have warm clothing but won't be irritated by the texture of it. If traffic noise drives him wild, make sure he brings headphones into the car with him. Think about the sensory culprits for your child.

Maggie started to laugh. "Kristen would kill me if she knew I was telling you this. When she was four, she was still yelling, 'Wipe my buns' because she didn't like the smell of the paper. I finally got her to do it herself by buying unscented toilet paper!"

If something drives your sensitive child wild and you can simply eliminate it or avoid it, then by all means, do it!

Brent gave me the eye again.

"Okay," I said. "Why would you bother to do this?"

"Because it feels so good to be believed and to be treated respectfully," Diane stated firmly.

"Because getting dressed isn't a hassle if the tags are gone and I'm not trying to get her to wear stiff jeans," Maggie replied.

"I'm thinking it's a case of choosing your battles," John offered. "There are so many other things to fight about, why hassle over the things that can simply be eliminated?"

I nodded, appreciating their insights. It's true, once you are aware of the triggers, you have a choice. You can choose to ignore them and try to force your sensitive child to chill out. Or you can respect the sensitive individual's reaction and find a way to work with it. Remember, the sensitive person does not choose to be sensitive. The bottom line is that he is experiencing a very uncomfortable sensation. Coping with it can be exhausting. Once that is understood, it's actually quite easy to work with the triggers and still meet the needs of everyone in the family.

Brent pretended to cover his head with his arms as though protecting himself from the crowd. "I get it, I get it," he joked in a tiny, high voice. Diane threw the empty bag of potato chips at him. She missed.

Eliminating and Avoiding Triggers

1. **Review the Sensitivity Triggers chart on pages 143 to 144.**
2. **Cross out those you could easily eliminate or avoid; note how you would do it.**
3. **Check your ideas with those from the group.**

Here are the group's answers, but remember, these are not the only answers. You may have thought of many ideas we missed, and that's great!

SENSITIVITY TRIGGERS

	Triggers	*How to Eliminate or Avoid*
SMELLS	perfumed toilet paper	buy unscented paper
	measuring sugar	have someone else measure it
	food or wrappers left in car	do not leave food or wrappers in car
	cigarettes	stop smoking
	perfume	avoid wearing perfume when with this person
	coffee	brew when kids aren't present
SIGHTS	uneven pictures	make sure pictures are level
	unmatched colors	match colors
	fluorescent lighting	provide lamps and other sources of light
TASTES	meat or lima beans	serve alternative foods
	licking stamps	buy self-adhesive or use a sponge
	food mixing	use plates with partitions
	licking envelopes	use self-adhesive or a sponge to seal
TACTILE SENSATIONS	seams in socks	buy socks without seams
	tags in clothing	cut them out
	playing in sand	eliminate sand play
	tight collars or wristbands	wear short-sleeved and collarless shirts
	hats	use hoods
	stiff jeans	select other types of pants
SOUNDS	alarm clocks	use clocks that play music
	hours of watching television	turn off television
	vacuum	vacuum when child is not present

	Triggers	*How to Eliminate or Avoid*
SOUNDS	whistling or tapping	stop whistling or tapping when this individual is around
	movies in theater	rent videos
EMOTIONS	sad movies	avoid sad movies

How did you do? Were you surprised at how obvious some of the answers were? Isn't it nice to know that you are already doing a lot of these things? I'm always amazed at how obvious some of the answers become once you are aware of the triggers.

It's also important to know that the younger the child or the more stressed, hungry, or tired the individual, the more important it is to simply eliminate the offending trigger. Stress reduces coping abilities. Things that may not typically bother you can suddenly become overwhelming when you are stressed.

3. REDUCE OR MAKE ADJUSTMENTS FOR TRIGGERS THAT CAN'T BE AVOIDED

Obviously there are triggers that can't be totally eliminated. For example, going to the grocery store is often very difficult for a sensitive individual. You can increase the likelihood of success by

- going midweek or during a slow time
- making a list so you know exactly what you're looking for
- limiting the time you are in the store, perhaps by shopping more frequently for fewer items
- shopping when everyone is well rested and fed

By making adjustments like these, you help the sensitive person to get through the store with less frustration—but you still get your groceries.

Sensitive infants are especially vulnerable to sensory overload. Babies on overload tend to fuss more, spit up, have more frequent bowel movements, and arch away from the adult holding them. Dr. T. Berry Brazelton suggests that touching and talking at the same time may be too stimulating for sensitive infants. He recommends that you slow down, soften your voice, and reduce the stimulation around your child.

Studies have also demonstrated that babies who are carried in kangaroo-style packs tend to fuss less and sleep more. The protective pack and close proximity to the caregiver reduce the stimulation levels for the baby.

When you are faced with sensorial triggers that cannot be eliminated, think creatively. How can you reduce them? What adjustments can you make?

Diane shivered. "I don't even want to remember this," she said. "Last fall Brandon started kindergarten. After the first day, he refused to get on the bus. It was a flat-out, absolute 'No way!' I couldn't drive him every day. He had to ride. It was awful."

"What did you do?" Maggie asked.

"First I figured out that he didn't like the smell—it wasn't the first time he'd complained about odors, and I remember the smell of the school bus myself. Anyway, I put a little dab of his dad's aftershave on him. That helped, and then I taught him to breathe through his mouth. It's gotten us through the year."

Diane was creative. Now it's your turn.

Making Adjustments for Triggers That Cannot Be Avoided

1. **Review the Sensitivity Triggers chart on pages 143 to 144 again. (Your job has gotten easier, since you've already crossed off those things that could be eliminated.)**
2. **This time cross out the items that could be reduced or those you could make adjustments to; note how you might adjust.**
3. **Check your answers with those from the group.**

SENSITIVITY TRIGGERS

	Triggers	*How to Eliminate or Avoid*
SMELLS	paint	paint with windows open or when the sensitive individual is not around
	bathroom smells	use a bathroom deodorizer
	garbage	take it out daily
SIGHTS	motion	have the child ride in the middle of the backseat so that he can see out the windshield
	sun	wear sunglasses, use visors
	monotony—same colors	bring along games to play in the car use color and texture in home designs
TASTES	toothpaste	try different brands of toothpaste
	spices	go easy on the spices season each piece separately
TACTILE SENSATIONS	shots	look away from the shot giver use bubbles or deep breathing
	wool hat/mittens	buy soft leather or fleece, not wool use pockets
	growing pains	use ice, heat, or a painkiller
	temperature changes	dress in layers
	haircuts	use deep breathing, allow child to say "Stop" for a second when the tickle gets to be too much

	Triggers	*How to Eliminate or Avoid*
SOUNDS	**sirens**	**teach child to cover ears with hands**
	knife scratching plate	**be careful cutting**
	traffic noise	**allow child to wear headphones**

The triggers that remain on your chart are now ones that cannot be dealt with by naming, eliminating, or reducing them. Now that the list is much shorter, they shouldn't seem quite so overwhelming. The final tool I want to offer you is take a break.

4. TAKE A BREAK

If you are the parent of a sensitive child or if you are sensitive yourself, it is essential that you give your child and yourself permission to take a break when you need it!

There are situations over which you have no control and yet must be a part of, like birthday parties for others or holiday dinners held at someone else's home. In these types of situations, one of the most effective coping skills is to simply teach your child to take a break *before* the stimulation levels become intolerable. If your child is three or under, you will have to monitor the situations and know when to take your child to the rest room, outside, for a car ride, or home. If your child is four or older, he'll need to start taking over this task. Teach him to come to you and say, "I need a break." Plan ahead what you might do so that he knows what to expect.

Next time your sensitive child complains about the onions you are cutting, the spices in your cooking, or that he doesn't like the new brand of bread or detergent you've bought, remember you have a sensitive child. Name the sensation or feeling. Teach him to think creatively. Is there any way to eliminate the offensive source of stimulation? Is there any way to diffuse it? If not, how can he take a break?

Helping Your Child Manage the Triggers

1. In order to organize your potential solutions, complete a picture of sensitivity for your child. On the chart below, list the most significant sensations that trigger her.
2. What strategies could she use to help herself cope?

Here's Sarah's chart for Cara:

Type of Sensation	*Key Triggers*	*Strategies*
SMELLS	sweaty people	avoid hugs after exercise breathe through the mouth
TACTILE SENSATIONS	certain lotions	try different lotions allow lotion to dry before dressing
	anything in her hair	avoid ribbons, bows, barrettes, cut hair short

Your turn:

Type of Sensation	*Key Triggers*	*Strategies*

PRACTICE, PRACTICE, PRACTICE

When you take the time to really think about the sights, sounds, smells, tastes, textures, and emotions that can trigger the members of your family, you are learning to pick up the cues. This information can help you avoid or prevent potential conflicts. Once you recognize those cues, you'll have an easier time developing successful strategies. The challenge, however, is that sometimes the fights aren't just about sensitivity. Other issues and needs can come into play. To bring harmony to your family, those interests have to be identified.

"Who has a sensitivity issue you'd like help with?" I asked the group.

"I've got one," Sarah offered. "My husband's brother is getting married next month. It's a formal wedding, and my husband wants Cara to wear a dress. Cara hates dresses. The issue is turning into a big fight, with my husband telling her she'll wear one or she won't go. Cara teeters between tears and fury. We all want to go, and Bob wants Cara to be there, but it really feels like we're backed into a corner now."

"Sarah," I asked, "what is each person saying or doing in this situation?"

"Bob says she has to wear a dress. That's it. Case closed. Cara says she can't. She hates the feeling of her legs exposed and says that dresses are too scratchy. She also doesn't like the way they look on her."

"What's Bob's response to Cara?" I asked.

"He says she's being ridiculous. Air won't kill her. Dresses aren't scratchy or women wouldn't wear them, and how would she know she doesn't look good in a dress if she hasn't worn one in years? Then Cara starts to cry. At first she wails, 'I can't. I just can't.' But then she gets mad and screams, 'I hate you!' Bob yells at her for talking to him that way."

As Sarah talked, I made our chart.

Bob	***Cara***
wants Cara to wear a dress	hates the air on her legs
tells Cara air won't kill her	dresses are scratchy

Bob	**Cara**
tells Cara dresses aren't scratchy	doesn't feel good in a dress
doesn't think Cara has tried a dress	just can't wear a dress

"Now look at your family's key-triggers chart," I directed Sarah.

Name	**Bob**	**Sarah**	**Cara**	**David**	**Sadie**	**Kim**
Key Triggers	sights	smells	smells	emotions		sights
Key Triggers	sounds	tastes	touch	sights		touch
Key Triggers		emotions			sounds	

"Looking at the charts, what do you notice?" I asked.

Sarah sighed. "That Bob and Cara are very different. He isn't sensitive to tactile things, and she is."

"It may be," I said, "that Cara is experiencing sensations that Bob has no awareness of, like Brent and Maggie's experience on our tour."

As parents we need to be aware of how we are similar to and different from our children. When we realize that we are different, it helps us remember that we may not be experiencing the same sensations.

For many people this simple awareness is enough to help them understand their child's point of view and find a solution that is acceptable to both of them. I doubted, however, that this information would be enough for Bob. I suspected he had an interest that was very important to him, one that had little to do with an awareness of sensitivity.

Turning to the group, I said, "Remember when we talked about persistence and the importance of considering interests?" They nodded. "What do you think is Bob's interest? What is really important to him?"

"I think he wants Cara to look pretty," Sarah responded.

I wrote this statement on the board.

"Any other ideas?" I asked.

"Maybe he wants people to know he can afford dress clothes for his kids," John offered.

I wrote it down and waited for others.

"Maybe he just wants her to do it because he said so!" Brent stated.

I added his idea to the list.

Since Bob wasn't present, we could only guess what might be important to him. Then we switched to speculating on what Cara's interests might be.

"I think she just wants to be comfortable and feel good. She hasn't worn a dress since she was three years old," Sarah said. "When she was fifteen months old she'd rip ribbons out of her hair or try to pull off the ruffles if I put her in a dress. She isn't a sloppy dresser. She cares how she looks. She just doesn't like dresses. And most of the time she does do what Bob says. I don't think she's trying to oppose him."

Identifying our individual interests is critical to finding solutions that work. If Bob's interest is simply to have Cara look pretty or to demonstrate that he can afford dress clothes for his children, there are many potential solutions that don't necessarily include dresses. If, on the other hand, he has decided that this is a situation in which he wishes to employ his parental authority, then a dress is a must. The interests determine the most effective solution.

"The best solutions are reciprocal," I said. "There is give and take. The interests of all involved are considered. So looking at the interests, what are potential solutions?"

"I don't like dresses either," Lynn stated. "I can really understand Cara's point of view, and if Bob just wants her to look pretty or be dressed up, there are beautiful flowing pant outfits in silky materials. They'd be comfortable for Cara and meet Bob's interests too."

"When Kristen made her First Communion she didn't want to wear one of those frilly dresses, so I made her a silky pants outfit and put flowers in hair," Maggie offered. "She looked darling. She was still in white and dressed up."

"There are culottes that look just like dresses," John said. "My wife wears those with tights all of the time."

We had three potential solutions in a matter of minutes.

"Now, what if Bob's interest is to express his authority?" I asked.

"Well, there are long dresses and silky dresses," Maggie said. "Maybe Cara could find something that would feel all right to her."

"Let her wear a dress for a minimal amount of time," Phil offered. "Don't have her put it on until the last minute. Then let her take it off as soon as possible."

"That just doesn't feel right to me," Lynn responded. "Shouldn't Cara be able to choose what she feels good in, as long as it meets social standards?"

There was a long pause.

John spoke up. "I'm wondering," he said, "if this is really where Bob wants to put his foot down. It seems like there are real viable alternatives available that could be satisfactory to everyone. Why do they need to fight?"

The others looked at Brent. He shrugged. "I don't like neckties," he murmured. "Maybe he should let her wear those flowing pants."

Lynn patted him on the back. "All right, Brent!" she cheered. He almost smiled.

We couldn't solve this problem for Bob and Cara. Only they could do that. We asked Sarah if she'd like to take our ideas home with her. She hesitated.

"They're both so angry," she said. "I just don't know if it will work."

"You know your family best," I reminded her. "You can choose to try the ideas, or you can leave them here." She nodded. Later she copied the responses and took them with her.

Trying new approaches isn't easy. We have to allow ourselves to be learners, to reflect on the lessons, test them, analyze what worked and what didn't, and try again. Each of us will do it when we're ready.

Now—if you're ready—it's your turn.

1. Select a common problem or issue that you think may be tied to sensitivity.

The problem: ______________________________

2. **Mark an *X* in each column in which the individuals involved are very sensitive.**

Name						
sights						
sounds						
smells						
tastes						
touches						
emotions						

3. **Are the areas of sensitivity similar or different? Circle one:**

Similar **Different**

4. **What strategies could you use to deal with this problem?**

How could you name it?

Could you eliminate it?

Is it possible to reduce it or make adjustments? If so, how?

Could you take a break?

---

5. **Choose the solution(s) that best meets the needs of everyone involved.**

---

6. **Evaluate how the strategy is working. If it doesn't seem to be effective, think about the other temperament traits we've discussed. Do you need to bring down the intensity? Are the individuals locked in? Make adjustments as needed.**

SAVOR YOUR SUCCESSES

I thought about Sarah as I drove to class the next week. I wondered if she'd found any of the ideas useful, but I also knew I needed to respect her privacy. Fortunately she was the first to arrive. She was juggling Kim on her hip and a diaper bag on her shoulder as she ushered in Cara, David, and Sadie. Sadie showed me her new necklace made of yellow glass beads.

Looking around the empty room, Sarah suddenly stopped. "Is this the right night?" she asked.

"Yes," I confirmed. "You're just the first arrival."

"That's amazing," she remarked. "I guess I was eager to get here. I've got a success story!"

I felt my pulse quicken. "Hurrah!" I cheered.

Later, when the entire group had gathered in the discussion room, she was ready to tell her story.

"I was afraid to talk with Bob," she began. "He'd been so angry about this whole thing. So I waited until the kids went to bed."

"Smart," Phil interjected. "Bringing down the intensity." I smiled, pleased he'd recognized the strategy.

Sarah paused, appreciating his comment too. "I showed him the charts I'd copied and talked about interests. At first he was angry that I'd brought up this issue in class. But when I told him we hadn't judged him, that we hadn't picked a solution for him, that we had just talked about interests and options, he settled down—especially when he saw Brent's suggestion, 'Just do it because I said so!'"

Brent gave a thumbs-up.

"But," she continued, "he also realized John and Lynn were probably right about choosing your battles. When he started thinking about it, he recognized that as the oldest child in his family he always feels pressured to set the standard. We ended up sitting down with Cara and explaining that her dad needed her to meet certain standards of dress. We asked her why she wouldn't wear a dress, and she repeated that she just couldn't. It didn't feel good. This time Bob listened and really heard her. Because of the chart, he realized she wasn't trying to be difficult. She always has been sensitive about her clothes. He agreed she could wear pants if they were dressy!"

"Cara and I went shopping the next day. I thought about asking Bob to go with us, but I thought that was pushing it. He hates shopping. We found a shimmering green tunic with flowing pants. Cara feels beautiful in it, and while Bob would only nod in approval, I could tell he thought she looked great too. Later he was kidding with her. That hasn't happened much lately."

We applauded. Sarah's eyes shone.

Your turn.

Record Your Successes

What sensorial triggers have you identified?

How have you helped your child name, eliminate, or reduce irritating sensations?

CORNERSTONE

Sensitive children need to hear

Statements that help them to feel good about their sensitivity:

- ✔ You are very caring.
- ✔ You are selective.
- ✔ You are tenderhearted.
- ✔ I appreciate how discerning you are.
- ✔ Someday you will make a great arbitrator.

Statements that help them identify their triggers:

- ✔ Smells really seem to bother you.
- ✔ Lighting is very important to you.
- ✔ You are very aware of the emotions around you.
- ✔ Noise can be very irritating to you.
- ✔ You are very sensitive to textures and temperatures.
- ✔ Tastes are very important to you.

Statements that help them manage their sensitivity:

- ✔ You can name that sensation or feeling and then decide what to do.
- ✔ You can choose to avoid or eliminate that sensation.
- ✔ You can figure out how to make adjustments so that sensation will not bother you as much.
- ✔ It's okay to take a break.

8

PERCEPTIVENESS

Helping Your Child Hear Instructions and Stay Focused

IN PREPARATION

- Read Chapter 9 in *Raising Your Spirited Child.*
- Find a partner for the drawing activity.

CHAPTER HIGHLIGHTS

- A new appreciation of perceptive kids.
- Information about the differences and commonalities between perceptiveness and ADHD.
- Strategies to help your child hear you and stay on task.
- Practice winning your child's cooperation.

THINGS TO OBSERVE

- What does your perceptive child notice that other people frequently miss?
- Does your child hear your instructions when you say them?
- Does your child pay better attention when your instructions include both visual images and words?

Our topic for the day was perceptive kids. I had just read *The Pearl* by John Steinbeck and had been enthralled by his keen descriptions. I was overflowing with enthusiasm for the richness perceptive people bring to our lives as I began to tell the group about Elizabeth, a very perceptive child I'd just recently met.

"Elizabeth is three," I began. "Twenty years from now I want to hire her. Elizabeth sees what others do not see. She notices subtleties that are hidden from others. She has the ability to discern what is not obvious. How do I know this? At her child care center, which is attended by more than a hundred children, Elizabeth can identify every child's blanket. After finding a cap on the playground, teachers ask Elizabeth who it belongs to—she always knows. Even pacifiers are Elizabeth's business. She knows that Rob's has a red spot on the end and that Bailey's has a piece of yarn. She recognizes every child's parents, can show a visitor where the coffee cups are stored, and finds the first worms on the spring field trip. Elizabeth is perceptive."

My face flushed as I rolled on. "Individuals who are perceptive tend to see things that others are unlikely to observe. While sensitive individuals experience sensations deeply, perceptive individuals experience sensations broadly, taking in a wide breadth of stimulation. As a result, perceptive children often gain an understanding and awareness of life beyond their years. Keen perception also forms the basis for a sharp sense of humor and a creative mind." I paused for a breath.

But before I could continue extolling the virtues of perceptive children, Lynn folded her arms across her chest and flatly remarked, "That's nice, but do you know what it's like to be Elizabeth's mother? Need I tell you that it takes twenty minutes to get her from the house to the car, that she has to look at every bug and leaf." Her voice grew louder. "And that she wants to collect those bugs and bring them into the car with her!"

"That's right," Brent agreed. "We want to talk about the kid who loses anything—gloves, toys, shoes—not firmly attached to his body."

I sensed strong emotions among the ranks as Lynn tapped the table, adding, "Yeah, the kid you send upstairs to get dressed. You think that's what he's doing, but actually he's stopped to pet the cat. When the school bus comes he still hasn't done his hair."

Maggie's voice was almost apologetic. "Could we talk about the kid who is so full of ideas that she just keeps talking to you and forgets to get dressed?"

I raised my arms, pretending to protect my head as Brent had the week before. "Okay, okay, I give up. I can see you're not interested in starting with the positive aspects of being perceptive. And I do have to agree, sometimes when a child is perceptive he may not hear instructions as they mix with the barrage of stimulation around him. It may be a struggle for him to decide which is the most important message or where his focus should be. As a result he often gets into trouble for not listening or for not staying on task. So, why don't we just start with the challenges of living with perceptive individuals. What else would you like to add?"

Lynn was ready. "They are slow, and they don't pay attention. They interrupt you to show you the bird or to listen to the sound. They get distracted, and they're forgetful."

Diane huffed as she turned to Lynn. "You think it's hard to live with perceptive people, you should *be* the perceptive person! I can forget my kids!"

John nodded, agreeing with Diane. "It is hard to be perceptive. Trying to concentrate in a room filled with people and decorations on the walls and ceilings is really tough. How can you listen to someone when you can see the spider climbing up the wall behind her or the frog swimming in the aquarium?"

Lynn's eyes opened wide. "I wonder if that's why Aaron gets so exhausted in school. He says it's so hard to pay attention. I thought he was just being lazy."

Silence fell in the room. The intensity that had fueled our discussion had diminished. Cautiously I looked around. It was Brent who finally said, "You're going to make us look at the positive side, aren't you?" I only grinned.

A NEW POINT OF VIEW

It's true. It can be challenging to live with the perceptive child. You do have to teach him the skills he needs to be able to hear the most important messages and to stay on task. Holding a positive vision will help you garner the patience you need to teach your perceptive child these important life skills.

I'm going to let you be honest too.

1. **Review the list of irritating, frustrating behaviors associated with perceptiveness—the "raw" resources.**
2. **Add your own.**
3. **Then ask yourself: What's the potential strength behind this behavior?**
4. **In the future, how might your child use this strength?**
5. **Check the next chart for possible answers.**

Challenges of Living with Perceptiveness	*Positive Aspects of Being Perceptive Today and in the Future*
has to look at every bug and leaf	
loses everything	
stops to pet the cat	
full of ideas	
slow	
notices people and decorations; interrupts	
exhausted from paying attention in school	

Here are some possible responses:

Challenges of Living with Perceptiveness	*Positive Aspects of Being Perceptive Today and in the Future*
has to look at every bug and leaf	**observant—a future scientist**
loses everything	**resourceful; can figure out how to "make do"—a future manager**
stops to pet the cat	**notices and enjoys the little things in life—a future photographer**
full of ideas	**exuberant and inventive—a future entrepreneur or writer**
slow	**methodical, observant—a future private investigator or scientist**
notices people and decorations, interrupts	**very aware—a future reporter**
exhausted from paying attention in school	**cognizant of stimulation levels—a future mediator, police officer, military officer**

It's important to remember that the engineer who invented Velcro did so after walking in the woods and noticing how burrs stuck to his clothing. He was perceptive, and because of him jacket sleeves with Velcro closures fit more snuggly, children's shoes with Velcro straps are easier to put on, and more. Take note of the perceptive individuals around you. Recognize the richness they bring to your life. Hold that positive vision.

"But how do you know if your child is perceptive or if he has attention deficit disorder?" Maggie asked.

Many people ask me the difference between being perceptive and having attention deficit hyperactivity disorder (ADHD). There isn't an easy answer. Children who are temperamentally more perceptive and energetic can learn strategies to help them stay focused and perform as necessary. For the child with ADHD, these strategies alone are not enough and at some point the child is unable to meet the expectations, responsibilities, and performance demands for a child his age. Ultimately ADHD interferes with schoolwork, sports, and everyday routine activities. If this is true for your child, it's time to look beyond temperament and consider additional medical concerns. Not all ADHD is alike—some kids are predominantly inattentive, some predominantly hyperactive-impulsive, and still others are both inattentive and hyperactive-impulsive. The symptoms attributed to ADHD may also indicate learning disabilities, hearing problems, or even anxiety or depression.

Determining whether a child has ADHD requires a thorough analysis. If you are concerned about your child, contact a clinic that both specializes in ADHD *and* understands temperament. Ideally the diagnostic process will include a complete physical, observations at home and in school or child care settings, testing by a psychologist or psychiatrist, and consultations with you. Keep asking questions and seeking information until you find adequate answers. Your child needs you to be his advocate.

In their book *Beyond Ritalin*, authors Stephen and Marianne Garber explain that when a child experiences problems with inattention, hyperactivity and/or impulsiveness, treatment should never begin or end with medication alone. Therefore, whether your child is more perceptive and/or has ADHD she will need help learning to sort out the most important messages. So let's get started.

EFFECTIVE STRATEGIES

In order to help perceptive children hear us and to stay on task, we have to make sure we are giving clear directions. "Find a partner," I directed the group. "We're going to work together."

"Isn't that asking a bit much?" Brent teased. I smiled at his joke and began reading aloud the instructions I'd written earlier on the board. You can do this with a partner at home.

1. **Grab a piece of paper and a pen or pencil.**
2. **Find a partner.**
3. **Sit back-to-back with your partner so that you are looking in opposite directions.**
4. **Draw a figure using five lines. Do not let your partner see what you have drawn.**
5. **Describe your figure to your partner so that he can draw the same figure.**
6. **Compare figures.**

How did you do? Were you able to match your partner's figure, or was yours very different?

Switch roles and try again.

Everyone reached in unison for the clipboards lying on the table. John stood and turned his chair back-to-back with Phil. Diane remained seated, scraping across the floor as she maneuvered into position behind Brent. Sarah and Maggie formed a team, leaving Lynn and I to work together. The room erupted in sound. Words mixed with laughter and groans of frustration. I heard Diane exclaim, "You know, I almost flunked geometry." Suddenly a howl from her caught everyone's attention. Chuckling, she leaned forward, comparing the figure on her clipboard to Brent's. "You're not even close," she informed him.

"You didn't do too hot yourself," he pointed out to her.

John remained quiet. Phil held up both of their clipboards to show a perfect match. Lynn and I had come close. Lynn's figure was much larger than mine, but the shape was the same. Sarah and Maggie, like Brent and Diane, were not even in the same ballpark.

"What helped you to be successful?" I asked.

Phil pointed at John. "He gave good directions."

"What are good directions?" I asked.

"He told me it was a five-point star pointing north."

"So he described a familiar image."

"Yes, and he said the figure was an inch tall."

"It was clear and simple," I pointed out. "What made it difficult to complete the task?"

Brent pulled his baseball cap down. "She didn't listen to me," he mumbled.

Diane poked him. "I did too. How was I supposed to know what an airplane rudder looks like!"

"He used words you didn't completely understand?" I asked.

"Well, I know airplanes have rudders, but I couldn't draw one," she retorted, scowling at him. "And he gave too many directions too fast. I couldn't ask questions. I couldn't see. Everybody was talking. I couldn't hear. It wasn't my fault. I listened!" She flopped back in her chair. I smiled to myself. I love spirited parents.

The frustration Diane experienced is common for people who are more perceptive. It's essential that we remember that perceptive kids really are trying to listen—the trouble is they are listening to everything. Our task is to slow down and help them discern the most important messages.

Perceptive children are able to hear us better and stay on task when we

1. CHANGE THE ENVIRONMENT

Perceptive kids are less likely to be distracted if there isn't anything to pull their attention away from the task at hand. It's also easier for them to sort out the most important messages if they aren't being bombarded with extraneous stimulation, as Diane was during the drawing exercise. Look around you. What can you do to reduce distracting stimuli? Can you turn off the television, close the blinds, or put extraneous toys, clothing, books, and pets in another room? And at your child's school can you ask to have him seated in front of the room so that the movements of the other children are behind him?

"That really does make a difference," John commented as I offered suggestions. Then he asked me, "Do you remember when my wife called you about our son, Todd?"

I was embarrassed to admit I didn't.

"It was four years ago," he said. That made me feel better. "He was in third grade and was really having trouble with math. We were confused because math had always been his favorite subject and he was very good at it. But suddenly he didn't get it and didn't like it. My wife called you looking for help. You told her to ask the teacher if she could come in and observe Todd. The teacher agreed. When my wife arrived, the teacher gave her a stack of exams to grade. The kids thought she was just working in the back of the room, but she was really watching Todd."

"Smart teacher," I commented.

"Yes, she was good," John agreed. "My wife realized Todd was sitting at a table with other kids who were distracting him. They were talking and goofing off, and Todd was getting pulled into it. He wasn't listening and as a result didn't understand the work."

"Where was his table?" Maggie asked.

"In the back of the room," John replied. "So my wife talked to the teacher. They moved him from his table to a study carrel in the room. I was afraid he wouldn't like it, but he loved it. A month later he moved to another table in the front of the room with different kids. His grades went up, and he loved math again. Now he's in seventh grade and entering the university's accelerated math program."

"Wow," I exclaimed. "What a great story. I can't guarantee that moving a child to a front table will result in accelerated math scores, but it certainly can help him stay on task. Does anyone else have an example?"

Maggie raised her hand. "I think I do," she said. "At the day care where I work we had a little guy who was constantly distracted at circle time by the trucks and cars outside the window. He kept interrupting. It was very frustrating, but instead of yelling at him, the teacher moved the circle so that her back was to a blank wall rather than the window. Then there was nothing behind her to distract him and he was able to stay much more focused and quiet."

"Great example," I affirmed. "And how about at home?"

"I play butler with Tara," Phil offered. "In the morning, we lay out on the bed all the clothes she's going to wear. The key is that she has everything—shirt, pants, underwear, socks, and shoes—right there in one spot. She can talk to me, but she stays put and gets on her clothes. Otherwise, she's going back and forth to her drawers looking for one thing, then another. She gets distracted and starts dawdling."

"Minimizing the trips is an important strategy," I confirmed. "The more you can group activities in one room or one spot, the less likely your child is to take off and get pulled into playing or doing something else. You might also try storing backpacks, coats, and shoes all by the door. Then your kids won't be running around searching for things when they're supposed to be getting on the bus."

Lynn had been listening attentively. Suddenly she sighed deeply. "I've been fighting with Aaron about where he does his homework. He always wants to work in my home office, and I want him to study in his room. He told me there were too many things in his room that he wanted to play with and the office was better because it was boring." Her voice dropped. "I guess he knows what he needs better than I do."

John perked up at Lynn's words. "Kids really do know what they need, don't they?"

"Many times," I confirmed. "Do you have an example?"

"Yes," he said. "My wife needs quiet when she's trying to focus, but Kelly always plays an instrumental CD while she is studying. My wife tried to get Kelly to turn it off because she thought it was distracting her. Kelly told my wife that she needed it, because it blocked out the distracting noise and helped her focus. We finally decided that we'd let Kelly's report card tell us who was right. When she came home with all A's, we quit hassling her."

Lynn smiled. "Tell your wife thanks," she said. "I needed to know someone else gets caught in these battles too."

Changing the environment to eliminate or reduce distracting stimulation can help your perceptive child stay on task and listen better. Look around you. What can you move, turn off, or put away that will help your child to focus on the most important information? And remember, your child may be able to tell you exactly what she needs—if you'll listen.

2. MAKE EYE CONTACT

I was leaving for class one night when I noticed there was a dirty cookie sheet, pitcher, and bowl sitting next to the kitchen sink. My son was standing with his back to me, on the other side of the room. As I passed him I told him to do the dishes before he left for his game that night. When I arrived home I found the dishes still sitting on the counter—dirty. I was not happy! When he walked in the door, I nailed him. "Not okay!" I said. "I asked you to do the dishes, and you walked out of here without touching them."

He sputtered, "What are you talking about? I did the dishes!"

I pointed to the cookie sheet, bowl, and pitcher still on the counter. "You call those done?"

He turned to look at the counter. "You told me to do the dishes. I thought you were talking about my dishes. When I ate, I rinsed my dishes and put them in the dishwasher. I thought that's what you meant."

I had started this conversation thinking my son was at fault. Instead I realized I had failed to follow the number-one rule of effective directions—make eye contact. Make sure your child sees you and is looking at you when you give instructions—perceptive kids hear best when they can see what they are hearing. You can even have your child repeat back the direction so that you know it has been clearly heard and understood.

Brent snorted. "That's Danny—if he can't see it, he doesn't hear it. If he's in the family room and I'm in the kitchen, I might as well be yelling at the moon. He doesn't hear a thing."

I agreed. "If you want your perceptive child to listen to you, you can save yourself a great deal of frustration by simply walking into the same room and making sure you have eye contact. You may also want to touch him, to insure you are being heard.

3. KEEP INSTRUCTIONS SIMPLE

Perceptive kids may be overwhelmed when given a big task. Rather than telling your child to get his backpack, lunch, coat, hat, and shoes, simplify your instructions by directing him to get his backpack. Once that is accomplished, he can get his hat. Then his coat and so on. Limit the number of directions to two or three steps at a time. Too many directions at once can overwhelm your perceptive child.

You'll also want to limit the number of words you use. In fact, if you talk less, your perceptive child will actually hear you better.

Maggie laughed. "That's true. This morning I said to Brian, 'Please go downstairs and brush your teeth.' He headed toward the bathroom, but five minutes later he was lying on the floor by my feet, playing with the dog. I asked him, 'Brian, did you brush your teeth?' He just looked at me. I knew he hadn't done it. This time I just said, 'Brian, teeth—*now*.' He got up and did it."

"Notice," I said to the group, "that when it was a specific task that Maggie wanted Brian to do, she didn't add *please* or *okay* to the message. If you say to your persistent and perceptive child, 'Brian, would you please go and brush your teeth,' you're liable to get a resounding no."

The best directions are simple, to the point, and include words that are easy to understand. Let's practice sending messages that are clear and simple.

1. Review the following list of directions.
2. Rewrite each one using a maximum of two words.
3. Check the words you selected. Would a child easily understand them?

Complicated Directions	*Simple, Clear Directions*
Brian, it's eight o'clock; you need to get ready for bed.	
Cara, if you hit your sister again, you're going to be in trouble.	
Jenna, put away your shoes, backpack, coat, and hat.	
Please come in for dinner, okay?	
Would you please be quiet?	
Don't do that again.	

Complicated Directions	*Simple, Clear Directions*
Brian, it's eight o'clock; you need to get ready for bed.	**Brian, bed.**
Cara, if you hit your sister again, you're going to be in trouble.	**Cara, stop.**
Jenna, put away your shoes, backpack, coat, and hat.	**Jenna, shoes, backpack. Jenna, coat, hat.**
Please come in for dinner, okay?	**Come, dinner. (If your child is slow to adapt, you'll need to have given her a forewarning; see the next chapter.)**
Would you please be quiet?	**Quiet.**
Don't do that again.	**Stop.**

4. TELL THEM WHAT THEY *CAN* DO

I grew up on a dairy farm. When I was ten, my two sisters—age twelve and seventeen, and I decided we wanted a horse. Considering where we lived, this was not an outlandish request. My father told us he would *not* buy us a horse. After a bit of discussion my sisters and I decided that Dad had merely told us he would not purchase the horse; he had not said we couldn't have one. We pooled our money and bought a fifteen-month-old registered quarter horse. When we brought him home, my father admonished, "You darn fools! That thing is going to grow." (His words were actually a little stronger than that, but this is a family book.) He was right. The horse did grow another foot at the shoulder. He was so tall we had to put him on the downside of the hill and stand on the upside in order to get a foot in the stirrup, but we got to keep him.

When giving directions to perceptive kids (and persistent ones too), tell them what they can do—not what they can't. There are three main reasons for this strategy:

1. If they're anything like my sisters and me, they'll think of what you failed to tell them they couldn't do and then do it. (You told them they couldn't play in the lake, but you didn't say anything about the creek.)

2. Kids are much more open to hearing what they can do than what they can't. And you've only got their attention for a few seconds, so focus on what's most important, what you want them to do—wash the pitcher, cookie sheet, and bowl—rather than saying "Don't walk out of here without doing the dishes."

Let's try a few.

1. Review the following directions.

2. Change each direction to tell the child what he can do.

Don't Directions	***Can-Do Directions***
Don't put your feet on the chair.	
Don't go in the street.	
Don't be naughty.	
Don't be noisy.	
Watch out.	
Don't be obnoxious.	
Don't be out too late.	
Don't leave a mess.	

Don't Directions	***Can-Do Directions***
Don't put your feet on the chair.	**Feet on the floor.**
Don't go in the street.	**Stay in the yard.**
Don't be naughty.	**Run outside; walk inside.**
Don't be noisy.	**Use a whisper voice.**
Watch out.	**Stand here by the door.**
Don't be obnoxious.	**Listen to Grandma.**
Don't be out too late.	**Be home by ten o'clock; call by eight.**
Don't leave a mess.	**Put books on the shelf.**

5. USE IMAGES AND ACTIONS AS WELL AS WORDS TO COMMUNICATE YOUR MESSAGE

During parent-child interaction time, Maggie's son, Brian, had been deeply engrossed in building a race-car track. "Will you watch him with me?" Maggie had asked.

"Of course," I answered. "What are you concerned about?"

"He just doesn't listen to me," she lamented. "I mean it. It's as though he doesn't even hear me, but I've had his hearing tested, and it's fine."

While we were talking the early-childhood teacher announced cleanup time. Brian continued playing. He never even looked up. The teacher then walked up to him and touched his shoulder, once again telling him it was cleanup time. Brian responded by adding more pieces to his track. It wasn't until the teacher went over, blinked the lights, and announced cleanup time again that Brian stood up, looked at his mother, and exclaimed, "It's cleanup time!"

I realized he had never heard the direction until the blinking light had caught his attention and helped him hear the words.

"Come on," I said to Maggie. Walking over to Brian, I held three fingers in front of him. "Brian," I said, "you can add three more pieces to your track, then we need to move it so we can have circle time." I suspected he had a picture of the completed track in his head, so I assured him that he could return to it when circle was over and the parents had left for discussion. He selected three pieces. Then I counted each one with him as he inserted them in his track. Finished, he stood up, brushed off his pants, and asked, "Where are we going to save it?"

I pointed to the red chair in the corner. "Let's put it by the red chair. It will be safe there." Together we moved it.

"How did you do that?" Maggie asked. "He never listens to anyone, especially people he doesn't know very well."

"It wasn't magic," I replied. "I suspect your son is a very perceptive child."

"He is," Maggie agreed.

"Perceptive kids are often visual learners," I continued. "I simply held up my fingers to indicate three more blocks and then pointed to the red chair so he could picture where it would be stored. When I added visual cues to my verbal instructions, he heard me better."

Companies spend millions of dollars each year creating images to help us "hear" their messages. Extensive market research has demonstrated that some people respond best when they hear a message, while others have to see it or feel it to remember it. They've also learned that if they want their customers to actually respond to their message, one exposure isn't enough. So they sing it to us, picture it for us on television and in magazines, and print it on buses and T-shirts. In multiple ways they send us their message. We are inundated until we "hear" them. Think about it: when you hear the Coca-Cola jingle, do you also form a mental image in your mind of happy people? They want you to. They want you to hear Coke, think Coke, and feel *good* so that you'll choose their product.

Observe your child. Is she like Brian? Does she need a visual cue, like the lights flickering, to "hear" your message? Does she respond to words alone? What happens when you sing to her or use a whisper voice? Experiment until you identify how your child "hears" best.

"What techniques help your child to hear you?" I asked the group.

"I've made charts," Diane replied. "It helps the kids and me."

"What did you do?" Maggie asked.

"I just made a list of all the things the kids needed to do in the morning. For the little ones I drew pictures. Then I created a row for each day of the week and tied a pen to the poster. The kids check off each task as they complete it. We use a different color for each day so that we don't get mixed up. It looks like this."

She got up and drew it on the board.

Task	***Sun.***	***Mon.***	***Tues.***	***Wed.***	***Thur.***	***Fri.***	***Sat.***
Use toilet	X	X					
Get dressed	X	X					
Brush hair	X						
Eat breakfast	X						

Task	*Sun.*	*Mon.*	*Tues.*	*Wed.*	*Thur.*	*Fri.*	*Sat.*
Put on shoes	X						
Get backpack	X						

"What else can you do?"

"We've used a timer," Phil replied. We figured out that it takes Tara about fifteen minutes to get dressed, so we set the timer. When it rings, she knows it's time to go downstairs for breakfast."

We continued brainstorming. Brent had his kids hop up the stairs or skip down the hall. By tying his directions to physical actions he was able to make his kids hear him better. Phil would point to the object he wanted the kids to pick up or put on. Seeing the object and hearing the words was enough to win their cooperation. John had taught his kids to close their eyes and make a picture in their mind of the tasks they needed to accomplish. And of course if the kids are old enough to read, you can write a note as well as tell them your message.

When you vary your techniques, you can also repeat your message without sounding repetitive.

Perceptive kids draw in every aspect of the stimulation around them. You can help them to sort out the most important messages. When you reduce distracting stimuli, make eye contact, give simple, can-do directions, and give visual and physical cues as well as verbal ones, it's much easier for them to hear you.

PRACTICE, PRACTICE, PRACTICE

"All right," Lynn said. "I'm ready. Help me figure out what to do with the kid who stops to pet the cat, forgets to get dressed, and misses the bus."

I wrote the five effective strategies for perceptive kids on the board.

1. Change the environment.
2. Make eye contact.
3. Keep instructions simple.

4. Tell them what they *can* do.
5. Use images and actions as well as words to communicate your message.

"Look at the list," I directed Lynn. "Which strategies could you use?"

"We definitely could change the environment," she said. "Right now he's running up and down stairs ten times. I could have him make sure he gets dressed and does his hair before coming down for breakfast. I could also lock the cat in my bedroom so he doesn't start playing with her. I can try to remember to make eye contact. I often yell from the other room, because I'm getting dressed too. I guess I could talk less. I know I'm constantly asking, where are your books, did you do your hair? Maybe I could try the single words—hair, books. And I think he'd be willing to create a checklist to review the night before, to make sure he's got everything he'll need in the morning."

I listed her suggestions on the board as she talked.

She sat back in her chair, reviewing the list. "I think that would help," she said and copied it down.

"But what if you try all of these things and they don't listen to you?" Sarah asked, shifting uncomfortably in her seat. "In the grocery store I tell Sadie to stay with me, but she's constantly dashing off to get a taste from the sample table or lagging behind."

John had gotten up to get himself a cup of coffee, but he listened attentively as he leaned against the back wall slowly mixing cream into his coffee with a stir stick. "When my kids were little I would tell them they had to be touching the cart or holding my hand. When they got a little older they had to stay within four feet or ask me if it was all right for them to go where they wanted to go."

"Did they do it?" Sarah asked. "Mine won't do it. When I'm trying to get the baby out of the car, Sadie will bolt across the parking lot. It's so hard to get it into her head that it isn't safe."

Maggie touched Sarah's arm. "Kristen would take off too. When she ran away, I went and got her. I told her it was *not okay* to run off. She had to listen. Then I told her that we were going to practice. I'd put the baby back in the seat and go through the whole thing again. I would say, 'Mom is getting the baby out, help me with the straps.' Then, 'Hold my hand when we walk in the lot.' It only took a couple of times before she got it."

Wanting to emphasize all of the effective techniques Maggie had used, I asked, "What did she do?"

"She told her what she could do, and she tied the words to actions," Phil replied. I nodded.

Suddenly Maggie seemed lost in thought as she twirled her hair around her finger. "I just realized I know how to use these strategies, but I haven't been doing it lately," she said. "No wonder Brian isn't listening to me. I guess I've been so stressed, with the divorce and everything. I just haven't been thinking about it. I can do this!"

Sarah exhaled. "I can too. I mean, I haven't been clear. I just said, 'Stay still.'" She paused, thinking. "I'm not sure she even heard me. I don't think I looked at her when I said it. I'm usually rushing to get the door open and the baby out before she's on the run." She paused again, then lifted her chin. "I guess there are some other things I could try." A look of determination shone in her eyes.

Now it's your turn.

1. Describe a situation in which your perceptive child has had difficulty sorting out the most important information.

---

2. Review the five strategies, create a plan that will help your child "hear" your instructions, and stay focused.

Strategy	***Action Steps***
Change the environment	
Make eye contact	
Keep instructions simple	
Tell them what they can do	
Use images and actions as well as words to communicate your message	

SAVOR YOUR SUCCESSES

It had rained before our next class, a cold drizzly rain, reminding us that winter still had a hold. But on Tuesday when we met, the sun was finally shining brilliantly. The hostas had surged from tightly wrapped points emerging from the earth to broad leaves gathering the light. Daffodils and tulips bloomed. Maybe, just maybe, spring was here to stay. The sunshine seemed to be reflected in everyone's mood—except Diane's. There wasn't any spring in her step. She was scowling, rubbing her neck, and twisting her head attempting to ease the tension that had gathered there.

She sighed. "I think I've got more stumbles than successes to share. I just can't get Andy to listen to me. I tried making my directions more visual. I made sure I had eye contact, but"—her voice dropped—"he didn't listen again. I needed a shower. He was in the kitchen. So I gave him a coloring book and crayons. I opened it up for him and told him I was going upstairs to shower. I told him to color this page and this page and this page. I turned the pages and showed them to him. I thought it would take him thirty minutes."

I glanced at my list to make sure of Andy's age (three years)—a very important piece of information.

"I went upstairs, but then the phone rang. By the end of the conversation I knew it had already been five, ten minutes, so I thought I'd better check on him. He was gone! I ran through the house, yelling for him. No Andy. I looked out the window. There he was, barefoot, no coat, standing in the rain.

"I dragged him in the house and timed him out, but when I said to him, 'Don't you know that's not safe, it scares Mommy,' he just smiled at me!"

"How many of you could take a shower and leave your three-year-old unattended?" I asked the group. No hands were raised. "How many of you could take a shower and leave a four-year-old unattended?" Four people raised their hands.

"You only have to wait a year," I told Diane. She groaned. "Seriously," I continued. "Andy at three doesn't understand safety. He's very perceptive, energetic, and persistent. I suspect he saw something outside. His desire to find out what it was and what he could make happen was much more powerful and desirable than staying in the house to color."

"The new swing set," Diane acknowledged. "We just put it up on Saturday. He loves it, and because of the rain we hadn't been outside that morning."

"You gave visual directions, but Andy didn't understand why they were important. You can't let Andy out of your sight—yet. Soon, but not now. It isn't safe," I said.

She drooped. I cringed inside. I didn't want to lose her.

"Look at it this way," I said. "You made eye contact. You made the directions visual. You told Andy what he could do. You did all of those things really well. You just have to wait until he grows up a little for that particular direction to be effective."

"This is so tough!" she exclaimed.

"Yes. That's why you read books and take classes. There is a lot to learn, and you're doing it."

She twisted in her chair. "Okay! Okay! I'll keep trying, but I need some help."

I turned back to the rest of the group. "How do you take a shower when you have a three-year-old?"

"You get up before he does," Maggie replied. "It's the only way you can get a few minutes to yourself with a busy, perceptive, persistent child."

Diane protested. "I like to sleep in too."

"Is it worth it?" Lynn asked.

Diane groaned. "Maybe not. I just used to take the others in the bathroom with me. Give them toys to play with, and shower. But Andy sees everything and has to try it. He tears apart the bathroom. I guess I could get up, but I've just been so tired."

Maggie patted her arm, reassuring her that it would get easier. Diane sighed deeply. Maggie waited a moment to be sure Diane was okay, then announced that she had a success story.

"What worked?" I asked her.

"Well, getting Brian ready for bed is always an issue. So I started by changing the environment. I turned off the television an hour before bedtime. Then I had him help me turn off the lights downstairs, and we went upstairs to change. I gave him three instructions at a time, holding up my pointer for pajamas, the middle finger for teeth, and the ring finger for pick a bedtime book. The strategies did seem to make a difference. It wasn't a miracle cure," she assured us, "but at least I felt like he was listening."

"It takes time," I reminded her. "Keep using the strategies we discussed, and watch closely. If you begin to realize that despite your efforts he is unable to follow directions or complete tasks that other children his age are, or if you find your frustration increasing and catch yourself screaming more, you may decide to have him tested for ADHD."

Maggie formed a pyramid with her hands under her chin as she reflected. "I won't forget," she said, then turned to Sarah and nudged her. "Tell them your story."

Sarah laughed. "Well, I have a sort of success. The kids and I were driving in the car. David was sitting in the back. He had a long reed in his hand and was tapping it on my head. I yelled at him to watch it. He kept doing it. That's when Cara, my ten-year-old, turned around and in her most stern voice stated, 'David, lay it down on the seat!' He did. I started to laugh. I realized immediately that she'd given a clear, physical direction. Mine was really fuzzy."

"Sarah, that's progress," I immediately declared. "You recognized an effective technique when you heard it."

"Yeah, I did," she admitted, her eyes twinkling. "And Sadie also stayed with me in the grocery store!"

As Sarah left that day, she paused to let me know again that she was really trying to be more positive. "It seems to be making a difference," she whispered as Sadie came flying into her arms.

How are you doing?

Savor Your Successes—and Your Stumbles

Think about your successes and your stumbles too—there may be mini successes hidden within your attempts, especially if you're catching yourself afterward or in the middle.

List directions you've given your child in the last twenty-four hours.

1. ______________________________

2. __________

3. __________

4. __________

5. __________

Which ones were most effective?

1. __________

2. __________

3. __________

Why were they effective? Did you reduce distracting stimuli in the environment? Did you make eye contact? Did you keep your directions simple and tell your child what he could do? Did you add visual or physical cues?

____

____

____

____

If your directions didn't work quite as you had hoped, what will you do differently next time?

____

____

____

____

Learning new skills takes time. It's important to enjoy the journey!

CORNERSTONE

Children who are perceptive need to hear

Statements that help them feel good about their perceptiveness:

- ✔ You are very observant.
- ✔ Someday you could be a scientist or an investigator.
- ✔ You are very aware.

Statements that help them recognize their triggers:

- ✔ Too many directions at once can confuse you.
- ✔ It's easier for you to "hear" when you can "see" the message too.
- ✔ Too much noise makes it hard for you to focus.

Statements that help them manage their perceptiveness:

- ✔ Be sure to look at the person who is speaking to you.
- ✔ You can turn off the television and other things that can distract you.
- ✔ You can ask to be seated in the front.
- ✔ You can form a picture in your mind of what you need to do.
- ✔ You can use your fingers to help you remember how many things you are supposed to do.
- ✔ You can make a chart or a list.

9

ADAPTABILITY

Identifying the Little Things That Can Make or Break the Day

IN PREPARATION

- Read Chapter 10 in *Raising Your Spirited Child.*
- Grab a highlighter.

CHAPTER HIGHLIGHTS

- A clear picture of transitions, those seemingly little changes or surprises that can make or break the day.
- Strategies to help slow-to-adapt children shift from one thing to another.
- Practice smoothing out the most challenging transitions like bedtime, cleanup, and leaving.

THINGS TO OBSERVE

- Which transitions, changes, or surprises trigger your child?
- What helps your child to cope successfully with transitions?

On the board I wrote:

Next week:

Raising Your Spirited Child, Tuesday evening class canceled

Rescheduled Wednesday 3:00–4:30 P.M.

Then I waited for the parents to enter the room. Lynn and Maggie, engrossed in a conversation, glanced at the notice on the board. Proceeding to their self-selected spots around the table, they pulled out their calendars and noted the change without interrupting their conversation. John paused at the doorway, his attention immediately caught by the words. His shoulders tightened, but he said nothing. Brent followed him. He stopped cold when he saw the announcement. Shoving his baseball cap up on his head, he turned to me and demanded, "What's that date?"

I told him. He pushed his cap off his brow, then pulled it back down low over his eyes. Dropping into his chair, he slouched as he folded his arms across his chest. If looks could kill, I was dead.

Phil, like Maggie and Lynn, simply noted the change. Sarah groaned, but it was Diane who proclaimed, "You can't do that!"

I grabbed an eraser and rubbed out the announcement. "I apologize," I said. "Class isn't canceled next week. We will meet Tuesday evening as scheduled. I just wanted to introduce our topic for today—adaptability to change. I admit I intentionally tried to trigger you, because I wanted to demonstrate how we unintentionally do it to kids all of the time."

John laughed. "You're right. We do surprise kids like that all of the time."

I looked at Brent and Diane. They were not ready to forgive me.

Lynn shrugged. "I wondered about it. I've never had any other classes changed like that."

Brent pushed his cap back up. He almost smiled as he admitted. "I'd already decided that I wasn't coming."

How we respond to change is affected by our ability to adapt.

"Who," I asked, "after reading the announcement thought, fine, I'll just come next Wednesday or skip if I have to?" Maggie, Lynn, and Phil raised their hands. "Who felt their intensity go up?" Sarah, Brent, Diane, and John raised theirs.

"This is a difference in adaptability," I explained. "When you are slow to adapt, any change or surprise triggers a stress reaction. You feel agitated and irritated. You don't like it! The same is true for kids who are slow to adapt."

Jim Cameron, Ph.D., a researcher with An Ounce of Prevention, a nonprofit preventive mental health organization in Berkeley, California, divides transitions into four categories:

- intrusions (such as scooping a baby up for a diaper change)
- shifts from one activity or geographical location to another (such as getting into the car)
- changes in ongoing routines (such as sleeping in a hotel rather than at home)
- expectations not met or changed (such as giving your child a blue bowl instead of his favored yellow one)

These are all transitions, the sneaky little shifts, changes, and surprises that can creep up and strike like a bee sting on a sunny day. You don't get to choose how adaptable you are, nor does your child, but you can learn to cope with transitions. Recognizing transitions and understanding your child's reaction to them is essential to winning his cooperation.

A NEW POINT OF VIEW

To help your child adapt more easily you have to identify the most common transitions she faces each day. Of course you can't predict them all, but the more you recognize, the easier life will be.

"Think about the last twenty-four hours," I directed the group. "Obviously, getting dressed, going to bed, and coming to meals are the big transitions your kids cope with every day. We will include those, but I also want you to think about the little transitions that can trigger your child and you. Let's start with the younger kids. What are transitions that can upset them?"

"Diaper changes," Maggie began.

"Different people holding them," Sarah added. "I remember when Cara was born. She was the first grandchild, and everyone wanted to hold her. The relatives passed her around one to the other, and she'd go nuts. People would complain that I was being overprotective when I took her away. It wasn't that I didn't want them to hold her, just not one after the other."

Diane jumped into the conversation with an entire list. "Moving from one room to another. Getting on a coat. A different pacifier or bottle. Being put down. Can you tell I have slow-to-adapt kids?"

"Yes," I agreed, "but I also notice that you recognize triggers."

She grinned and nudged Phil. "Got any?" she asked.

"Flushing the toilet," he said. "T.J. loses it if you flush the toilet when he wants to, or if you open the drain on the tub when he wants to do it. For that matter, if you open the door, turn off the light, cut his toast wrong—any of these things can send him into orbit."

The others laughed, recognizing situations they too had hassled with. We added a few more.

Washing hands
Getting in a car seat
Running errands
Pizza deliveries
Getting off or on an elevator
Being woken from a nap

"What about preschoolers?" I asked.

"Picking up at day care." Phil groaned. "Tara will run away or won't put on her coat. Sometimes she gets furious because it's me and not my wife picking her up. The other day I came early. I thought she'd be happy to see me, but she didn't want to leave. When I tried to get her going she ran away and climbed under the jungle gym. I couldn't reach her. I had to stand there like an idiot, fuming until she came out."

"Leaving can be especially difficult," I remarked. "Kids don't want to leave, parents are usually in a hurry, and there are often other people watching."

Phil nodded in agreement.

"What else?" I continued.

"Visits with the other parent," Maggie murmured, her voice tight and intense. "Both my kids have a terrible time before visits and after them. I know that when the kids have been with their dad for the weekend, Sunday night and Monday morning will be terrible." She shifted, suddenly noticing Phil and Brent flanking her. "It isn't that he's a bad dad; it's just the change."

"Switching homes is often stressful for children," I agreed. "Even if they're not the ones moving back and forth, the comings and goings of stepsiblings can be very challenging for children who are slow to adapt."

Brent listened carefully, then he asked, "Is this why Katie was so rotten last weekend? On Saturday night we took the kids out to eat. She didn't want to go. We told her we'd go to one of her favorite restaurants. She got in the car. But then we decided to go to the Mall of America after dinner, so we changed restaurants."

I knew immediately that he was talking about a major transition and disappointment. It didn't surprise me when he said, "She had a fit. After the restaurant we went to the mall. But she complained that we had parked in the wrong place and we went in the wrong door. She was right, we usually do park on the other side, but so what? Finally, to settle her down a little bit, we bought her something to drink, but the cup was different from the one she had gotten last time and it had ice in it and she didn't want ice. She got so mad she ended up dumping the whole glass!"

"Think about each of those situations. What is the commonality?" I asked.

"Changes?" Brent questioned.

I nodded. "They are the little things that can ruin an evening out."

"But Sonja and Danny didn't act that way," Brent said.

"Are they slow to adapt?" I asked.

"No," he responded.

"Is Katie?"

"Yes."

"That's why," I answered.

"But she really went overboard," he retorted.

"Brent, how did you feel about my announcement to change class?" I asked.

"That's different," he said. "I couldn't come Wednesday. What did you expect?"

"Did Katie expect you to go out to eat on Saturday night?" I asked.

"No," he replied. "There just weren't any groceries in the house, and we thought it would be fun."

"Did she expect a restaurant different from the one where you ended up?"

"Yes."

"Was the glass different?"

"Yes, but . . ." Then he paused, sitting back to contemplate.

I shifted gears, wanting to respect his space and pull the attention away from him for a moment.

"What about older kids and adults?" I asked.

"I've got one," Maggie said. "In January Kristen's teacher, Mrs. Kelly, cut back to half time and Ms. Davis took over the afternoons. Kristen's first reaction was 'No way is this going to work.' It took two weeks before she decided Ms. Davis was nice. Now, two months later, Mrs. Kelly is taking a full leave of absence, and even though Ms. Davis is taking over full time and Kristen knows her, she has fallen apart. When she told me, she wailed, 'Mrs. Kelly is leaving for good—for good.' When I tried to talk to her about it, all she could say was, 'I've told Mrs. Kelly about important things, and Ms. Davis doesn't know them, and how will I tell her?' She was so distraught this morning I could hardly get her to school."

"Changing teachers midyear can be very stressful for slow-to-adapt children," I agreed. "She's going to need more support and patience from you."

Maggie groaned. "I know."

When we finished, our list looked like a minefield for slow-to-adapt kids.

TRANSITIONS THAT CAN TRIGGER SLOW-TO-ADAPT INDIVIDUALS

Younger Children	***Older Children and Adults***
diaper changes	losing a game
different people holding them	stopping play to start homework

Younger Children	***Older Children and Adults***
moving from one room to another	changing teachers midyear
getting on a coat	wearing boots
different pacifier or bottle	not getting to play as expected
being put down	field trips
a change in child care providers	dentist and doctor appointments
flushing the toilet	surprise parties
being woken from a nap	pop quizzes
opening the drain	turning off the television
turning on the light	someone unexpectedly getting sick
yellow bowl instead of red one	canceled outings
toast cut the wrong way	not getting a date
washing hands	getting in the car and finding the gas tank empty
getting into a car seat	kids falling apart unexpectedly
running errands	meetings canceled or changed
pizza deliveries	emergencies at work
getting off and on an elevator	sick child care provider
being picked up at child care	relatives dropping in
visits with other parent	Monday mornings
phone ringing	first day after vacation
changing clothes for different seasons	getting ready in the morning
daylight saving time	different restaurant
parent returning from trip	being asked to stop and do something
different parking spot	coming inside from outside
bedtime	late arriving home
coming to dinner	turning off the television

Reviewing the list of transitions, it quickly becomes apparent how challenging it is to help young slow-to-adapt children cope. The mere ringing of the telephone or the delivery of a pizza can set them off. Without strong language skills to communicate their frustration, they are vulnerable to eruptions.

Older kids have gained skills that help them deal with the little things—pizza deliveries don't throw them anymore. Once they are able to tell time, going places or shifting from one activity to another may not be quite as difficult. But losing a game, cancellation of an event, or unexpectedly turning off a favorite television show can still be very difficult to manage.

By becoming aware of the transitions in your child's life, you can more easily help your child cope successfully with them. The fewer the surprises, the more cooperative your child will be.

Now it's your turn.

1. **Review the list of transitions. Highlight those that are triggers for your family members.**
2. **Think about the transitions in your family's day. What are the intrusions, shifts, changes in routines or expectations that can trigger your family members? Add them to the list.**
3. **Fill out the chart below to get a complete picture of your family's transition triggers.**

As an example, here's Sarah's chart.

TRIGGER TRANSITIONS

Bob	*Sarah*	*Cara*	*David*	*Sadie*	*Kim*
kids falling apart unexpectedly	phone ringing when making dinner	losing a game	getting up	getting in car seat	diaper change
kids refusing to go out the door	Bob coming home late		errands	leaving preschool	

Bob	*Sarah*	*Cara*	*David*	*Sadie*	*Kim*
	Monday morning		**leaving friends**	**changing clothes**	
			changing seat assignment	**different bowl**	
			being asked to do something		
			different movie		

Your turn.

TRIGGER TRANSITIONS IN THE LAST 24 HOURS

Name:					

TEACHING YOUR CHILD TO TAKE OVER THE TASK

As you become aware of the transitions in your day, point them out to your child. Teach her to identify those surprises, intrusions, and changes that are likely to trigger her. You can say things like, "Prepare yourself—transition coming—bedtime." Or call out, "Transition alert! I just heard the garage door; Daddy's coming in." Yes, it will take years for your child to figure this out, and you may feel a bit foolish using a word like *transition* with a two-year-old, but sooner than you might think she will figure them out. That knowledge will help take the sting out of those transitions for her.

I remember one day when my daughter, then thirteen, broke a wire on her braces. She asked me to make an appointment to get it fixed, which I did. The only time the orthodontist could see her, however, was right after school. I admit I got distracted and failed to call school to forewarn her. When she arrived home, I was caught off guard and said, "Grab a snack. Your appointment is in fifteen minutes. We've got to go." She stopped, gritted her teeth, and with hands on her hips informed me, "Mother, you didn't transition me!"

Kris knows a transition when she feels it, and fortunately for both of us, that information helped her cope with the change in routine. If she hadn't been as skilled, my direction may have triggered her. If she had gotten upset and I didn't know about transitions, I would have wondered why.

Here's your opportunity to test your skills. Read the following scenario, and see if you can identify the transitions. Use a highlighter to mark them.

The room was darker than usual at this hour, the rising sun smothered by black clouds. Jeanne, the mother of three, snuggled deeper under the covers. She didn't want to get up. The previous evening had been rushed and harried. Nothing had gotten done. Then the baby had woken twice during the night. Now a "to do" list ran through her head: gotta make lunches, pack the kids' backpacks, get out of the house by seven-thirty. Why, of all days, did she have an early meeting today? She grimaced at the thought.

Down the hall, five-year-old Michael awoke. He crawled to the end of his bed, pulled up the shade, and lay back under the covers, thinking about his day, just as he did every day. Later he'd go in and cuddle with his mom in her bed. He was the family's early riser and always managed to sneak in a few minutes alone with his mom before his sisters woke up.

But right now he wanted to think about his new bicycle. Just last night he'd ridden it for the first time, by himself! He smiled, remembering the good feeling. Today he wanted to ride his bike all day. A thought flashed in his mind, bringing panic to his gut.

Was this a child care day or not? He tried to remember, but he couldn't. He looked at his doorknob, where his mom hung his backpack on child care days. It wasn't there. Relief flooded through him.

Crawling out of bed, he pulled his favorite blanket out with him. His thumb and finger stuck through the holes in the corner, rubbing against the bump of stitching, just the way he liked it. He loved it when his mother cuddled him, and today he couldn't wait to tell her about his plans to ride his bike. Maybe she'd even want to take a ride with him.

Heading down the hallway, the *whoosh* of her shower brought him out of his reverie. Entering her room, he found her bed empty, the door to the bathroom shut, and his sister standing there. Disappointment struck hard.

His wail assaulted Jeanne. Long and shrill, it pierced the bathroom walls. Automatically her body jerked back away from the "monster" outside the door.

What were the transitions for Michael? Here's what I think.

- He woke up (shift).
- He didn't know if this was a day care day or not (change in routine).
- He'd planned to cuddle with his mother, then found her bed empty (expectation).
- He'd expected to talk with her about his bicycle but found her in the shower (expectation).
- He found his sister there (intrusion).

Seen from his point of view, his distress doesn't seem quite so incomprehensible. With each shift, surprise, intrusion, or change you can practically feel his intensity rising.

He's not alone. His mom is facing her own challenges.

- Her plans the evening before were disrupted (change in routine).

- She didn't finish some things that usually ease her morning transition (change in routine).
- She has an early meeting, which changes her schedule (change in routine).
- The baby woke her twice during the night (intrusion).
- She hoped to get a shower in before the kids woke up (expectation).
- Michael is screaming, she doesn't know why, and she didn't expect it (intrusion).

Kids aren't the only ones who are triggered by unexpected transitions—that's why it's so important to try to anticipate as many as possible.

EFFECTIVE STRATEGIES

Every time there is a transition, we have choices to make. If the transition is anticipated, we can

- choose to avoid it (we really don't need to sign up for one more dance class or run one more errand)
- work through it (we need to get to work and school)

If the transition is unexpected we have to

- bring down the intensity (the child becomes upset by the surprise or change; we have to calm her before we can do anything)

Then we can decide to

- avoid it (Oh, I didn't realize the yellow bowl was so important to you. We can wash it.)
- work through it (Oh, it is disappointing that the movie is sold out. Take a few minutes to slow down, and then we can figure out what else we'd like to do.)
- just do it (a fire drill)

Let's talk first about responding to the predictable transitions, and then we'll tackle the ones that catch us off guard.

When you can anticipate a transition, you can choose to avoid it or work through it. Avoidance is frequently a good policy, especially in a busy household with little kids.

"Who has an example of predicting a transition and choosing to avoid it?" I asked the group.

"I think I do," Maggie replied. "I've actually been feeling a little guilty about it. I probably shouldn't have signed my kids up for a class so soon after school, but I did."

I mentally made a note to emphasize Maggie's awareness of scheduling for success.

"On Monday afternoons," she continued, "my kids take karate lessons. On that day, I pick them up at the bus stop instead of letting them come home. We actually would have time to come in and eat snack, but I know that if Brian gets his coat and shoes off, it'll be a fight getting him going again."

"Smart plan," John mused.

"Well, I don't have the energy for a fight after working at the day care," Maggie replied. "I'm drained. So I bring them a snack they can eat in the car and drive straight to karate. Usually we arrive early and sit there talking for a while until they finish eating."

I was amazed by her organization even after a full workday.

"Is that choosing to avoid a transition or just being lazy?" She laughed.

"I'd call that insightful avoidance!" I exclaimed. And wanting to emphasize all the effective strategies she had used, I asked the group, "Why does this work?"

"She's eliminating about ten transitions by doing it that way," John answered.

"Like what?" I asked.

"Going in the door," he said. "Going out the door. Coats off. Coats on. Shoes off. Shoes on. Sitting down. Standing up. Deciding on a snack. Putting away backpacks. Starting to play. Stopping play. Going to the bathroom. Changing their typical routine once they're in the house. I wrote his answers on the board.

"Whew," I remarked. "Maggie, look at all the work you're saving yourself."

"It's a matter of survival," she replied.

"Any other examples?" I asked.

"If I want to stop for gas or grab something at a store, I do it before I pick up Tara," Phil said. It isn't worth it to try and stop on the way home with her."

Brent threw up his hands. "You know I have to say this," he said. "Life isn't like this. You can't pussyfoot around, putting off errands or picking them up at the bus stop all of the time. Their teachers aren't going to do that."

I agreed with Brent. "Life is full of transitions, and slow-to-adapt kids do have to learn how to cope with them. But as a parent, it is also important to choose your battles. There are lots of times you can't avoid the transition. The kids will get plenty of practice. And actually, most effective teachers do try to avoid unnecessary transitions. The last thing they want to do is trigger a room full of kids."

Brent played with his cap. "Think about your own experience," I prodded. "Were you angry at me when I told you I was changing the class time?"

"Yeah. We signed up for this class on Tuesday nights because it fit our schedules. You shouldn't change it."

"So as a group leader, it would be better if I thought about how changes I make could affect the others in the group?"

"Yeah."

"And if possible, it really would be better for me to avoid changes?"

"Yeah. If you can," Brent replied.

"And that would feel better and be more respectful to you as a participant who signed up and made plans for a specific night?"

"Yeah."

"I think so too," I said.

"And you think kids need the same thing?" he asked.

I nodded and said, "If we can."

Review your list of transitions. Cross out any you can avoid or eliminate. Promise to ask yourself, Is this transition really necessary? Think carefully before you change a routine, surprise your child, or add another transition to her day. Understand that transitions rob energy from your slow-to-adapt child and generate intensity. One too many can send her into an overload tantrum.

Sometimes making the decision to avoid or eliminate a transition forces us to set priorities. If a child is going to before-school child care, then going to school, then going to after-school child care, then to dance, then to scouts and so forth, there simply may be too many transitions in his day. Sometimes our slow-to-adapt children are the family's emotional barometer, helping us to realize when we are overscheduled and rushing too much.

Now let's talk about the transitions that cannot be avoided. Spirited children do need to learn how to handle them successfully. It's an important life skill.

In my experience effective transitions include four steps:

1. Forewarning
2. Adjusting
3. Refocusing
4. Moving through the transition

"If I had forewarned you, perhaps given you a handout on the first day alerting you to a future change, would it have been easier for you to handle?" I asked the group.

Heads nodded. "We would have had time to plan," Phil said.

"Yeah," Brent agreed. "And it would have been even better if you'd consulted with us about what time to switch the class to, instead of springing it on us as a done deal."

"So you'd prefer a warning and a chance to negotiate?"

Brent scowled, "Yeah, is that asking too much?"

"I don't think so," I concurred. "And kids are just like us. They like to know things ahead of time and they need a chance to adjust. Let's start with preparation and forewarning.

"Some kids need lots of preparation. They need to know days ahead or at least hours in advance of changes. Other kids, if you told them two days ahead of time, they'd be upset for the entire two days. Each child is different. Effective forewarnings are a bit of an art. You have to decide what fits for your child. Who has an example of an effective forewarning?"

John was first to respond. "Todd and Kelly are older. Transitions aren't too tough for them, but for some things I have to give them enough warning, especially if it involves a weekend. Like last weekend. My wife and I decided we'd all work on the house on

Saturday. We told Todd and Kelly on Wednesday so they couldn't tell us they'd already made plans."

"What exactly did you say?"

"My wife said to them, 'On Saturday we need to clean the house. Do you want to get it done first thing in the morning, or sleep in and work from one o'clock to three?' They complained, of course, but chose the afternoon."

"Great!" I remarked. "You gave them enough time to prepare and room to negotiate. Who has another one?"

"Last night Bob was late getting home," Sarah said. "Sadie wanted to know when he was coming. I told her about seven o'clock. She asked when is that? I told her it was when she would be taking her bath."

"Yes!" I exclaimed, raising my hand in a sign of victory. "What did Sarah do that is so important for young children?"

Blank stares and silence from the group.

"She answered in kid terms," I explained. "Little kids can't tell time, which makes changes in routines or shifts from one activity to another especially difficult. Sadie doesn't understand seven o'clock, but she does understand bath time. Sarah gave her a frame of reference she could comprehend. Who has another example of kid terms?"

Maggie jumped in, her confidence growing. "At day care, when I work late afternoons, I tell the kids that their moms will come when we read stories, which is between four-thirty and four forty-five. Or, Dad will come when we move up front, which is about five-thirty. Have I been doing it?"

"Yes," I confirmed. "Again, you've made time something the kids can comprehend. Little kids don't understand five more minutes, but if you tell them they can have three more jumps, or stack six more blocks, you are making time concrete and understandable."

Children wake up with expectations and plans for their day. Transitions often intrude upon or change those plans. Effective forewarnings include: allowing your child enough time to prepare for an upcoming transition (how much time depends on the child), and using kid-friendly terms or examples (words and ideas that are easily understood).

1. FOREWARNING

1. Read the following scenarios. How might you forewarn the child in each situation?
2. Record your answers. Then read on about adjusting, refocusing, and helping the child through. After each section, come back to this chart and write your response.
3. You can check your responses against the sample answers after each step or continue until you've completed all four.

Transition	*Responses*
Your child is four. She's working on a puzzle. You need to run an errand.	Forewarn: Adjust: Refocus: Help move through:
Your child is ten. You've scheduled a dentist appointment for 4:30. He gets off the bus at 3:30.	Forewarn: Adjust: Refocus: Help move through:
Your child is sixteen. You're making plans for the weekend. You need to find time to visit grandparents.	Forewarn: Adjust: Refocus: Help move through:
Your child is two. It's time to get dressed.	Forewarn: Adjust: Refocus: Help move through:

Transition	*Responses*
Your child is eight months. She is playing with a toy. Her diaper needs to be changed.	**Forewarn:** **Adjust:** **Refocus:** **Help move through:**
Your child is six. He is determined to make an airplane out of Legos. You need to leave for a family outing.	**Forewarn:** **Adjust:** **Refocus:** **Help move through:**

2. ADJUSTING

Once a child is engaged in an activity or has an expectation in mind, even if you have forewarned him, it may still be difficult for him to stop what he's doing and shift to something else. It is essential that you allow your child time to adjust and find a stopping point.

In order to help your child adjust you need to

- read cues
- acknowledge feelings
- solve the problem together

Reading cues

If your child is completely engrossed in an activity even though you have told her that you will be going to the store at four o'clock, she's not likely to take your announcement that it's time to leave calmly. Read the situation. Note her focus. Is she unaware of other things in the room? Is she lost in her project?

Are her shoulders hunched as she works? If so, a sudden demand to stop will surprise her and cause her intensity to rise.

Consider your own body language as well. Is your jaw clenched? Are you breathing fast? Do you feel rushed? If your child is focused, your intensity will fuel hers. It's worth it to both of you to stop, take a deep breath, slow down, and then slowly, calmly approach her, recognizing that she is going to need a few minutes to shift. Pausing may seem difficult, but that moment can actually save you time in the long run and definitely reduce the hassle.

Acknowledging feelings

Transitions can be very frustrating and disappointing. By taking a second to read the cues, you can approach your child more empathetically. You might say, "I can see you're really working hard on that puzzle" or "You're having a great time in that fort, it's hard to stop" or "You probably didn't expect Daddy to be here this early." Remember that acknowledging feelings doesn't mean your child won't fuss, it simply helps to reduce the intensity of those emotions.

Solving the problem together

You might say something like, "I'm sorry we don't have time for you to finish your puzzle. Dad is waiting. What can we do? Can we save this? Could you take the puzzle with you? Can you fit in two more pieces, then stop?"

By allowing your child to adjust, you keep intensity levels down. You can't easily transition a child when intensity is high. Reading cues, acknowledging feelings, and problem solving help to diffuse strong reactions and keep you working together.

Go back to the transition work sheet. Add the steps you would take to help the child adjust in each situation. Consider what feelings need to be acknowledged. If you're unsure, point out what you see. For example, you might say, "I notice how intent you are right now" or "Your jaw is clenched." Once you've acknowledged the feelings, think about the problem you need to help your child solve in order to help her transition.

3. REFOCUSING

As the time to shift draws closer, help your child refocus to the next activity. It's especially helpful if the next thing includes something he enjoys. You might say something like:

"It's time to go. You can bring your favorite stuffed toy with you."

"Grab your headset for the car."

"Let's set a date for you to play with your friend again."

"Is your next game Tuesday?"

"Do you want to crawl up the stairs like a turtle or hop like a bunny?"

Using your imagination is a great way to help young children refocus.

As you talk, start putting away toys, turning off the television, and shutting down any activities that may make it difficult for your child to let go and shift. Refocusing is not bribery. Bribery involves a power play, for example, "If you get in the bathtub, I will give you a toy." Refocusing assumes cooperation, for example, "Which toy do you want to take into the tub?" The assumption is you are working together and simply talking about what comes next. The feeling is very different from that of a bribe.

Go back to the transition work sheet. This time add the words you would use or the actions you would take to help the child shift his focus to the next activity.

4. HELPING THEM MOVE THROUGH IT

Expect your slow-to-adapt child to need your help moving through the transition. Even if you have forewarned her, allowed her to adjust, and helped her refocus, it's very likely that she will still need help—even if she's the oldest. You might feel frustrated when you realize you are helping your slow-to-adapt six-year-old get dressed, while your quick-to-adapt four-year-old dresses herself. But if you recognize that your slow-to-adapt child is struggling and needs help, you won't feel as frustrated. You'll stay cool and so will she. The transition will go much more smoothly and quickly. Ultimately your slow-to-adapt child will learn to cope with the transitions on her own. It will just take longer.

In the examples below, note which children will probably need a parent's help moving through these transitions.

Compare your responses with the following suggestions. Remember, there are many possible answers. These are only examples.

Transition	***Responses***
Your child is four. She's working on a puzzle. You need to run an errand.	"It's almost time to stop. We need to run an errand." (forewarning; if possible, forewarn her earlier in the day that you'll need to go to the store) "You are working very hard." (adjusting; acknowledging feelings) "How many more pieces until you can stop?" Or "What do you have to do before you can stop?" (adjusting; problem solving) "Did you want to drive past the construction crane again? We could go that way." (refocusing)
Your child is ten. You've scheduled a dentist appointment for 4:30 Thursday. He gets off the bus at 3:30.	On Monday tell him, "You've got a dentist appointment on Thursday at 4:30. (forewarning) That will change your routine. It's always difficult for you to change." (adjusting; acknowledging feelings) On Wednesday remind him, "Tomorrow is your dentist appointment." (forewarning) "What do you need to do to be ready?" (adjusting; problem solving) "After the dentist, do you want to invite Todd over?" (refocusing)

Transition	***Responses***
Your child is sixteen. You're making plans for the weekend. You need to find time to visit grandparents.	"What's your schedule for the weekend? We're trying to find a time to go to Grandpa and Grandma's." (forewarning) "I know you have a busy schedule." (adjusting; acknowledging feelings) "When are you available?" (adjusting; problem solving) I bet Grandma will make your favorite brownies again. (refocusing)
Your child is two. She's having a great time jumping on the trampoline she received for her birthday. It's time to stop and get dressed.	Avoid this transition by getting her dressed as soon as she gets up and before she starts playing with anything. Bring out the clothes. (visual forewarning) Then say, "Three more jumps and then it's time to stop jumping and get dressed." (refocusing) "You are really having fun jumping." (adjusting; acknowledging feelings) "When you're dressed we'll play . . . " (refocusing) or "you can jump again." "Can you pull up the zipper?" (helping move through)
Your child is eight months. She is playing with a toy. Her diaper needs to be changed.	With a diaper in your hand, reach out toward her but do not touch her. "Time to change your diaper." (forewarning) "Can you give me that toy?" Wait until she drops the toy or turns to you. If she doesn't gently tug on the toy, wait for her to loosen her grasp. (adjusting; problem solving) Pick her up for diaper change. (helping move through)

Transition	***Responses***
Your child is six. He is very persistent. He has just started building an airplane from Legos. He loves to play with his Legos. You need to leave for a family outing.	"We will need to leave in thirty minutes. You may not have enough time to finish your airplane; think about where you could stop in case you have to quit." (forewarning) "We'll be leaving in ten minutes. You probably have time to add ten more pieces." (forewarning) "One more minute, or two more Legos." (forewarning) "You have lots of plans. It's hard to stop. When we come back you can start again." (adjusting) "What do you want to see at the zoo today?" (refocusing) "Where do you want to put this so it can be saved? I'll help you move it there." (helping move through)

How did you do? Did you allow enough time in your forewarning? Did you notice that one forewarning usually is not enough? You have to be careful not to nag, but if a child is slow to adapt and persistent, he may need at least two or three forewarnings. Were your words and actions kid-friendly? Did you acknowledge feelings? And did you acknowledge those feelings again? How about problem solving? Were you able to work together and negotiate a solution? How did you help your child refocus? Did he need your help moving through the transition? Keep practicing, and take note of what words or actions seem to make transitions go more smoothly for you and your child.

All this thinking and talking may seem like a great deal of work. It is. But as you incorporate the techniques into your day, you will be establishing a respectful way of communicating with your child. You will be laying the foundation for success today—and tomorrow.

ESTABLISH ROUTINES

Ultimately, you will want your child to be able to move through transitions independently. Routines are the key to independence for slow-to-adapt kids.

Review your list of transitions. Select those that happen every day or at least once or twice a week. Then plan specific, consistent steps, and allow enough time to achieve them. For example, your routine in the morning might look like this:

Alarm goes off or music starts to play.
Lie in bed and slowly wake.
Get up.
Go to the bathroom.
Get dressed.
Eat breakfast.
Brush teeth and hair.
Put on coats.
Get in the car.

Try to keep the steps to a minimum and as simple as possible. After doing this exercise, Phil realized that Tara's bedtime routine was a page and a half long!

Allowing enough time is important for routines to be successful. Rushing will always trigger slow-to-adapt children. Take notice of how long it *really* takes your child to brush her teeth or eat breakfast or how long she *really* needs to lie in bed before getting up. If it's a battle to get your child out of the shower in less than fifteen minutes, *don't fight it—plan for it.* (If she's using up all the hot water, let everyone else shower first. Or set a timer to help her adjust.) Slow-to-adapt kids don't hurry. You might wish they would, but short of sending them to boot camp, it's unlikely you will get them to speed up. And if you think about it, do you really want to teach your child how to rush?

Of course your child does live in a family and needs to be considerate of others, so once you've figured out how long it really takes your child to do the things she needs to do, establish your start time. If your child needs to be up and moving by seven but needs twenty minutes to lie in bed first, the alarm should be set for 6:40 A.M. (Remember, if she's sensitive to sound, find an alarm that doesn't trigger her. Many kids use a boom-box alarm that awakens them to their favorite CD.) Because slow-to-adapt kids are often groggy in the morning, it's tempting to let them sleep longer. But rushing causes their intensity to rise and puts them over the edge faster than anything else.

If you find the amount of time you need does not match the time available, go back and look at the steps. Try to eliminate as many as you can until the steps fit the time available. For example, showers may need to be taken the night before. Breakfast may need to be cold cereal instead of pancakes. Try packing backpacks and lunches the night before.

As you review your routine, figure out what time you would need to start it in order to avoid rushing. Then you can decide if the plan is realistic for your family. If it doesn't seem feasible, think about what changes you need to make.

Reviewing Routines

Take a look at your most troublesome routine. Record all of the steps involved. In the right-hand column, record the time you need to allow for each step.

Challenging routine: ______________________________

____

Steps	***Time Allowed for Each Step***

Steps	***Time Allowed for Each Step***

Changes that need to be made: ______________________

____

Once you've established your routine, your child will be able to take over much more of the transition herself. She'll know what to expect, what comes next, and how much help she can expect from you. Soon those regular transitions will become simpler.

WHEN THE TRANSITIONS ARE UNEXPECTED

No matter how organized and tuned in you are to the transitions in your day, you and your child will still encounter unexpected transitions. These put the body on alert, ready for flight or fight. Intensity shoots up. In order to help your child cope, you have to bring down the intensity *before* trying to move through the transition.

Go back and review the chapter on intensity. Think about the calming activities you can use on the spur of the moment and in any environment, such as acknowledging feelings, taking deep breaths, and stepping back from the situation to take a break. All of these techniques can help you bring down intensity—no matter where you are. Remember too that every unexpected transition provides an opportunity to learn how to manage strong feelings. As you work with your child, you are not wasting time or just surviving. You're teaching life skills.

Once the intensity is down, then you can decide to

- avoid the transition

- move through it (allowing your child to adjust and refocus, as in a predicted transition)
- move your child through it because there is no other choice—such as when there are ten people behind you in line or you've got to get to the emergency room *now*!

If you have to move through the unexpected transitions immediately, your child will be upset. But if most of the time you've predicted the transitions and managed them smoothly, you and your child will cope with the few emergency situations. The reality is that sometimes we don't get to use our preferred style. But it helps to recognize that working out of our preferred style is exhausting. When you have to do it, try to slow down the rest of your day and plan more activities that will soothe both you and your child.

PRACTICE, PRACTICE, PRACTICE

Phil and Brent got up to refill their coffee cups. Diane and Lynn rolled their heads from side to side and stretched. John pushed back his chair, extending his legs. It had been an intense session. Now it was time to practice.

"Think about some of the most challenging transitions you've faced in the last two or three days," I directed the group.

"Unexpected doctor's appointment," Diane offered. "When Andy woke up from his nap, I noticed he had pinkeye. I wanted to get him in right away. The doctor could see him at three forty-five. That meant I'd have to grab Justin off the school bus and go. Justin had no idea this was coming, and I knew he wouldn't like it."

"So going to this doctor's appointment was unpredicted?" I confirmed.

"Yes."

"What's the first thing you have to deal with, then?" I asked.

"Bringing down the intensity?"

I nodded.

"His or mine?" Diane laughed.

"Both," I responded.

"Well, I didn't think of that," she said, "but I did think about avoiding it. I called my husband to see if he could come home and be with Justin, but he couldn't. Then I thought that I'd call school to warn him, but I felt silly doing it, so I didn't. I did make him a snack so he could eat in the car."

"You worked hard in those few minutes," I replied. "You thought about avoiding the situation. You thought about forewarning. You made a snack, which can be soothing. Look at how well your intuition was working for you!"

Diane smiled, "Yeah, but I didn't follow my gut. I met him at the door and told him we had to go. He said, 'No! I'm not going.' I said, 'I'm sorry, but you have to.' He asked to go to a friend's. I thought about it, but then I was too embarrassed to ask someone to watch him, so I didn't let him. I took him with me. He wasn't happy about it."

"Now you have more information than you did yesterday when this happened," I said. "What might you do next time?"

"Well, bring down the intensity."

"How?"

She shrugged.

Maggie stepped in. "Sometimes I'll tell Kristen, 'This is going to be tough. I'm sorry, I know you don't like surprises, but we don't have a choice.' I usually talk about her disappointment or frustration. It does seem to help."

"Why does that work?" I asked them. "What's Maggie doing?"

"Acknowledging feelings," John answered.

"Right," I said. "After bringing down the intensity, then what?"

"Well, I could have negotiated for a different time with the doctor and avoided the whole thing in the first place."

"Yes," I agreed.

"I guess I could have called school."

"Anyone ever call school?" I asked the group. Heads nodded. "Anything else?"

"I could have problem solved with Justin and let him go to a friend's. Or I could have taken him with me, like I did, and made it easier by bringing something to do, expecting that he'd still complain some."

"Yes," I confirmed. "And notice how many options are available to you. When you recognize transitions, you can select the one that fits for you and your child at that moment."

"But what if you do all that and they still start screaming and won't work with you?" Sarah asked.

"Do you have a story?" I asked.

"Yes," she said. "Last Sunday everything was going fine. We got up, played a little, had breakfast, and then it was time to put on coats and go to church. Sadie fell apart. I did too," she admitted sheepishly.

"What did you do?" I asked.

"I stepped away."

"Great, you brought down the intensity."

"My husband stepped in."

"Nice to have a partner who'll work with you," I replied.

"I was standing at the door with my coat on; Sadie was a screaming heap at my feet. I started to lose it. My husband took one look at the two of us and said, 'Just go to church.' So I did, and he stayed home with Sadie."

"So you chose to avoid it?" I remarked.

"Yes, but I feel controlled by her," she replied wearily, brushing back her hair.

"What happened before eleven o'clock on Sunday morning?" I asked.

Sarah thought for a moment. "Well, in the end we were rushing. We'd been out on Friday, so she had had a sitter. She was having fun with her dad. I was pretty stressed out all week."

"So her intensity level was high?" I asked.

"I guess." She sighed.

"Recognizing you didn't have time to bring it down, and your husband was willing to stay home, you chose to let go. Sometimes that is a very appropriate response. What could you have done if Bob didn't want to or couldn't stay home with her?"

Straightening her shoulders, Sarah stated, "We could have just hauled her out into the car. I've done it before."

"And sometimes you have to," I said. "If you have forewarned your child and allowed her an opportunity to adjust, the odds are in your favor that the transition will go more smoothly. But there are the times, especially with a younger child, when you may simply have to say, 'I'm sorry. I know it's hard to change,' and then do what you need to do. No matter how conscientious you are about preparing for transitions, there will still be a few that end in tears. Just remember, our motto is Progress, Not Perfection."

She looked straight at me.

"Next week I'm not rushing," she declared. "That always gets her."

Now it's your turn.

Smoothing Out Transitions

Think about the most difficult transition you've faced this week. Knowing what you now know, plan your response for next time.

Challenging transition: ________________________________

IF IT IS PREDICTABLE:
How could you *avoid* it?

If you decide to work through it, how could you

forewarn:

adjust:

refocus:

help your child move through it:

IF IT IS UNPREDICTABLE:
How could you bring down the intensity?

Could you avoid it or just let it go?

If you need to work through it, how could you

adjust:

refocus:

help your child move through it:

If you need to just do it, what will calm your child afterward?

Our time was up. I was tired, and I suspected others in the group were too. We had worked really hard. Helping kids cope with transitions does take a great deal of thought as well as patience. As the group members moved out, I caught Brent.

"Did I push you too hard today?" I asked.

"Nah," he replied.

"Good. I didn't mean to. Was any of it helpful?"

"A little," he said, I think to be nice to me.

"Have you ever noticed a boss or your wife forewarning you?" I asked.

"Not something I've been looking for lately," he replied, the corners of his mouth twitching.

"Well, if you get a chance, think about it," I said.

He nodded and left.

SAVOR YOUR SUCCESSES

It was a glorious June evening. A warm breeze gently ruffled the petals of my peonies, and the hummingbirds had returned to my feeder. I had to admit it was a little difficult to walk into the building. I wondered if everyone would come or if they would choose to luxuriate in the evening. But they all came, ready to share their stories.

Diane was giddy. "I've got a success! Brandon was at the neighbors' and Justin and Andy were playing upstairs. I noticed Justin sneaking down the steps, laughing to himself. Minutes later Andy, the three-year-old, appeared steaming! I recognized this was a transition.

"I said to Justin, 'You can't just sneak out. Andy needs a transition. He needs you to give him a warning that you want to quit and then play a few more minutes.'

"'But I told him I wanted to quit, and he wouldn't,' he complained.

"'Well, let's try again,' I said.

"'How long do I have to play with him?' he asked.

"I knew Justin would want to bargain—he's very persistent. So I said ten minutes. He immediately came back with five, as I expected. I accepted it, since that was what I really wanted anyway. So they went back upstairs and played. Then I went up and gave the one-minute warning. I mean, I told Andy there could be two more races, then it was time to stop." She corrected herself, remembering the kid-friendly terms. "At the end of that time, they stopped playing, no hassle, no name calling. It worked!"

"What did she do?" I asked the group. We created a list of all the strategies Diane had used.

Recognized a transition (stopping play)
Explained to the kids what was needed for a successful transition (you have to give a warning)
Negotiated with Justin to help him shift—and predicted his persistence (ten minutes reduced to five)
Gave a forewarning (five more minutes)
Went up and worked with them
Gave a one-minute warning (final forewarning: two more races)

Diane raised her arms in victory. We all enjoyed her success.

Then Sarah tentatively raised her hand. "I didn't answer the phone," she said. "It was dinnertime. It had been a hectic, stressful day again. I was cooking, getting things ready. Bob was in the kitchen too. I stopped to help Kim into her high chair. The phone rang. I felt my body tense with the ring. I noticed that and remembered from our list—a transition. I told Bob, don't answer it. He wanted to know why, but I just said, 'Don't.' I knew the answering machine was on, and I just couldn't take one more thing. We didn't answer the phone, and I felt better. That's it." She shrugged.

We gave her a thumbs-up. I paused once more, waiting. Brent pulled on his cap. I turned to him.

"Maybe it's a success," he said. "I'm not sure."

"Try us," I encouraged him.

"The cousins had been with us for the weekend," he said. "The kids had played outside and had been up late the night before. I took Katie in the house to put on her pajamas. She went berserk, screaming, falling limp on the floor. I picked her up and started to wrestle her into the pajamas, but then I thought about the intensity stuff and the transitions. So I stopped. I sat down on the couch with her and started reading her bedtime book. She stayed there, sucking her thumb. When I felt her body go limp, next to mine, I put on her pajamas and she went to bed."

"Wow," I remarked. "That sounds terrific. What's the problem?"

"I told her to put on her pajamas," he said. "She didn't do it. Instead of making her, I read her books. She won. If that's not spoiling her, what is?"

"What was your goal?" I asked quickly.

"To get her to bed," Brent responded.

"Did you do that?"

"Yes."

"What did reading books do?"

"Calmed her down."

"Did she still get on her pajamas?" I continued.

"Yes."

"Did she still go to bed?"

"Yes."

"It was just in a different order?" I asked.

"Yes."

"Did she fall right to sleep?"

"Yes."

"Did you achieve your goal?"

"Well, I guess," Brent said. "I got her to bed, if that's what you mean."

"That's not spoiling," I said softly. "It's respect. It's working with your child's temperament. That's what this class is all about."

Record your success. Then look at it and analyze why it worked.

1. SUCCESSFUL TRANSITION:

What did you do?

What did you say?

How did your child respond?

2. WHY DID IT WORK?

Did you identify the transition?

Did you avoid it?

Did you forewarn your child?

Did you allow time for your child to adjust?

Did you help your child refocus?

Did you help your child move through it?

3. DID YOU BRING DOWN THE INTENSITY?

CORNERSTONE

Children who are slow to adapt need to hear

Statements that help them feel good about their adaptability:

- ✔ You like routines.
- ✔ You like to know the plans.
- ✔ You like to allow enough time.
- ✔ You can be flexible.

Statements that help them recognize a transition:

- ✔ Rushing is stressful to you.
- ✔ You weren't expecting that.
- ✔ Surprises upset you.
- ✔ It's hard to shift from one thing to another when you're having a good time.
- ✔ It's difficult to leave.
- ✔ That was disappointing to you.

Statements that help them manage a transition:

- ✔ Think about it, do you really need to do this?
- ✔ What would you like to take with you?
- ✔ What are your plans?
- ✔ What do you need to finish before you leave?
- ✔ You have ten more minutes to do what you want to do.
- ✔ Breathe deeply—that was a surprise.

10

REGULARITY, ENERGY, FIRST REACTION, AND DISPOSITION

Fertile Ground for Power Struggles

IN PREPARATION

- Read Chapters 11, 14, and 15 in *Raising Your Spirited Child.*
- Gather together your family and friends.

CHAPTER HIGHLIGHTS

- A more detailed look at the cues that indicate the traits of regularity, energy, first reaction, and disposition.
- Responses that encourage understanding.
- Successful strategies for reducing or eliminating power struggles.

THINGS TO OBSERVE

- What is your child's first reaction to anything new?
- How predictable is your child's eating, sleeping, and elimination schedule?
- How energetic is your child?
- What is your child's prevailing disposition or mood?

Going on vacation with my husband is like going to boot camp. He thinks it's fun to go to our cabin where he can jog a few miles, then mountain-bike, swim, water-ski, and relax in the evening with a little hike. I think some of these activities are just fine, but I'd just as soon have a few hours to lounge on the beach reading a good book, taking a nap, and just "being." Going to the cabin is relaxing, but to me a real vacation means an adventure—like to the mountains of Jamaica, where tourists don't typically go. Our differences don't stop there. When we bought our present home, I saw what it could be. He saw what it didn't have and needed and what it would cost. (In the end we were both right.)

Even in the little things of daily life, we have our differences. No matter where I am or what time zone I'm in, my body tells me at six o'clock Minnesota time that it's time to eat. If I don't get something to eat right then, I get rather testy—my children will attest to that. Actually, I get a headache and a bit nauseous. My husband eats whenever he feels like it. It doesn't matter if it's six o'clock or nine. And then there's bedtime. At ten o'clock I wilt. You could set your clock by it. If I know I'm going to be up late, I need a nap during the afternoon to keep me going. He, on the other hand, might stay up until midnight one night and hit the sack at ten the next. It really doesn't matter to him.

People are different. Understanding those differences is critical to bringing harmony to our families. My husband and I have chosen to be together. In fact, we were attracted to each other by those very differences. It's taken a great deal of work to figure out how to operate together, but we realize our lives are richer because of those differences.

Children, whether they come to us biologically or through adoption, are people too. Although we might have expected that they'd be just like us, they turn out to be their own individuals, adding more complexity to our family's relationships. In my experience, the temperament traits of regularity (how predictable our biological rhythms are), energy (how energetic we are), first reaction (our first and most natural response to anything new), and disposition (our prevailing perspective of the half-full, half-empty glass) provide very fertile ground for power struggles. It is easy to believe that our children are out to get us when they put their innate traits on display—but actually they are doing what comes most naturally to them.

I call these four temperament traits the "bonus traits" because not all spirited children will score a 4 or 5 in each of these categories. So if your child has already scored high on intensity, persistence, sensitivity, perceptiveness, and adaptability *and* now picks up more points on regularity, energy, first reaction, and disposition, you get a bonus!

When it comes to how regular or energetic we are or how we approach new situations, our differences can be very challenging to deal with. In order to help people work together more effectively I like to give them an opportunity to see those differences lined up in front of them.

You're going to have to gather your family for these exercises, and if you can find a few neighbors or friends who are willing to join in the activity, it will be that much more fun. Once you have everyone together, decide on an imaginary line across your living room or, if you like, go ahead and put down a strip of masking tape.

We'll start with regularity and continue with energy, first reaction, and disposition. After we've had a look at differences, we'll practice using our new knowledge.

A NEW POINT OF VIEW: REGULARITY

Looking at Our Differences

Designate one end of your imaginary line or tape as the spot for the "regular" individuals to stand. These are the people who *need* to have dinner at a specific time every night, say five-thirty or six o'clock—not because their life requires it but because they *need* it.

The middle of the line is for the "grazers"—those who eat and snack throughout the day.

The end of the line is reserved for the "irregular" individuals, those who have eating and noneating days or who may eat one meal and skip the next.

Ask each group the following questions:

1. **What's positive about your type?**
2. **What triggers your type?**
3. **What do you need?**

The regulars tell me they are predictable. They know exactly when their dinner is served and that it will usually last twenty to thirty minutes. If dinner will be late for some reason, they have to eat something at the usual time in order to be able to "wait." It's upsetting to them if they can't eat when their body says it's time. Delaying a meal or snack even fifteen minutes can be a painful endurance test for them. What they need more than anything is predictability and good, nutritional food. Feed them at regular times, and they'll be happy.

The grazers tell me they are flexible. Their dinners can be anytime between five-thirty and nine and last ten minutes to an hour. They can snack, then sit down and eat a meal. They can also eat a meal and then start grazing again. Grazers are triggered when someone tries to close the kitchen and stop them from nibbling. What they need is good nutritional food easily available and a flexible schedule. Allow them their spontaneity, and they'll be happy.

The irregulars also tell me they are flexible. Their dinnertime varies—sometimes they don't eat dinner at all. On any given day three-fourths of them will have skipped breakfast. If forced to eat when they're not hungry, they feel bloated and uncomfortable. They're triggered when someone tries to force them to eat or tells them they're ungrateful because they're not eating a meal that's been prepared. They need good nutritional food and choices about when they eat.

What's most amazing to me is that every body type and weight is included in each one of these groups. There isn't a "bad" or a "good" group—a healthy or unhealthy one. And no matter what their style, members of all three groups worry about good nutrition and family mealtimes.

EFFECTIVE STRATEGIES

What can you do when your family members have very different body rhythms?

1. Recognize those differences.
2. Teach good nutritional guidelines.
3. Make nutritious foods available, then allow flexibility.
4. Develop family rituals and routines.

1. RECOGNIZE THOSE DIFFERENCES

Take a good look at where you are standing on the continuum. Then check where the rest of your family is. Who needs regular meals and bedtimes? Who is irregular? Who is a grazer?

A Look at Regularity

1. List each family member.
2. Place an *X* in the column that best describes each person.

Here's an example from Sarah's family.

Name	*Regular*	*Grazer*	*Irregular*
Bob	X		
Sarah		X	
Cara	X		
David		X	
Sadie	X		
Kim		X	

Now it's your turn.

Name	*Regular*	*Grazer*	*Irregular*

If you're very regular and have an irregular child, her eating habits may scare you. It's very difficult for you even to imagine skipping a meal. When your child refuses to eat, you may worry that her growth will be stunted, but in reality she merely has a style different from your own. Kids with irregular eating habits do get what they need. Your job is to make sure nutritional food is available.

If you are a grazer or irregular, it may be very challenging for you to understand your regular child, who demands to eat at very predictable times and finds it extremely difficult to delay a meal or snack. When you identify the preferred style of your family members, it will help you to predict their needs and understand their actions. You'll quickly realize their behaviors reflect their temperamental styles and see that they are not deliberately trying to drive you crazy.

2. TEACH GOOD NUTRITIONAL GUIDELINES

Contact your local county extension office to order a good guide pyramid for daily food choices (and see the appendix for other options). Put it on your refrigerator, and plan your meals and snacks around it. Remember, your children can't eat junk food if you don't buy it. In a now classic study conducted by Clara Davis, it was found that when children are offered nutritional food choices, they will, over time, eat a balanced diet. The key is making those foods available. You control what comes into your home.

It is critical that you teach your child good nutritional guidelines. You can start when she's just a toddler. When your child asks to eat, take her to the food chart and help her select a snack from it. If your child asks for a soda, review the food chart with her, helping her to decide if she's met her nutritional needs for the day. If she has, soda may be an acceptable choice. If she hasn't, it isn't. Obviously she won't completely understand at first, but ultimately she will. Then when she's older and off at a friend's house, you know she will be able to make good food choices for herself.

3. MAKE NUTRITIOUS FOODS AVAILABLE, THEN ALLOW FLEXIBILITY

I hope this exercise has allowed you to see firsthand that people are different. If nutritious food is available, they will eat when they are hungry and keep their energy levels up. Ellen Satter, author of *How to Get Your Kids to Eat . . . But Not Too Much,* says, "Parents take responsibility only for *what, when* and *where* food is served, leaving children responsible for *how much* they consume or *whether* they eat at all."

You don't have to be a short-order cook. Teach your child how to make his own snack. Buy small plastic pitchers so he can pour his own juice. Teach him to help himself.

4. DEVELOP FAMILY RITUALS AND ROUTINES

This may sound contradictory, since I've just recommended flexibility, but family rituals and meals aren't just about food. In a survey of National Merit scholars the one thing these outstanding students had in common was eating a meal each day with their family. It's been suggested that the discussion at the table enhanced their vocabulary. Mealtime conversations allow us to share thoughts and feelings, plan family outings, exchange news, and discuss world events. The kids learn manners, family values, and most of all have their parents' attention.

So even if your child is irregular and not hungry, invite her to the table. Let her know she can choose how much to eat but that you want her to be part of the conversation.

If your family's schedule prevents you from sitting down for dinner, consider breakfast or a bedtime snack. Be creative, and somehow, some way, take time to connect as a family.

Younger children may not want to sit at the table. A typical three-year-old may last only five to ten minutes, but if the adults continue to sit and converse, ultimately that child will come back. Setting a good example creates a lasting impression. One day you'll find yourself sitting around the table for thirty, forty minutes discussing with your teenagers the day's events. Build those family traditions.

Routines are also important for sleeping. Even if a child is not tired, he can learn to rest or play quietly in his bed until he is ready to fall asleep. Often children who have irregular sleep patterns become sleep-deprived. A predictable routine helps the irregular child to unwind and rest. See Chapter 9 on adaptability for effective transitions that can help your child fall asleep.

Eating, sleeping, and eliminating commonly lead to power struggles for parents and children. By understanding and respecting differences in normal body rhythms, families can find ways to work together and stop those struggles before they ever start.

A NEW POINT OF VIEW: ENERGY

Differences in Energy

Gather your family and friends again. This time ask the high-energy people to stand on one end of the continuum. These are the people who crave exercise and *need* to move. The low-energy people, those who may exercise but don't necessarily crave it, should stand on the opposite end of the line. I've found that exhausted parents of spirited children will place themselves on the low-energy end but realize as we talk that they actually have a high need for exercise and movement. Their need is not being met,

and as a result they feel even more fatigued. When doing this exercise, think about your days before spirited kids. Where would you have placed yourself on the line? Disabilities should not automatically place you on the low end either. I have a colleague and friend who uses a wheelchair, but his energy level is very high. He needs to lift weights and do other exercises every day.

Ask each group:

1. **What's positive about your energy level?**
2. **What triggers you?**
3. **What do you need?**

The low-energy people tell me they can travel long distances easily. They do not need to get up and move. They are quiet and sedate. Their parents loved that when they were little because they didn't get into lots of mischief or have accidents climbing trees. They are triggered when others try to rush them or get them to move faster. They need understanding that constant physical activity is not relaxing for them and that they do get many things accomplished during the day. They simply do things at their own pace.

The high-energy people tell me they get things done. They're always busy and on the move. They're triggered when they are confined or when they are told not to move or touch anything. They desperately need to exercise, to be active, and to be able to take things apart and examine them.

There's a little irony to this trait. Many people praise kids who are more sedate. However, when it comes to adults, we tend to prize energy.

EFFECTIVE STRATEGIES

What do you do when the members of your family fall along the entire continuum?

1. Recognize those differences.
2. Plan kinesthetic activities.
3. Create safe environments.

1. RECOGNIZE THOSE DIFFERENCES

Take note of where you are on the continuum and where the rest of your family is standing. Who needs to move? Who is a bit more quiescent?

A Look at Energy Levels

1. List each family member.
2. Place an *X* in the column that best describes each individual's energy level.

Here's Sarah's chart.

Name	*Low Energy*	*Medium Energy*	*High Energy*
Bob		**X**	
Sarah	**X**		
Cara			**X**
David			**X**
Sadie			**X**
Kim			**X**

Your turn.

Name	*Low Energy*	*Medium Energy*	*High Energy*

If, like Sarah, you are a low-energy parent with a high-energy child, you're going to need extra help keeping up with this child. If you're a high-energy parent with a high-energy child, plan regular exercise for both of you.

2. PLAN KINESTHETIC ACTIVITIES

Exercise is important for everyone, but it is essential for high-energy individuals. Whether you are a low- or high-energy person, exercise is good for your health and creates the natural soothing agents that help you to manage intensity. Exercising is time well spent. The challenge is to find a balance for those family members of differing energy levels.

Exercise has to be consciously pursued. Instead of driving six blocks to the store with your child, consider walking, biking, or roller-blading there. If your energy is lower than your child's, think about things you can do in which she can be active and you can watch, like going to the park or enrolling her in gymnastics or swimming lessons. *Timing is important.* If you put off exercise until late in the day, your high-energy child may already be in a frenzy or unable to settle.

If you know your child will need to sit still, think of a funnel. Let him use his large muscles *before* you expect him to settle down and use his small muscles. For example, before a family holiday dinner, plan to take your child outside to play ball, ride a bike, or run. Once he's had a chance to whirl around, the odds will be in your favor that he will be able to sit still through the meal. Always plan frequent breaks for your high-energy child, knowing that he is using his nonpreferred style when he's still. It takes a great deal of energy for him to keep his body quiet. The effort can be exhausting.

When selecting a school, look for classrooms in which kids are allowed to work standing at tables or lying or sitting on the floor. Seek a teacher who plans physical methods of teaching, such as jumping, sorting, or stacking, so that kids are busy and on the move. Observe to see what happens to the child who is balancing on the back legs of his chair. Does he get into trouble? Or does the teacher encourage him to move in a safe, appropriate way?

As you plan appropriate outlets for your high-energy child, don't forget about her hands. High-energy kids frequently get into trouble for picking at or fiddling with things. If you know you will be going to the store, riding in the car, visiting a friend, or in another situation where your active child will need to refrain from touching, think about what she *can* do with her hands. In the checkout line, rather than grabbing candy off the rack, can she get your checkbook out of your purse? Can she help pack groceries? While riding in the car, have you brought along hand-held games so she's not fiddling with the heat or window controls or pulling the hair of the child sitting next to her? If you know that her hands will be on the move, plan something acceptable for them to be doing.

3. CREATE SAFE ENVIRONMENTS

Take a good look at your home. Does it allow active children to move about and to touch things? If your active child is a toddler, it is essential that you childproof your home to keep her safe. Remove sharp objects, cover electrical outlets, and so forth. Rather than punishing your child for climbing on your dining room table, tell her she may not climb on the table, and then find a place where she *can* climb. Reconsider large furniture purchases that take up all the space in a room, preventing children from rolling, tumbling, or jumping. Remember that when the weather is bad, your energetic child will need room to actively play indoors.

When you consciously plan appropriate outlets for your high-energy child, it's much easier for her to manage her intensity and to be still when the situation requires it.

A NEW POINT OF VIEW: FIRST REACTION

Differences in First Reactions to Anything New

Gather those friends and family members again. This time give them the following scenario: You have won a trip from a local radio station. The hitch is, to get it you have to go onstage with the disc jockey at a community fair.

Then ask each participant if his reaction would be

"Great! Let's go!"

"Tell me more."

"Tell me a lot more because right now I'm thinking, 'Forget it.'"

Form your continuum with the "Great!" people on one end, the "Tell me more" people in the middle, and the "No way" folks on the other end. Then ask

1. **What's positive about your reaction style?**
2. **What triggers you?**
3. **What do you need?**

The individuals who jump right into things tell me they have exciting lives. They like new things and seek them out. They are triggered when they are forced to hold back, wait, or are told to not be so impulsive. They crave excitement and love having someone to share that excitement with.

The more cautious participants tell me they are wise. They are not gullible, nor are they easily persuaded to try risky behaviors. They think before they jump, and as a result they rarely end up in trouble. They're triggered when they're pushed to do things *now* or teased that they're afraid. Before trying something new, they need time to think, lots of information, a chance to watch others, and, most important, support.

So, what do you do when some of the members of your family want to go horseback riding and camping in the mountains, while others say, hold on, partner? Work together.

1. Recognize those differences.
2. Help your child understand her feelings.
3. Prepare your child.
4. Support your child.
5. Allow time.
6. Remind your child of past successes.

EFFECTIVE STRATEGIES

1. RECOGNIZE THOSE DIFFERENCES

Look at where you are standing on the continuum. Where is the rest of your family? Who likes to jump right into things? Who experiences a cautious first reaction?

A Look at First Reaction

1. List each family member.

2. Place an *X* in the column that best describes each individual's first reaction.

Here's an example from Sarah's family.

Name	*Jumps In*	*Tell Me More*	*No Way*
Bob	X		
Sarah			X
Cara	X		
David			X
Sadie			X
Kim		X	

Your turn.

Name	*Jumps In*	*Tell Me More*	*No Way*

If you and your child are on opposite ends of the continuum, it is easy to misunderstand his reactions. The individuals who jump into things quickly tend to have a slower flight-or-fight response. Their bodies typically do not respond to new situations as stressfully. As a result, their intensity does not rise. Their pulse rate and heartbeat remain stable.

The more cautious individuals have very finely tuned flight-or-fight reactions. In new situations their bodies quickly go on alert. Their heart starts to race. Their breaths come fast and furious. The result is that "jumpers" and cautious individuals have very different physiological experiences when facing new experiences and may find it difficult to understand one another.

Working together is just that—work! But it's really worth it. The cautious individuals in your family can help you learn to think before doing something that may get you into trouble. They will also plan more relaxing vacations. The jumpers in your life will lead you to new, exciting adventures. By operating together you can create a very enjoyable and healthy balance, even if your styles are different.

2. HELP YOUR CHILD UNDERSTAND HER FEELINGS

Cautious kids need to know they are not the only people to ever feel uncomfortable facing new situations, people, or activities. If they are experiencing anxiety, name it and let them know it is a very common emotion. If they are experiencing headaches or stomachaches, assure them that they do not have the flu. Teach them to use soothing techniques like deep breathing, chewing gum, smiling, or, for the little ones, thumb sucking to help them feel more comfortable. Talk about other members of your family or friends who share these feelings.

The kids who jump in need to know they seek excitement. Teach them to stop, think, then act.

3. PREPARE YOUR CHILD

It is essential that cautious children be prepared for new activities. Give your child as much information as possible about what to expect. Read books, watch videos, arrive early, and observe others. Many parents find that their cautious child is more comfortable when he's the first arrival. Then he can watch as others enter.

Whenever your child is facing a new situation, ask, "What will make it better?" Give your child tools to feel more comfortable and in control. On one of our family vacations we rode horses in the mountains of Montana. It was a brand-new experience for my cautious daughter. Things were going relatively well until our guide stopped on a narrow segment of the trail to allow us to view eagles taking off *below* us. Kris's horse turned to munch on a bush, its rear legs resting about six inches from the cliff's edge. Kris was terrified. Her ashen face and teary eyes gave her away. The guide led us to a meadow, then stopped. He went to Kris and said, "You know, my wife hates that path too. Bridges scare me." He reassured her that she was not the only one to ever feel frightened. He then told her that she could call a stop at any point. She could also get off of her horse and lead it or ask him to lead it. He assured her that before we took any more steep or narrow paths he would consult with her and let her decide if she was comfortable taking them or not. Reluctantly Kris remounted and continued the ride, but as Dan kept checking with her and allowing her to help him choose routes, her confidence grew. By the end of the trip, she was begging to come back again.

I don't know if Dan knew about spirited kids, but he did know how to acknowledge feelings, and he helped Kris understand that although she couldn't stop herself from a cautious first reaction, she could do things that would help her cope with her discomfort and ultimately enjoy the activity. He gave her tools that helped her feel more in control.

Think about what you can do for your cautious child. Can you allow her to say "Stop" if she needs to stop? Perhaps she would be more comfortable if she took along a picture of your family, invited a friend, went early to practice privately, or stayed late to ask questions individually of the instructor. By preparing your cautious child and helping her find tools to help her cope, you'll enable her to successfully handle new situations.

4. SUPPORT YOUR CHILD

Your cautious child needs your reassurance and support when facing a new situation. You cannot expect to drop a cautious child off at a first practice, new dance class, or new child care center and simply drive away. Plan to stay with him and support him as he moves into the new situation. Let him know who can help him after you leave. Let him know this is a safe place and that he will be okay. He needs your support to be successful.

5. ALLOW TIME

Teach your cautious child to say, "Let me think about it" rather than "No" when faced with a new situation. Allow him plenty of time to think through the situation, gather information, and quell his fears. Do *not* push. You don't teach a child to swim by dumping him into the deep end of the pool. You start in the shallow end and let him build on his successes before moving him into deeper water. The same is true for new situations.

6. REMIND YOUR CHILD OF PAST SUCCESSES

—and point out progress. Talk with your child about past situations he has learned to handle comfortably. You might say something like, "Remember at the beginning of the school year you didn't like Mr. Jones, but now you do." Or "Remember when you couldn't swim and didn't even want to get in the water, but now you are a fantastic swimmer."

Kids who learn to recognize their cautious first reactions are much more willing to tackle new situations because they understand their feelings and feel confident that they have the tools to help them cope.

A NEW POINT OF VIEW: DISPOSITION

Disposition

Gather those friends and relatives one last time. Ask them to form a continuum based on how they would describe a day with a few clouds in the sky. Would they see themselves saying, "A glorious day! The sun is shining. It's warm. It's beautiful"? Or "It's partly cloudy and eighty-two degrees today."

Then ask

1. **What's positive about your style?**
2. **What triggers you?**
3. **What do you need?**

The debates about this trait rage. The sunny-day people describe themselves as cheerful and fun to be around. They're triggered when others don't take them seriously. They need people who enjoy life the way they do.

The more serious group (partly cloudy and 82 degrees) say they think like Barbara Walters. They see themselves as analytical, thoughtful, practical, and realistic. They can see what presently exists and what needs to be fixed. They're not afraid to ask the tough questions. They're triggered by people who won't be serious and are frustrated when others refuse to see the drawbacks of a situation. They need others who appreciate quality and aren't offended by their questions. But more than anything, they want others to know that they are happy.

EFFECTIVE STRATEGIES

How can you work together, enjoying those who see the sunny side of life and appreciating those who are more realistic, practical, and analytical?

1. Recognize those differences.
2. Slow down.
3. Teach kids to be optimistic.
4. Take note of how your child expresses enthusiasm.
5. Teach your child social graces.

1. RECOGNIZE THOSE DIFFERENCES

Look at where you're standing on the continuum. Where is the rest of your family? Who is more serious? Who is more light-hearted?

A Look at Disposition

1. List each family member.

2. Place an *X* in the column that best describes each person's disposition.

Here's an example from Sarah's family.

Name	*Sunny*	*Somewhere in Between*	*Serious*
Bob			**X**
Sarah	**X**		
Cara			**X**
David			**X**
Sadie	**X**		
Kim	**X**		

Your turn.

Name	*Sunny*	*Somewhere in Between*	*Serious*

2. SLOW DOWN

Jim Cameron, Ph.D., from An Ounce of Prevention in Berkeley, California, calls disposition the "downstream trait." Disposition is tied to other temperamental experiences. Frequently a child's mood deteriorates to downright nasty when there have been too many transitions, too much stimulation, or too many nos. If you catch issues tied to your child's adaptability, sensitivity, or other temperament traits earlier, you can help your child to cope and be less fretful. Learning to read cues is essential for every child, sunny or serious. The earlier you can catch emotions that are moving toward negative, the more likely you'll be able to head them off. So slow down your interaction with your child, and look for those cues.

You'll also want to make sure your child is getting enough sleep. When a child's mood is more cranky than serious, it may be a sign that she's sleep-deprived. Tired kids can't cope. They end up acting out and losing it much more frequently. If you're unsure whether or not you child is getting enough rest, try including a twenty-minute quiet time in her afternoon. She can read, listen to music. If she's tired, she'll fall asleep. If not, she can get up and go after the twenty minutes.

3. TEACH KIDS TO BE OPTIMISTIC

Be your child's historian. Remind him of past struggles and problems and what he has done to cope with them effectively.

In *The Optimistic Child*, Martin Seligman, Ph.D., stresses the importance of teaching kids that good events are generated by their own actions, while bad events are isolated exceptions. For example, when your child gets an A on an exam, talk about the fact that she isn't just lucky or smart but that she worked hard. She *did* something that made this happen. When she experiences a difficult situation, ask her to tell you what happened. You can agree with her that it was disappointing to fail the exam, but it doesn't mean she's dumb or that she's going to flunk out of school. It's an isolated event that is not likely to happen again. Later you can help her figure out what she needs to do next time to improve her grade. Does she need to work with a tutor? Could she ask for more time? Does she need a quieter testing space? Knowing there are things she can do gives your child a sense of hope and lets her know she can make good things happen.

4. TAKE NOTE OF HOW YOUR CHILD EXPRESSES ENTHUSIASM

When my son was in middle school, he won a major writing award. His accomplishment was announced over the public-address system to the entire school. His teacher was amazed at his reaction: he smiled slightly. That was it—no cheers, hoots, or hollers, no bows, no victory dances. If you have a serious child, especially an introverted one, he may rarely be overtly enthusiastic. It is essential that you recognize that when this child chatters or says something like "It was fun," this is a major drumroll, exclamation-point WOW! The more you catch these subtle "enthusiastic" responses, the more you'll realize this kid really is happy—he's just serious.

5. TEACH YOUR CHILD SOCIAL GRACES

You can count on the serious child to point out flaws, so it is essential that she learn the social graces. Otherwise you might find yourself cringing when she informs Grandma that the banana bread is really lumpy and tastes funny, which is what you thought too but had the sense to keep to yourself. The serious child needs to learn that although something may be less than perfect, she does not always have to share her point of view. Or, if she needs to say something, a simple "No, thank you" is always preferable to an "Oh, yuck!"

PRACTICE, PRACTICE, PRACTICE

I'd moved the group from the classroom to the lobby to give us lots of space for our continuums. Now it was time to move back to the discussion room. The parents shared stories and chuckled as they returned to their seats. I divided them into four working groups.

"Today you get to be me," I informed them.

Brent pushed up his sleeves. "I doubt your husband would appreciate that."

"*Pretend* you're me," I clarified.

I then explained that when I conduct training sessions for large audiences, I encourage parents to anonymously write questions down on index cards. Many people, especially introverts, don't like to ask questions in front of a large audience. The index cards provide a way for me to hear from them and also to sort out the most common questions. I had selected four cards and attached them to the clipboards. "Your task," I informed the group as I passed around the clipboards, "is to read each card, decide which bonus trait(s) is(are) being described, review the suggested strategies that we've just discussed, and select the ones you could use to help the child cope with the situation."

Brent and Diane both grabbed for the top clipboard. I wasn't surprised. Phil and Lynn took the second. Maggie selected the third. A minute later I noticed everyone had started working except John and Sarah. They were both waiting for the other one to pick up the last clipboard. Finally realizing neither one of them was going to do it, John turned to Sarah. "Let's not rush into this," he advised. It was apparent he had a sound understanding of cautious first reaction!

I've included the cards so that you can try this exercise too.

Read each card, and circle the bonus trait(s) being described. Review the suggested strategies that we've just discussed, and select the ones you could use to help the child cope with the situation.

Card 1

My child is six years old. Whenever he's faced with a decision, he says no. Then later he'll say yes, he wants to. Should I let him change his mind a certain number of times, or do I need to teach him to stick with his first stated choice?

Bonus Trait(s)	***Strategies***
energy	
regularity	
first reaction	
disposition	

Here are a few recommendations from Diane and Brent. Remember, if your answers are different, you may have picked up on something we missed.

Diane read the card for the entire group, then asked, "Are these decisions about *new* situations or just decisions?"

I shrugged. "We don't know. This is all the information we have. Which is pretty typical, because often parents who attend the large lectures have not yet read *Raising Your Spirited Child* or attended a class. They haven't studied temperament, so they don't recognize the pattern of new situations. They simply know they have a child who is constantly saying no, then changing his mind, and they can't figure out why."

Diane turned back to the clipboard. "With the information we have, we think the temperament trait is first reaction."

"What strategies are you going to use?" I asked.

Diane listed the following answers, and I filled them in on the chart as she spoke:

Card I	***Temperament Trait***	***Strategies***
Faced with decisions	First reaction	Give him more information
		Talk about fears and feelings
		Tell him to think about it, then ask again later
		Remind him of things that have been fun in the past, even though initially he had wanted to avoid them

"Anything else?" I asked the group.

"What about teaching him to say, 'Let me think about it' rather than 'No'?" Lynn offered.

"Good suggestion," I said as I added it to the list. It is essential that we teach kids the skills to be able to manage their temperament traits themselves.

"We still haven't answered the question," Brent pointed out. "Should she let him change his mind?"

"What do you think?" I asked the group.

Maggie gripped her pen confidently. "Sometimes I have to say, 'I'm sorry that you said no, but the deadline has come and gone. Maybe next time.'"

Lynn agreed. "If Aaron signs up for something, then wants to quit halfway through, I tell him he has to finish."

"Those are both important lessons," I confirmed. "When you have a child with a cautious first reaction, it's essential that you and your child understand it and believe that he isn't trying to be indecisive. Be careful not to trigger him by rushing him or pushing him to act too quickly. When he's making decisions, you can give him information and time to think before he has to commit. For example, you could say, 'If you sign up for soccer, you'll be practicing two nights a week and have games every weekend. You may know kids on the team, or you may not. It can be an opportunity to make new friends. Your cousin played last year; you could call him and ask him what it was like.' Give your child the information he needs to fully understand what the activity entails, then he can decide if he would like to try it. Once he's committed, if the experience is not what he thought it would be, you can help him figure out what will make it better. But unless it's an extremely negative experience, you will want to help him to fulfill his commitment. This is especially true if your child is school age. Developmentally, school-age kids need to learn the importance of finishing things. It's a key to establishing a sense of competence.

"If your child is a preschooler, it's important not to start with activities that require a very long commitment. The preschool and early elementary years are a time to explore interests. For example, you might try gymnastics for six weeks, then swimming. Dance might be the third option, then your child can decide what he'd like to do again."

"But what do you do if your child always says no?" Sarah asked. "David doesn't even want to try."

"If your cautious child is reluctant to try any new activity, you may have to encourage him to select one," I advised. "If he's just started a new school year, or you've just moved, these changes may be enough for the cautious child to handle. But once his life has settled down, help him select one activity. It could be dance, music, athletics, scouts, a social-service group, or whatever else interests him, but trying one thing allows him to identify and develop his interests. Once he's made his selection, help him to figure out what he needs to feel comfortable."

Suddenly the room erupted in side conversations. I heard Diane say, "Sometimes I feel I'm negligent because I haven't signed up my kids for a million activities like my neighbor has."

"But I think too many activities are stressful," Lynn responded.

Maggie joined them, saying, "Kristen has scouts on Monday, church school on Wednesday, and basketball on Thursday. It is just too much, especially when I have to haul Brian too. Kristen finally told me, 'Mom, we've just got to cut out these religion classes.' We cut, but not religion."

"Being a sensitive parent is the wisest action," I recommended while attempting to pull them back. I could see the next class I offered had to include more on development and stress.

How did you do? Did you select similar strategies? Did you think of others that would fit you and your child better? Now try the next one.

Card 2

What do I do with my son? On Wednesday he refused breakfast. He said he wasn't hungry. He ate a big lunch but only a light dinner. Then he wanted a bedtime snack. I want to tell him the kitchen is closed after 6:00 P.M. But I'm so worried about him. He's got to eat. How do I know he's getting the right nutrients?

Bonus Trait(s)	***Strategies***
energy	
regularity	
first reaction	
disposition	

Phil flipped his clipboard, indicating he had Card 2. "We think it's an issue of regularity. We also don't think it's a big deal. Mom is regular, and the child is irregular. It seems to scare her when he doesn't eat. We're going to have her do a continuum with him, so that she recognizes their differences. Then we're going to suggest she teach him good nutritional guidelines, only buy nutritional food so she knows when he does eat that it's good stuff, and"—he paused, and Lynn took over.

"She should still plan her meals and encourage him to come to the table, sit, and talk, but she can stop hassling him over how much he eats or if he eats."

Maggie pointed at the chart. "Don't we need to know if he's growing okay?"

"Yes," I responded. "If he's consistently following his line on a growth chart, he's doing fine. It's important to remember that in the first year of life kids triple their weight. During the second year, growth slows down tremendously and so do kids' appetites. A two-year-old may eat less than a one-year-old."

"I want to know if his mom has to be a short-order cook," Diane replied.

"What do you think?" I asked.

Phil, the irregular adult in our group, replied, "Just teach him to make things himself, and keep the kitchen open."

Brent held up the food pyramid I'd given him. "Where's the category for beer and chocolate?" he asked straight-faced.

John leaned over to him, pointing at the bread and cereal section, the largest box in the pyramid. "They must have meant to put it here, you know—hops and barley."

Diane laughed and said, "Maybe fruits and vegetables." We looked at her quizzically. "Cocoa beans!" she clarified.

Nine weeks into class, and this group had definitely become comfortable with one another.

What suggestions would you add?

Card 2	***Temperament Trait***	***Strategies***
Refusing to eat	Regularity	Recognize different styles
		Teach nutrition
		Teach to prepare simple foods
		Keep kitchen open
		Plan meals as family rituals

Card 3

I am the mother of a three-and-a-half, almost four-year-old. She refuses to sit and eat dinner. She gets up a million times during a meal, and although I take lots of time in making meals from scratch, thinking of her likes and dislikes as much as possible, it is always a battle. Two bites and she's done. I do not use dessert as a bribe to get her to eat.

Bonus Trait(s)	***Strategies***
energy	
regularity	
first reaction	
disposition	

"Who wants to try this one?" I asked. "I think it might be a little tougher."

John read the card to the group, then said, "We thought it was regularity, but after listening to Phil, we've decided it's energy with a little bit of regularity thrown in. We think this is a high-energy kid. At least to me she sounds a lot like my son, Todd. In college I worked as a waiter in a sorority house. I ate standing up, walking around. I still do. My wife thinks we should all sit down, especially with the kids. When Todd was little he'd constantly get up from the table, so I made him the waiter. He's really good at it."

"Oh, oh, I know," Diane exclaimed, almost jumping out of her chair. "You buy a cookbook for kids and let them help prepare the meal." Then she started to laugh. "I let Andy, my three-year-old, put peanut butter on a hot-dog bun and then add a banana to it. He called it a boat. A week later I asked him what he wanted for lunch. He insisted he wanted a boat, but for the life of me I couldn't remember what a boat was. I went crazy trying to figure it out." She giggled, enjoying her own story.

Maggie recommended exercising before the meal. Lynn added purchasing swivel chairs and teaching the kids to sit down in them, so that they don't fall out.

What ideas do you have?

Card 3	***Temperament Trait***	***Strategies***
Leaving the table	Energy	Recognize her energy
		Plan for her energy:
		—Do something active before the meal
		—Make her the waiter
		—Involve her in cooking
		Set rules to keep her safe
	Regularity	Provide nutritional foods
		Let her choose how much she eats

Card 4

I feel like I'm living with my father, but actually it's my ten-year-old son. I'll take him shopping, and he'll say things like, "We need to go home now, you've spent enough money." Or when we're driving in the car he'll ask me how fast I'm going when we both know I'm going 45 mph in a 30 mph zone. Why does he think like this?

Bonus Trait(s)	***Strategies***
energy	
regularity	
first reaction	
disposition	

This time Maggie started. "I'll take this one," she said. "This kid is my daughter's clone. The trait is disposition, and the child has a serious and analytical point of view. What do you do? You get used to it!" She laughed. "Okay, okay, you teach him to be tactful. You use humor, and sometimes you tell him, 'Thank you, you're right.'"

I added her comments to the chart.

Card 4	***Temperament Trait***	***Strategies***
Telling his mother to stop shopping	Serious mood	Teach him to be tactful Use humor Tell him he's right

How did you do? Did you select the same temperament traits? If not, what bits of information led you to another trait? We may have missed something that you noticed, especially if you're analytical. What strategies did you select? Notice that you don't have to use all of them. You can select one or two that are most helpful or useful in that situation.

Extra Practice

In case you feel like you need more practice with the bonus traits, I have another exercise for you. I rarely have time to cover this in class, so I send it home with parents and invite them to bring it back if they have questions.

1. Select and use a different-color marker for each member of your family.
2. Mark an *X* on the continuums for each of your family members.
3. Fill in the examples of behavior for each family member.
4. Select strategies for each person.

SAMPLE

1. Regularity

CHILD 1	CHILD 2	MOM
X	X	X
regular	grazer	irregular

Examples of Behavior Tied to This Trait	*Effective Strategies*
CHILD 1: Gets very intense when her food isn't ready at usual time	Have little snacks ready
CHILD 2: Seems to be either constantly hungry or not hungry at all for half of the day or better	Stress the importance of eating nutritional foods
MOM: Tends to be overoccupied with feeding and cleaning up for others; by the time I realize I haven't eaten for *hours,* I'm nowhere near food	Sit down, relax, and enjoy food at convenient times Listen to my body's hunger pains

YOUR TURN.

1. Regularity

regular	grazer	irregular

Examples of Behavior Tied to This Trait	*Effective Strategies*

SAMPLE

2. Energy

CHILD 2		CHILD 1 and MOM
X		XX
low energy quiet/quiescent		high energy on the move

Examples of Behavior Tied to This Trait	*Effective Strategies*
CHILD 1 AND MOM: *Have* to burn up energy in order to function; we eliminate stress through activity	Sign up for physical sports such as swim/dance/softball
CHILD 2: Is overwhelmed by a full day of constant activity that includes a lot of interaction	Allow time alone Give her space Do not push into being too active

YOUR TURN.

2. Energy

low energy quiet/quiescent	high energy on the move

Examples of Behavior Tied to This Trait	*Effective Strategies*

SAMPLE

3. First Reaction

CHILD 1	MOM	CHILD 2
X	X	X
jumps right in		cautious

Examples of Behavior Tied to This Trait	*Effective Strategies*
CHILD 1: Not intimidated by others; loves to just have fun	Enjoy it Teach to stop, think, act if necessary
CHILD 2: Slow to adapt to new situations and surroundings	Prepare ahead of time Remind of past successes
MOM: Sometimes I jump right into things; other times I am very cautious	Give myself time when I need it

YOUR TURN.

3. First Reaction

jumps right in — cautious

Examples of Behavior Tied to This Trait	*Effective Strategies*

SAMPLE

4. Disposition

CHILD 1 X — CHILD 2 X — MOM X

sunny — serious

Examples of Behavior Tied to This Trait	*Effective Strategies*
CHILD 1: Typically very happy; bounces back to a good mood easily	Slow down and watch for cues
When overstimulated or over-tired, screams with frustration	Teach her calming activities
CHILD 2: Observes everything; analytical and perceptive	Allow time and space Help her see what she *can* do
MOM: Uptight about little things that are only important to me, not others, such as housecleaning	Slow down Focus on what's working

YOUR TURN.

4. Disposition

sunny ——————————————————————— **serious**

Examples of Behavior Tied to This Trait	*Effective Strategies*

Take the time to complete this chart. It is well worth it. From it evolves a picture of your family's preferred style of interacting *and* the best strategies for you.

Working with the bonus traits takes effort. It is essential to recognize that people are different. That doesn't mean, however, that you excuse poor behavior. The information simply helps you to understand the issue and then figure out the most effective strategies to work together harmoniously and respectfully.

SAVOR YOUR SUCCESSES

It had been two weeks since we'd last met. The thermometer read 80 degrees Fahrenheit. Wild geraniums were crowned with purple blooms in the woods, and pots of geraniums, impatiens, alyssum, and pansies decorated everyone's doorsteps. The odds were we'd finally seen the last frost.

We didn't even have to wait for discussion time to share success stories; during family time we saw one success in progress. Sadie was crying when she and Sarah arrived. It had been a tough day, and she hadn't wanted to come. She clung to Sarah and cried, "Don't leave me!"

Sarah stayed calm. She wasn't embarrassed. She knew now that Sadie was often quite cautious. She found a familiar book and started reading it to her, adding, "I'll stay with you until you're comfortable." Sarah also took time to talk to the children's teacher and let Sadie know that she could ask the teacher for help too. Sadie stopped crying, but at the end of circle, when it was time for separation, she panicked again. Clinging to Sarah, she screamed, "No! Don't GO!"

"I'll stay," Sarah replied. The other parents left. Sarah remained, now a security post simply sitting on the floor, available to connect with Sadie but not interacting. Sadie started to play with the modeling dough. After ten minutes she hadn't come back to check in, so Sarah stood up, said good-bye, and without wavering walked out the door. Sadie didn't protest.

When Sarah entered the parent discussion room, the group spontaneously broke into applause. She looked startled, then presented us with a heartwarming grin.

"Wow! That was beautiful!" I exclaimed.

Sarah laughed. "I was just doing what we talked about."

"And doing it well," I continued.

Brent handed me a marker. "Aren't we supposed to analyze why it worked?"

"Of course," I replied, just a bit embarrassed. I hadn't realized I was so predictable.

I turned to the board as Maggie spoke. "She supported her."

"Told her she wouldn't leave until she was comfortable and that the teacher could help her too," John added.

"Gave her time," Brent offered. "She was really patient."

Sarah soaked it all up as we added to the list. The mood was light. Everyone could see the kids had made progress and so had we.

"Any other successes?" I asked, turning back to the group.

This time John leaned forward. Since he usually listened more than he talked, I caught the movement quickly and invited him to share his story.

"It isn't a kid story," he said. "It's a me story. My wife and I went to buy a coffee table. I had a type in mind, but when we got to the store, my wife kept saying, 'What about this one? What about that one?' I needed time to think. I caught myself saying, 'No, no.' Then the salesperson got involved, and the two of them were both trying to convince me. Finally I sat down in a chair and said to my wife, 'Would you please go with the salesperson and stand over there while I sit here and just look for a minute? I need time to think about it.' She did. I did, and then we made a decision. In the past we would have ended up real frustrated with each other."

I pointed out the respectful phrases John had used:

I need to think.
Please go with the salesperson.
I want to just look for a minute.

These are important phrases for cautious first-reaction people to learn.

It was a fun check-in. Lynn had been working with her kids on nutrition. When she cut a brownie for her oldest daughter's lunch, her daughter said, "Mom, that's full of fat. Give me the skim-milk pudding instead!"

Brent and his kids had gone outside and played before going to visit grandparents. The visit had been much calmer.

Maggie had realized Kristen's chatter was really her way of showing excitement, and even though she never used words like *fantastic* or *super,* Kristen was pleased and happy.

Diane recognized that while Andy was regular with sleeping and eliminating, he wasn't when it came to eating. "I didn't think regularity was a problem for us, but then I realized we'd butt heads about his not wanting to eat lunch all the time. It's still a problem, but I step back more quickly."

I sat back, savoring their successes. Slowly but surely everyone—at his own pace—was making progress. Next week would be our last class. I ran down the attendance form, stopping to reflect. Was there anything else I wanted to talk about? Did anyone need a referral for a medical or counseling consultation? Everything was in order. It was almost time to say good-bye.

Next week was an ending. It also needed to be a beginning.

Savor Your Successes

How are you doing?

Think of challenging behaviors you've experienced that you now realize are tied to the bonus traits. Record them here.

What strategies did you use to help your child be successful?

Reflect on your progress. Are you pleased? Is an understanding of temperament answering your questions? Do you need additional information or support? If so, call that friend who knows and loves your child and can provide you with the encouragement you need.

CORNERSTONE

Children who are irregular need to hear

Statements that help them feel good about their irregularity:

- ✔ You are flexible.
- ✔ You can wait if a meal is late.
- ✔ You can be very spontaneous.
- ✔ You'll make a great traveler.

Statements that help them identify their triggers:

- ✔ Being forced to eat upsets you.
- ✔ You are not always hungry at mealtimes.
- ✔ Having food available at all times is important to you.
- ✔ Choices are important to you.
- ✔ Sometimes it's difficult for you to fall asleep.

Statements that help them manage their irregularity:

- ✔ Join us just to talk, if you're not hungry.
- ✔ You can lie quietly and rest if you're not ready to go to sleep.
- ✔ You can learn to make your own snacks.
- ✔ You can learn to select nutritional foods.
- ✔ Routines can help you.

Children who are energetic need to hear

Statements that help them feel good about their energy:

- ✔ You have lots of energy.
- ✔ You can accomplish many things.
- ✔ You have the energy to be a great athlete or dancer.
- ✔ I like your energy.

Statements that help them identify their triggers:

- ✔ Being able to move is important to you.
- ✔ Sitting still too long is very difficult for you.
- ✔ You learn best when you can move your body.
- ✔ Being able to touch things is important to you.
- ✔ Traveling on a plane or in the car can be challenging for you.

Statements that help them manage their energy:

- ✔ Getting exercise every day is important to you.
- ✔ You need room to move.
- ✔ You learn best when you can touch things or use your body.
- ✔ You can lie on the floor when you're doing your homework.
- ✔ You can stand at a table to work.
- ✔ Taking frequent breaks when you have to be still is important for you.

Children who are cautious in new situations need to hear

Statements that help them feel good about their cautious first reaction:

✔ You think before trying things.
✔ You are not impulsive.
✔ You like to watch before trying something new.
✔ You are not easily persuaded to try risky behaviors.
✔ I'm really going to appreciate your style when you're a teenager!

Statements that help them identify their triggers:

✔ Being pushed bothers you.
✔ New situations or people may be difficult for you.
✔ You like to take your time to make a decision.
✔ You like to know what to expect.

Statements that help them manage their cautious first reaction:

✔ You can choose to go early.
✔ You can ask for information.
✔ What will help you feel more comfortable?
✔ It's all right to watch first.
✔ You can change your mind.
✔ Remember when you were successful with. . .
✔ You can ask for support.
✔ You are feeling anxious, but you are not sick.
✔ You can take your time.

Children who have a serious and analytical disposition need to hear

Statements that help them feel good about their serious disposition:

- ✔ I appreciate your analytical point of view.
- ✔ You are practical and realistic.
- ✔ You see what needs to be fixed.
- ✔ You're not afraid to ask tough questions.
- ✔ You set high standards.
- ✔ You'll make a great evaluator or judge.

Statements that help them recognize their triggers:

- ✔ Seriously considering all factors is important to you.
- ✔ Getting enough sleep is essential for you.
- ✔ It's upsetting to you when others do not see what needs to be fixed.

Statements that help them manage their serious disposition:

- ✔ You can say what you like, as well as what needs to be fixed.
- ✔ It's important to be tactful.
- ✔ How can you make it better?
- ✔ You really worked hard on that.
- ✔ I appreciate it when you tell me what you liked.

11

PLANNING FOR SUCCESS

Predicting and Preventing the Trouble Spots

IN PREPARATION

- Read Chapters 13, 17, 18, and 19 in *Raising Your Spirited Child.*
- Grab a pen or pencil.
- Pull out your wallet.

CHAPTER HIGHLIGHTS

- Steps to help you plan for success.
- Strategies to help you predict the potential tough times and avoid or minimize them.

THINGS TO OBSERVE

- Think about the next twenty-four hours. What trouble spots can you predict? What about next week? Next month?

I cut a bouquet of peonies to take with me to class and picked up a batch of brownies. I hoped that flowers and chocolate would help me ease into the last class. I always approach it with mixed feelings. I'm sad. I hate to say good-bye to the parents and kids. I'm happy because I believe—no, I'm certain—the parents have gained some insights and learned strategies that have enhanced their relationships. I'm frustrated because I always wish I could have done more, and I'm challenged to review the curriculum and make it better for next time. So I take my deep breaths, open the door, and get ready to plan for success.

Sadie made me smile the minute she walked in the door. "Do you know *stupid* is not a good word?" she asked me very seriously.

I flashed back to when Joshua was three and a half. I'd let him ride his Big Wheel along a Minneapolis parkway. He stopped when he saw a motorcyclist lounging against his bike. The man cut an imposing figure, feet and arms crossed, chains hanging down from his leather vest and pants, forearms heavily tattooed. Carefully perusing the man's equipment, Joshua suddenly asked, "Where's your helmet?"

"Don't have one," the man growled, uncrossing his arms and pulling himself to his full six-foot, two-hundred-pound-plus frame.

Joshua looked at him quite seriously. Then, hands on hips, he loudly announced, "My mom says anyone who doesn't wear a helmet is stupid." Blood rushed to my face as the man spat on the ground, then turned to stare at me. Silently, ferociously, he let me know what he thought of my advice. Gingerly I stepped back, vowing to never use the word *stupid* again!

"Oh, yes, Sadie," I agreed. "*Stupid* can get you into trouble."

Brent and Danny arrived next. I noticed they both had new Oakland A's caps and each had a shiny flashlight attached to his belt loops. Phil entered with T.J. on one arm and swinging a diaper bag in the other hand.

Diane stopped when she saw me. "This is it! Isn't it? Our last class. We need a reunion!" she declared dramatically.

So our discussion began with plans for a picnic to include the group's spouses, partners, and all the kids. Diane felt better knowing she could continue to connect with others who understood spirit. Now it was time to plan for success.

"Please take out your wallet and lay it on the table in front of you," I directed the group. Brent and Phil looked at me suspiciously. "Is this going to cost me?" Brent wanted to know.

"Depends," I told him, enjoying the moment of intrigue. "We're going to do a little gambling here."

Maggie laughed. "You're assuming I have money in it?"

Sarah started to squirm. I leaned over to her and whispered, "It's only pretend." She relaxed.

"Who," I asked, "is willing to bet me the contents of their wallet that your child will be successful at dinner tomorrow night?"

Lynn's hand shot up. Maggie's wavered. Brent grabbed his wallet. "No way!" he stated, absolutely confident of his prediction.

"How about getting ready for school?" I asked. Three hands shot up. "What about the next party? Vacation or trip to grandparents?"

With each of my questions hands flew into the air or exclamations of "Forget it" resounded. They each felt they could reasonably predict whether or not their kids would be successful.

Of course the predictions are not a perfect science. No one can foresee the future, but when you learn to predict your child's *typical* reaction, you can plan for success. You don't have to feel like a victim, waiting for the next explosion. Understanding temperament is the key. It allows you to step into the driver's seat and take a different route.

Next time you walk into a store, school, or family celebration, stop and ask yourself, would I be willing to bet the contents of my wallet that my child will be successful in this situation? If you can't say yes, maybe you need to take a few minutes and plan for success!

A NEW POINT OF VIEW

Planning for success requires that you to stop and think about the next twenty-four hours, the coming week, the next vacation, holiday, party, dentist appointment, shopping trip, school start or end, dinner, bedtime, or any other event in your child's life and ask yourself: *What does my child need to be successful in this situation?*

Ultimately your child will take over the responsibility of asking this question for herself. But until she does, you are the one who has to do it, and you are the one who has to teach your child how to do it for herself. It begins by predicting.

"Think about the next twenty-four hours, the next week, or the next month," I directed the group. "What situations do you expect to encounter that are potential trouble spots for your child?" I created four categories on the board.

Routines	Social Situations	Vacations/Travel	School

"Dressing," Diane and Sarah responded simultaneously.

"My father's birthday party," Lynn added. "It's the big sixty, and all the relatives are coming. I know Jenna will have trouble with it."

"Yeah, anything with holidays or birthday parties," Diane agreed. "We really have to talk about them, and traveling too. I don't want vacation to be a nightmare this year."

Brent started twisting paper clips. "Is there something you'd like to add?" I asked him.

"School," he said. "I think we'd better find a better match for Danny or he's going to get labeled as a bad kid." I added it to the list.

Sarah raised her hand. "We need to talk about games. David goes ballistic every time he loses, and the neighbor kids are getting sick of it."

I looked around. "Is that it?" I asked.

Phil checked the list. "Looks good," he said, reaching for another brownie.

POTENTIAL TROUBLE SPOTS

Routines	***Social Situations***	***Vacations/Travel***	***School***
dressing	Grandpa's party	vacation	finding the right school
	losing games		

Now it's your turn.

1. **Think about the next twenty-four hours, week, or month.**

2. **Review the following categories. What potential trouble spots can you predict for your child?**

3. **List them in the appropriate category.**

POTENTIAL TROUBLE SPOTS

Routines	*Social Situations*	*Vacations/Travel*	*School*

EFFECTIVE STRATEGIES

Once you've predicted the potential tough spots, you have a choice. You can simply choose not to take your child into that situation, or you can choose to help him work through it. The younger your child, the more often you may simply realize it's better not to include him. Otherwise you can drastically reduce the intensity of the tough times by thinking about what your child will need to be successful in that situation. This approach moves you from a reactive position to a proactive one—you hedge your bets. In the process you also teach your child self-awareness and coping skills that ultimately he will be able to use to plan for his own success.

In *Raising Your Spirited Child* I offer a four-step process for planning for success.

1. **P**redict the reactions.
2. **O**rganize the environment.
3. **W**ork together.
4. **E**njoy the **R**ewards.

The POWER approach.

I'm choosing to slightly change that process for two reasons. First, the POWER approach has proven to need a bit of fine-tuning. If it's working for you, don't worry; keep using it. The steps are correct, I'm simply choosing to simplify it and focus more on temperament triggers and strategies. The second reason is a bit whimsical. I thought it would be more fun to have an acronym that would go along with the "betting on success" theme. I came up with PAID.

1. **P**redict the tough spots.
2. **A**nalyze the temperament traits involved.
3. **I**dentify the triggers—what sparks the troublesome behaviors.
4. **D**evelop strategies for success.

Use the PAID process, and chances are you'll enjoy the payoff of your efforts. You'll be rich in your sense of harmony, joy, and satisfaction as your child successfully manages potentially troublesome situations.

Here's how it works.

1. PREDICT THE TOUGH SPOTS

Think ahead, and select a potential tough time you'd like to manage better or maybe even eliminate. You can start with an easy one, like getting your child to pick up his toys or schoolbooks. If you're feeling full of energy, you might want to put your efforts into a tougher issue, one that really drives you nuts, like getting your child to bed or to do homework. Review the list you just completed for ideas, and decide which you're ready to tackle.

2. ANALYZE THE TEMPERAMENT TRAITS

Think about each of the temperament traits. Decide which ones are key traits for your child in this situation. For example, if the potential tough time is summer camp and your child is cautious in new situations, first reaction will be a key trait to consider.

3. IDENTIFY THE TRIGGERS

Once you've identified the key traits involved in this issue, think about the triggers for this trait. What will set your child off? For example, if you've selected cautious first reaction as a key temperament trait, then you can predict that your child will be triggered by new things, being teased about her caution, or being pushed. Don't worry if you can't remember them all. The temperament summary chart on the next page will help you.

4. DEVELOP STRATEGIES FOR SUCCESS

Knowing what will trigger your child allows you to select strategies that will help him avoid those triggers or reduce their impact. For example, if a key temperament trait is cautious first reaction, your first strategy would be to prepare your child:

Involve your child in selecting the camp.
Visit the camp before enrolling.
Obtain a video or pictures of the camp.
Talk with someone who has been to the camp.
Arrive early to check out the camp before others arrive.
Talk about what to do if he becomes homesick.

Next, support your child:

Ask what will make it better.
Send along favorite pictures, snack foods, and other comfort items.
Sign your child up with a friend.

In other words, begin by thinking about who your child is and what will likely be her first and most natural reaction in that situation. Then teach him strategies that will help him manage that reaction and be successful.

Here's the temperament summary chart. There's space for you to add triggers and strategies that are especially important for your child.

SUCCESSFULLY GUIDING YOUR SPIRITED CHILD: TEMPERAMENT SUMMARY

Temperament Trait	*Triggers*	*Effective Strategies*
INTENSITY strength of emotional reactions	being ignored being told not to be so intense intensity of others disappointment rushing fatigue hunger	Manage the intensity * plan soothing activities, like modeling dough, reading, water play * exercise * keep your sense of humor * breathe deeply or blow bubbles * take a break or change the scene * do something repeti tive like chewing gum, rocking, or swinging * find positive outlets for intensity: music, athletics, dance
PERSISTENCE commitment to one's goals	being told no unclear limits or limits that keep changing not having a choice being forced to quit not being listened to not being allowed to do things for oneself	Teach your child to be an effective problem solver * let your child know you are listening and trying to understand * offer choices) * ask what's important * look for multiple solutions * evaluate solutions together

Temperament Trait	*Triggers*	*Effective Strategies*
Persistence *(cont.)*		* allow time to finish activities * set clear, consistent rules * involve your child in the planning process
SENSITIVITY depth of one's awareness to sights, sounds, smells, textures, and emotions	too much stimulation tags, bumps, seams, noises, smells other people's anger or hurt feelings being too hot	Teach your child to manage stimulation levels * find ways to eliminate offensive stimulation: remove tags, turn off lights and TV, buy cotton clothes * finds ways to reduce stimulation that cannot be eliminated: take a break, be selective about food and clothing Believe your child
PERCEPTIVENESS how easily outside stimuli interfere with or change the direction of one's behavior	too many directions at once unclear directions directions that are only verbal too much distracting stimulation in the environment no routines	Minimize distractions * make changes in the room * make eye contact Keep directions simple and clear * break tasks into simple steps * tell your child what he *can* do

Temperament Trait	*Triggers*	*Effective Strategies*
Perceptiveness *(cont.)*		Make directions visual and tactile as well as verbal * use charts * use fingers as reminders * place objects in view * tie directions to physical objects or movement * write notes
ADAPTABILITY ability to adapt to intrusions, shifts from one thing to another, changes in routines, and surprises	being rushed surprises expectations not met unexpected changes	Teach your child to be aware of transitions and to eliminate or prepare for them eliminate transitions * avoid unnecessary transitions * avoid overscheduling Prepare for transitions * let your child know what to expect * allow time to adjust * help your child refocus on the next activity * plan to help your child through transitions Create routines

Temperament Trait	*Triggers*	*Effective Strategies*
REGULARITY predictability of eating, sleeping, and eliminating patterns	not getting enough sleep inflexibility lack of routines	Teach your child how to cope with social norms of mealtimes and bedtimes while providing flexibility * teach nutritional guidelines * teach your child self-help skills * establish routines for mealtimes and bedtimes
ENERGY how active one is	confinement rainy, cold days no exercise sitting too long	Teach your child to plan for physical activities every day * involve your child in sports, music, or dancing * seek teachers who encourage hands-on learning * find ways for your child to move throughout the day
FIRST REACTION how one first reacts to anything new	anything new being pushed being teased about caution being forced to decide too quickly	Teach your child to recognize that the first reaction may not be the final decision Prepare your child * give information * allow time for observing and thinking

Temperament Trait	*Triggers*	*Effective Strategies*
First Reaction *(cont.)*		Allow a second chance * teach your child to say, "Let me think about it" instead of automatically saying no Support your child * help your child figure out what will make it better: taking a picture of Mom, going with a friend
DISPOSITION one's general mood	missed cues of other traits lack of sleep others not taking things seriously	Teach your child to see what can be done as well as what needs to be fixed * slow down your interactions with your child * make sure your child is getting enough sleep Take note of how your child expresses enthusiasm Teach your child social graces: thanks, I appreciated that, it was nice
INTROVERSION tendency to recharge by going within	too many people crowding too much activity no time alone	Teach your child to recognize his need to recharge by taking time alone or with one special person * provide space and time alone for your child * allow your child time to think * limit interruptions

Temperament Trait	*Triggers*	*Effective Strategies*
EXTROVERSION tendency to recharge by going outside of oneself	too much time alone boredom inactivity not being able to talk	Teach your child to recognize her need to recharge by being with people and doing things * allow your child to talk through problems with you * provide opportunities for your child to be with others and to be actively involved in a variety of experiences * give your child lots of feedback

PRACTICE, PRACTICE, PRACTICE

Let's try our hand at planning for success. I told the group, "Select one tough time you'd like to focus on, and find a partner who is willing to work with you."

"Only one?" Diane lamented.

"Yes, only one," I responded. "It's important to set your priorities and focus your energies. If you try to handle everything at once, you're more likely to become overwhelmed. It's better to select one and enjoy that success."

The group quickly broke into pairs and threesomes. They perused the temperament summary chart and came up with strategies. Their groans intermixed with exclamations of "My kid does that too!" and "Great idea!"

"Hang on a minute," I called to the group.

"You are going to let us finish, aren't you?" Brent growled at me.

"Yes, I am. I just wanted to point out that as you plan for success right now, you are not stressed, you are working with someone else—you are not in isolation—and you have resources in hand. All of these things help you to be successful. Remember them when you go home. You can plan for success by yourself, but it's really nice to have help and support."

As the parents went back to their work I drew another chart on the board. Ten minutes later they were ready to present their plans for success.

Diane and Sarah had tackled dressing. Both had kids who ran around when it was time to get dressed. Their children were easily distracted and really poky.

1. Pretend you are part of Sarah and Diane's group. Work with them on this example.
2. Write your answers in the chart below.
3. Compare your suggestions with those of Diane and Sarah.
4. How are your plans similar?
5. What makes them different?

PLANNING FOR SUCCESS

Predict Potential Tough Spots	***Analyze Temperament Traits***	***Identify Triggers***	***Develop Strategies***
dressing: kids run around, get distracted, and are poky			

Reviewing the temperament summary chart, Diane and Sarah selected energy, adaptability, and perceptiveness as the key temperament traits fueling the challenging behavior. I wrote them on the chart on the board. Maggie, who was sitting next to me, pointed to sensitivity. "Wouldn't this be the most important trait? My kids complain that the cuffs are too tight or the material doesn't feel right."

I looked at Diane and Sarah. "No," they responded in unison. For Andy and Sadie sensitivity isn't a big issue.

"This," I pointed out, "is why it is so important to look at your own child's temperament. If you just select a strategy without understanding why the behavior is occurring—what temperament trait is being triggered—it's unlikely that the strategy will work. For example, if your child has difficulty getting dressed, you could just cut out the labels and always buy cotton, but if sensitivity isn't the issue, these strategies won't help at all. You have to know which temperament traits are being triggered in order to select the most effective strategies."

"Wow," Diane responded. Then, after identifying the key temperament traits, she described the triggers she and Sarah had selected. Finally they created strategies using the suggestions from the temperament summary chart as guidelines.

Here's their chart.

PLANNING FOR SUCCESS

Predict Potential Tough Spots	*Analyze Temperament Traits*	*Identify Triggers*	*Develop Strategies*
dressing: kids run around, get distracted, and are poky	perceptiveness	too many directions and distractions	make a dressing chart lay out clothes keep blinds down dress in bedroom—no TV pick up distracting toys

Predict Potential Tough Spots	*Analyze Temperament Traits*	*Identify Triggers*	*Develop Strategies*
dressing: kids run around, get distracted, and are poky	energy	being confined	let kids stand in front of mirror while dressing have kids run around between items of clothing but stay in bedroom
	adaptability	being surprised and rushed	set up a routine allow enough time get dressed before any other activities refocus to what's next be available to help

Remember, there isn't one right plan. What's most important is knowing your child's temperament so that you can predict what will trigger him. Then you can avoid those triggers by selecting strategies that help your child cope successfully.

Lynn reached for another brownie. "Let's do one for the older kids."

"Yeah—losing a game," Maggie suggested.

John volunteered to read the plan he developed.

"I thought the key temperament issues were intensity, adaptability, and disposition.

"Why disposition?" Maggie asked.

"Because Todd's very serious. When he loses he becomes critical of himself. I thought teaching him to be optimistic would help him to cope better."

"I like that," Maggie said as she offered John a brownie. "And I wouldn't have thought of it. Tell us what you put down for triggers and strategies."

Here's his plan for success.

PLANNING FOR SUCCESS

Predict Potential Tough Spots	*Analyze Temperament Traits*	*Identify Triggers*	*Develop Strategies*
losing a game	intensity	disappoint-ment	teach him to breathe deeply
		fatigue	help him recognize when he needs a break
		intensity of others	encourage him to chew gum while he's playing
		being told not to be intense	tell him to smile, make jokes, and keep his sense of humor
			teach him words to to describe his frustration
	adaptability	being surprised—he never expects to lose	talk about the possi-bility of losing
			remind him that he can play again
	disposition	missing cues of rising intensity	teach him to congrat-ulate the winners
			focus on what he has done well
			plan what he wants to do next time
			ask Mom or Dad for help

"Could you do it?" I asked the group.

"This stuff is fantastic!" Diane exclaimed. "Why didn't we do this the first week? It really makes you think about each kid and what he needs so you don't have to feel like you're walking on eggshells all the time."

Lynn laughed. "I don't know about you, but I couldn't have started here."

"Speaking of starts," John interceded, "let's help Brent select a school for Danny."

"Can we do it together?" Lynn, the great extrovert, wanted to know.

I looked at Brent. He shook his head. "Fine with me."

"Start with the key temperament traits," I suggested. "Remember when I first introduced temperament? We selected key temperament triggers. Do any of those come into play for Danny at school?"

Brent paused, rubbing his chin. "Let me see that summary chart again," he said, gesturing to Lynn. "Definitely energy, and he's a pretty strong extrovert, so he gets into trouble for talking out of turn. I think persistence is an issue. He tends to lock in."

"Knowing Danny is a high-energy extrovert who tends to lock in, what can you predict will be his triggers?" I asked.

"Being forced to sit still," Brent said, glancing through the chart. "The extrovert in him is triggered when he can't talk, and he needs to have a lot of stuff happening."

"What about the persistence?" I asked.

"He doesn't want to be told no, and he needs someone who will listen to him."

"Let's look at the strategies," I said. "What will he need in a classroom to be successful?"

Brent slouched in his chair. I sensed he was uncomfortable figuring out the strategies.

"What helped you in this class?" I asked him. "You're high-energy too, aren't you?"

"Yeah," he responded. "Being able to get up to get something to drink was nice, and I liked the nights we worked in the lobby. That was the best for me."

"And you're persistent?" I asked.

He smiled. "Maybe a little, but everybody listened"—he glanced warily at Lynn—"even if they didn't always agree with me." Then he pointed at Diane. "I'm not an extrovert, but you let her talk enough." Diane gasped.

"But not too much," Maggie immediately assured her.

"Now think about Danny. What will he need, what strategies will help him be successful?" I turned to the group, inviting them to help Brent. Here's the summary of their responses.

PLANNING FOR SUCCESS

Predict Potential Tough Spots	*Analyze Temperament Traits*	*Identify Triggers*	*Develop Strategies*
selecting a classroom	persistence	being told no not being listened to having no choices	Find a teacher who * listens for understanding * offers choices * looks for multiple solutions * sets clear, consistent rules * involves kids in planning process
	energy	confinement sitting too long	Find a teacher who * has lots of hands-on activities * allows kids to move around the room
	extroversion	boredom inactivity not being able to talk	Find a teacher who * allows kids to talk through problems * provides opportunities for kids to work together * gives lots of feedback

By using the chart, we saw that Danny needs a teacher who is comfortable with and plans for energy, who listens, and who gives the kids many opportunities to talk and do things together. But the teacher also cannot be a pushover. She must have clear rules and let the kids know what is and what is not negotiable.

Brent can take this information to the principal and ask her to help him find the right teacher for Danny. If for some reason that's not feasible, he can ask other teachers or parents for recommendations. But he has to be careful doing that, because the best teacher for one child may not be right for your child at all.

"Think about Katie," I pointed out to Brent. "She is an introvert who is sensitive and slow to adapt. The best classroom fit for her would be one where there's harmony, the stimulation level is low, and transitions are clear and limited in number. Most important, she needs a class where there are many opportunities for the kids to work alone, where they are not crowded and can choose their partners.

"It is possible that a fabulous teacher for Danny would be skilled enough to create a setting where all types of kids thrive. Or she may be perfect for Danny, but Katie would do much better in the room next door. Each child is unique. That's why the puzzle is always so interesting and fun."

Now it's your turn.

1. Think about selecting a classroom or child care program for your child.
2. What are key temperament traits in this setting for your child?
3. What will trigger those traits?
4. What type of strategies do you need to see employed in the classroom for your child to be successful?
5. If you have more than one child, do this for all, and note the similarities and differences.

PLANNING FOR SUCCESS

Predict Potential Tough Spots	*Analyze Temperament Traits*	*Identify Triggers*	*Develop Strategies*
selecting a classroom			Find a teacher who

Brent copied down the chart we'd made and sat back. I waited for him to say something, but he didn't.

I was surprised. "Brent," I said, "you haven't asked the thought-provoking question." He lowered his eyebrows at me. "You know, Why do we have to do this? And what do you do if you can't do this—if there aren't any choices?"

"Oh, yeah. Why do you have to do this?" he asked in a mock grumble.

"Thanks for the opening," I said and went into my little speech. The better fit you find for your child in the classroom, the better he will do. By talking with the principal, seeking recommendations from others, and observing in schools, you can find the teacher who can work with your spirited child very well. Spirited children can excel both academically and socially. There really are wonderfully committed, creative, caring teachers out there. Find them!

In situations where there is only one teacher for each grade or little or no choice for you and your child, it is crucial to know your child's temperament traits and triggers. This way you will have greater awareness of potential issues and will have the tools to talk about them with the teacher and suggest changes within that environment. In this situation your child really needs you to be his advocate.

"I think we've got time for one more," I said to the group.

"We have to do the birthday party!" Lynn demanded.

"And my vacation!" Diane cried.

"We can do the birthday party quickly," I offered, "but vacation is more complex because your child doesn't go alone." Diane gave me her best exaggerated pout.

"Okay," I agreed. "We'll try to do both."

I'm going to let you help Lynn.

When I asked Lynn what Jenna's key temperament traits were, she answered, "She's an introvert, slow to adapt, and very sensitive, especially to smells and people chewing loudly.

1. Review the temperament summary chart.

2. Identify triggers for each of these traits.

3. Suggest strategies Lynn might use to help Jenna be successful at Grandpa's birthday party.

PLANNING FOR SUCCESS

Predict Potential Tough Spots	***Analyze Temperament Traits***	***Identify Triggers***	***Develop Strategies***
Grandpa's sixtieth birthday party	**introversion**		
	sensitivity		
	adaptability		

Here's an example of a plan for success.

PLANNING FOR SUCCESS

Predict Potential Tough Spots	***Analyze Temperament Traits***	***Identify Triggers***	***Develop Strategies***
Grandpa's sixtieth birthday party	introversion	crowding too many people no time alone too much activity	discuss need for time alone teach to tell Mom when she needs a break plan breaks ahead of time * take a walk * go for a car ride * play a game
	sensitivity	smells people chewing	eat before the party be selective about where she sits bring mints

Predict Potential Tough Spots	*Analyze Temperament Traits*	*Identify Triggers*	*Develop Strategies*
	adaptability	surprises	review together plans for the day
		expectations not met	plan how to take breaks and where to sit
		being rushed	arrive early
			allow enough time
			plan what to do in case of surprise or disappointment
			* take deep breaths
			* count to ten
			* chew gum

How did you do? There is room for creativity in this scenario. If the party is held in a home with just family members present, the plan for success may look quite different from one developed for an event held in a restaurant or hall with hundreds of people attending. The most important factors are to find a socially acceptable way for Jenna to take a break when she needs it, to avoid unpleasant smells, and to know what to expect and what is expected of her.

Planning for Success in Social Situations

1. **Think of a future social situation for your child.**
2. **What key temperament traits will be significant in this situation?**
3. **Identify the triggers for those traits.**
4. **Develop strategies for her success.**

PLANNING FOR SUCCESS

Predict Potential Tough Spots	*Analyze Temperament Traits*	*Identify Triggers*	*Develop Strategies*
social situations			

Last but not least, it's time to think about vacations. You have to consider not only your spirited child's key temperament traits and triggers but those of other family members too. Here's the picture from Diane's family.

PLANNING FOR SUCCESS

Name	*Predict Potential Tough Spots*	*Analyze Tempera-ment Traits*	*Identify Triggers*	*Develop Strategies*	*Final Plan for the Family*
Bob	vacation	introversion	crowding too much activity too many people	needs space and some time alone	
Diane	vacation	extroversion	boredom having no one to talk to	needs people and activity	
		intensity	intensity of others	needs exercise	

Name	Predict Potential Tough Spots	Analyze Tempera-ment Traits	Identify Triggers	Develop Strategies	Final Plan for the Family
Justin, 8	vacation	intensity	intensity of others	needs exercise	
		sensitivity	conflict	needs harmony	
Brandon, 5	vacation	extro-version	boredom inactivity	needs people and activity	
		sensitivity	smells, sights, sounds	ways to reduce or eliminate offensive stimuli	
Andy, 3	vacation	persistence	being told no	choices	
		percep-tiveness	too many distracting stimuli	ways to reduce stimuli	
			too many directions at once	simple, clear directions	

Looking at the chart for Diane's family you can see that their plan needs to include

1. time and space for Bob—Diane's family will enjoy vacations more if they do something that allows for choices and opportunities to do things together, in pairs, or individually. In that way, Bob can have a break when he needs it and keep his energy level high.
2. exercise and a variety of activities for Diane and the boys.
3. harmony for Justin, who needs to know everyone is working together.
4. choices for Andy.
5. someone on duty with Andy. Diane and Bob have to be aware that Andy is very perceptive, persistent, and three

years old, which means that if they are in a crowd and he sees something, he may take off. One of them must be responsible for him at all times.

6. avoiding being confined together for hours and endless sight-seeing without any active involvement.

So what could Diane's family do? They really could do anything—they just have to agree that they will consider each individual's needs and find solutions that work for everyone.

If this is a driving trip, the family can plan to exercise before getting in the car, then make frequent stops, especially at parks or playgrounds. Those who choose to do so can move and play, and those who want to sit and enjoy the space can.

If they are going to an amusement park, they may wish to select a hotel within walking distance so that they can take a break at lunch, swim in the pool, then go back to the amusement park later. This plan allows for both activity and breaks. They may also choose to go when crowds are smaller and it's easier to keep track of Andy. In fact, they may even decide to wait for their trip to Disney World until Andy is older and is able to understand the importance of staying with his parents, even when he sees something interesting.

They might choose a quiet getaway at a lake. A wide choice of physical and quiet activities should keep everyone happy as long as side trips, board games, and family reading times are planned for rainy days or evenings.

By working together—making sure that there are opportunities for both introverts and extroverts to recharge and planning activities that respect the needs of the various temperament types—a spirited family can have a *great* vacation.

That's it. By planning for success, you will be PAID for your efforts with more success and, most important, more joy in one another's company.

SAVOR YOUR SUCCESSES

We were down to our last fifteen minutes together. I still had ten weeks' worth of work to summarize, and I also wanted to create a sense of closure. I wanted everyone to walk out recognizing what they'd learned. But more important, I wanted them to feel good about themselves as parents. I suspected this last wish might be a little tough.

Given our state's heritage, it was very unlikely the group would feel comfortable publicly patting themselves on the back or even acknowledging what they'd learned. I got out my now infamous index cards and tossed them in the middle.

"Here's your question," I said. "What's the most important thing you learned about your child or yourself?"

As the group grabbed for the index cards, I heard groans intermixed with jokes.

When they were done, we read them out loud to commemorate the time we had spent together. I don't know who authored each card. Your guess is as good as mine. But here they are.

I came to this class to learn how to deal with my child's intensity. I never expected to learn about my own.

I learned I was more like my child than I initially thought and that my wife's temperament is very different from ours—which finally explains why we react in opposite ways.

I learned that I'm a high-energy extrovert. I also learned that my husband is probably spirited.

Hang in there. There's hope!

I'm getting to know my children and appreciating their differences.

I think I've been given a new perspective and tools to work with. I'm actually more patient and more understanding. I am try-

ing to plan ahead and think about what works and what is too much. I've even figured out how to calm situations that before the class I felt helpless to deal with.

I found out I don't adjust easily to changes—and there've been lots of changes in my life lately. I'm also intense and sensitive. Learning this was as beneficial to me as what I learned about my child.

That's the exciting thing about spirited kids. As we learn how to work with them, we get to learn about ourselves and our partners too. It is a process that includes great days and some that might be downright rotten. Yet even on those lousy days there is the hint of potential, the glimmer of possibilities.

I remember in particular one very stressful day. It was 95 degrees Fahrenheit with humidity to match. We'd just moved, and the air conditioner wasn't working because Charlie the carpenter was tearing down five walls and the kitchen. I'd had it. When Joshua started to tease his sister, I have to admit that twenty years of training and experience working with spirited kids went out the window. I yelled at him. "Joshua, stop being a *jerk*!" (Now you know why Progress, Not Perfection is our goal!) Then I stomped toward my bedroom, one of the few spaces that wasn't a pile of sawdust. Behind me I heard Joshua merrily wisecrack, "So, Mrs. Parent Education, in which chapter do we refer to our children as jerks?" My frustration dissolved in laughter.

That's Joshua, a spirited child, who is now almost an adult. Spirited children learn to deal with their own intensity. They learn to diffuse yours too. Until they get there, they make you laugh. They make you cry. They make you work harder than other parents. But when you take the time to help your child understand his temperament and teach her skills to be successful, you are teaching essential life skills. You are helping a child who is more to be more, and you are creating a family in which spirit thrives.

So what was the most important thing you learned about your child or yourself?

If you'd like, please let me know. Write to:

Mary Sheedy Kurcinka
c/o HarperCollins Publishers
10 East 53rd Street
New York, NY 10022

SOURCES OF FOOD PYRAMID POSTERS

COMPILED BY MARY DARLING, UNIVERSITY OF MINNESOTA

Comer Para Vivir: No Vivir Para Comer Spanish poster
NASCO Fort Atkinson
901 Janesville Avenue
P.O. Box 901
Fort Atkinson, WI 53538-0901
(800) 558-9595

East African Pyramid poster
Seattle–King County Department of Public Health
Health Education Materials Distribution
110 Prefontaine Place South, 2nd floor
Seattle, WA 98104
(206) 296-4354

East Indian Pyramid
Los Angeles Project Lean
P.O. Box 802-864
Santa Clarita, CA 91380-2864
(213) 250-8621

Native American Pyramid poster
Yakima Indian WIC Program
401 Buster Road
Toppenish, WA 98948
(509) 865-2102

Russian or Eastern European Pyramid
Department of Health Warehouse
P.O. Box 47905
Olympia, WA 98504-7905
(306) 586-9046

Southeast Asian Pyramid
Seattle–King County Department of Public Health
Health Education Materials
110 Prefontaine Place South, 2nd floor
Seattle, WA 98104
(206) 296-4354

Vegetarian Food Guide Pyramid
The Health Connection
55 West Oak Ridge Drive
Hagerstown, MD 21740-7390
(800) 548-8700

Chinese, Italian, and Mexican Pyramid handouts
The American Dietetic Association
P.O. Box 97215
Chicago, IL 60678-7215
(800) 877-1600

You may also try your local county extension office.

INDEX